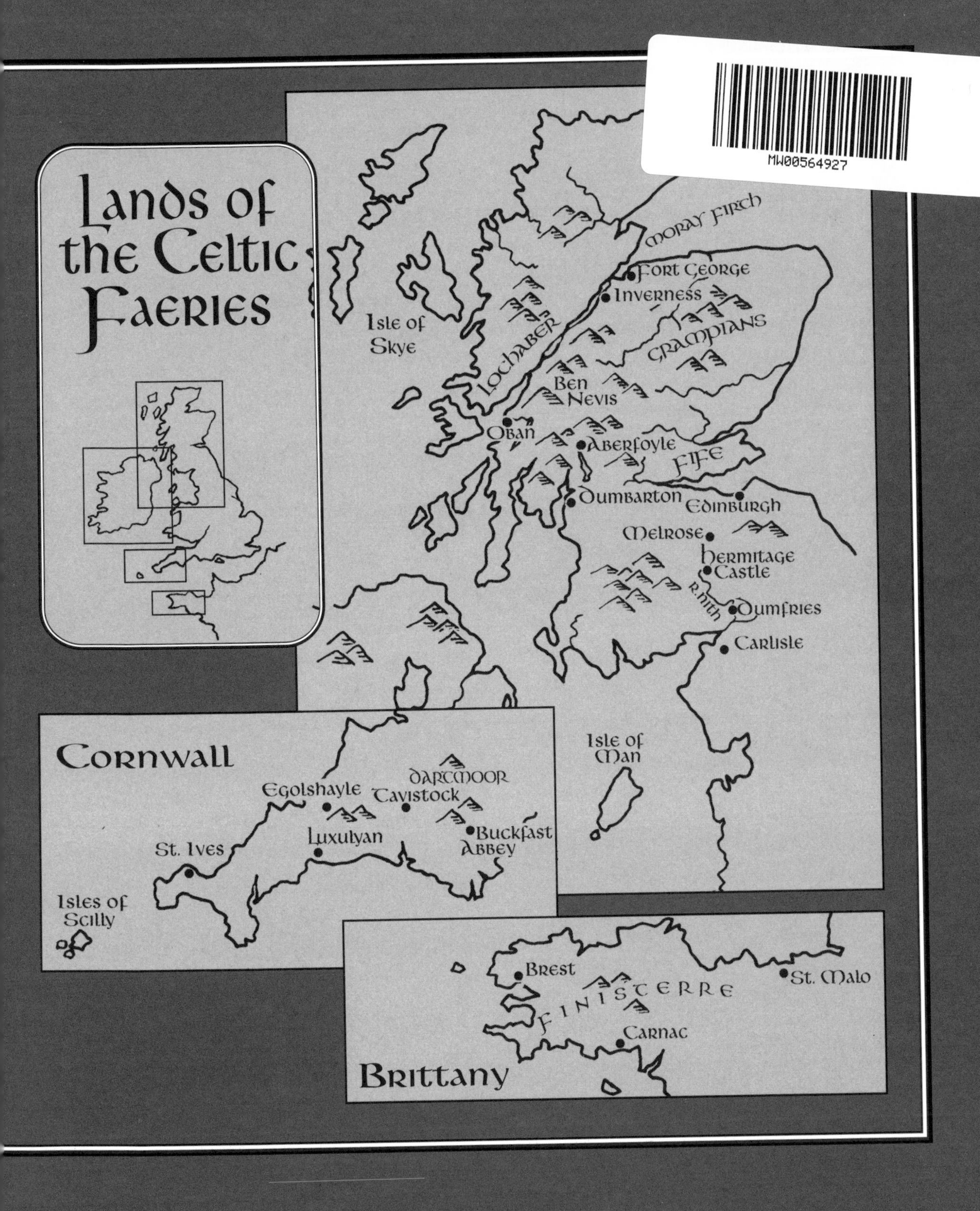

Lands of the Celtic Faeries
Isle of Skye
Moray Firth
Fort George
Inverness
Lochaber
Grampians
Ben Nevis
Oban
Aberfoyle
Fife
Dumbarton
Edinburgh
Melrose
Hermitage Castle
R. Nith
Dumfries
Carlisle
Isle of Man
Cornwall
Dartmoor
Egolshayle
Tavistock
Luxulyan
Buckfast Abbey
St. Ives
Isles of Scilly
Brest
Finisterre
St. Malo
Carnac
Brittany
MW00564927

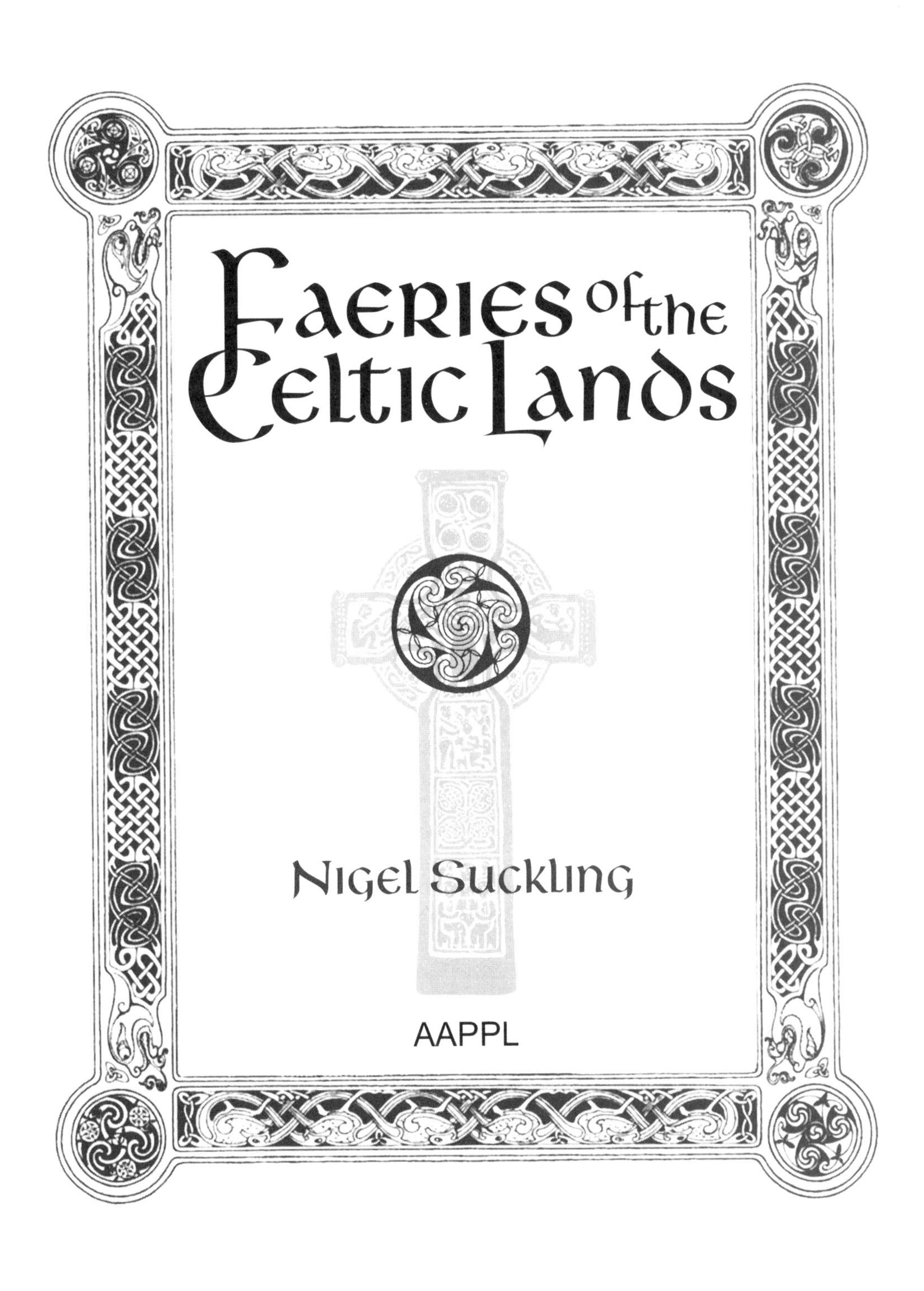

Faeries of the Celtic Lands

Nigel Suckling

AAPPL

Faeries of the Celtic Lands

Published by
Facts, Figures & Fun an imprint of
AAPPL Artists' and Photographers' Press Ltd.
Church Farm House, Wisley, Surrey GU23 6QL
info@ffnf.co.uk www.ffnf.co.uk
info@aappl.com www.aappl.com

Sales and Distribution
UK and export: Turnaround Publisher Services Ltd.
orders@turnaround-uk.com
USA and Canada: Sterling Publishing Inc.
sales@sterlingpub.com
Australia & New Zealand: Peribo Pty.
michael.coffey@peribo.com.au
South Africa: Trinity Books.
trinity@iafrica.com

A catalogue record for this book is
available from the British Library.

ISBN 13: 9781 904 332749

Printed in Thailand
by Imago Publishing info@imago.co.uk

Contents

Introduction

THIS IS A BOOK I've wanted to write for over half my life, ever since I first stumbled into the strange and wonderful, if often baffling realm of Celtic mythology, with its legacy of faerie-faith that has carried a certain magical perspective from ancient times right through here into the present day. It is a distinctly different view from that of mainstream Europe because seen from its western fringes, though preserving many ideas and traditions that once prevailed over most of the continent.

It is as distinct in fact as Celtic art is from the mainstream, as seen in the angelic illuminated manuscripts like the Books of Kells and Lindisfarne, which in their design are actually much closer to Islamic art than their equivalents in the rest of Europe, though through no very direct connection.

What is the reality of faeries? I have a friend who is famous for his faerie paintings, using the term in its broadest possible sense. When asked once if he had ever actually seen one he had to admit disappointedly that no, unfortunately he hadn't – yet. What he did was paint the beings he felt should be there in certain magical places, especially in Cornwall where he lives; but they always hover just off the edge of vision, or are slightly out of focus.

Only a few gifted seers like William Blake have ever claimed to be able to see faeries naturally, but there are many more who, like my artist friend, can sense them with the eye of imagination, piercing the veil of invisibility faeries long ago raised around themselves; and even more who have a lingering conviction that such things should and possibly even do exist in some closely parallel dimension that occasionally intersects ours.

What was lacking, it seemed to me when I first stumbled into this whole field, was some clear and simple guide to its dazzling intricacies, some kind of guiding thread through the maze. I still haven't found such a primer or guide, despite having read mountains of endlessly fascinating books on the subject, so here is my attempt to fill that gap, addressed to those who find themselves in the same position today – curious, and even possibly quite well acquainted with much of the material, but daunted by the chaotic wealth of it on offer.

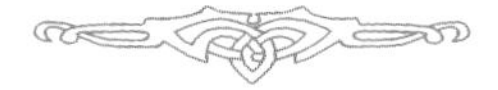

Celtic beliefs about faeries were never exclusive to them. Similar ideas have been held by neighbouring and even far distant people, either through contact or simply because there are some supernatural beliefs that all humans share, even without any direct lines of communication. Australian aboriginals for instance, cut off from the rest of humanity for thousands of years, nevertheless shared with the Chinese, Europeans and many others a conviction that the stars of the Pleiades had once been seven sisters. In different places the legends vary in the details of who the maidens were and how they came to be placed in the heavens, but the essential notion is the same, probably hatched tens of thousands of years ago when the handful of ancestors of the whole human race sat looking up at the stars over north Africa and wondered what they were all about.

So it is with faeries. Along with scarier beings such as vampires, witches and werewolves, people everywhere have believed in them in one form or another since the beginning of time. What is special about Celtic faerie lore is that it is much more vividly documented than most; and widespread belief in the reality of faeries lingered much longer on the Celtic fringe than in the more prosaic neighbouring lands.

An enormous debt is owed to the early Christian scribes of Ireland in particular, who earned the country its nickname as the Land of Saints and Scholars back in the first millennium. Without them very little would be known directly about the supernatural beliefs or mythology of the ancient Celts, because none of it had previously been written down. The Celts had an alphabet but only used it for rare inscriptions – it being a point of honour among their bards and druids that all lore should be carried in their heads. So when, as happened across most of Europe, they were swamped by others such as the Romans, Goths or Huns, most of that lore simply disappeared.

In Ireland lucky conditions prevailed for saving at least a glimpse of the ancient Celtic world view, in which faeries played a leading role. To begin with the Irish were never conquered by the Romans and most others in the first millennium, apart from the partial success of the Vikings. Also their conversion to Christianity was a remarkably benign one. The Irish welcomed St Patrick as a breath of fresh air, not least because he was ready to challenge the druids and other pillars of the old order on their own terms, with little more than his own courage, wit, imagination and humility – even winning many of his enemies over to his own point of view.

The Christianity that flourished in Ireland was very different to that of Rome, much more tolerant of the native traditions and pagan past of its converts. There was of course some censorship involved in writing down the old legends. Gods were often presented as historical figures and scribes often distanced themselves from the pagan tone of what they were writing when it became too magical or rude; but still, their willingness to record the old legends for posterity is far more striking than their occasional tinkering. There were even noble attempts to tie the legendary history of Ireland in with that of biblical and classical European history, the brave scholars making heroic efforts to include as much as possible of their old traditions instead of just trying to bury them, as happened too often elsewhere.

So it is in the *Book of Invasions (Lebor Gabala Erenn)*, one of the epics they painstakingly transcribed from the bards, that we learn of the arrival of the faerie-folk in Ireland, apparently descending from the sky in flying ships amidst a great storm cloud that covered the island for three days and taking possession of the land from the mountain tops rather than the coasts. More like gods than the general modern idea of 'fairies', they were very much like Tolkien's elves – tall, graceful, wonderfully talented in music, poetry and all the arts and sciences. They also understood the secrets of magic.

These are the beings that inspired the tales of faeries, their size shrinking as they were pushed ever further from consideration in the everyday world, though never quite so much in the surviving Celtic lands as elsewhere. These faeries are where we begin this book, looking at the tale of their arrival in this world and then after a time retreating from it into another parallel one, from where they continued to influence and interact with humans right into the modern age.

Note: Regarding the proper spelling of Celtic names of both people and places I must at this point ask some indulgence. There are so many inconsistent variations around that in the end I have simply and subjectively chosen those most familiar to me, on the grounds that at least they should then be more or less consistent within this book, if not with each other. Also I have sometimes used anglicised versions of names (banshee, brownie) where these are likely to be more widely recognised than the Gaelic spelling. A similar thing goes for the versions of famous stories that I retell. What I have done is, wherever possible, gathered three or four direct translations of original ancient manuscripts and then told the story that seemed to be hovering behind them all.

PART 1

When Faeries Ruled the World

CHAPTER 1

The Coming of the Tuatha

so it was that the tuatha de danann came to ireland. in this manner they came: in dark clouds. they landed on the mountains of conmaicne rein [co. leitrim] in connacht; and they brought a darkness over the sun for three days and three nights.

Book of Invasions (ch. 55)

The clearest account of the origins of the Celtic faerie folk comes from the tale of their arrival in Ireland in probably the oldest collection of Irish legends called the *Book of Invasions*, found in the twelfth century *Book of Leinster* and other medieval collections, though mostly based on much earlier documents probably dating back to the eighth or ninth centuries.

This book tells how a race of more than human talents, gods in fact, came and took possession of the island from its previous inhabitants. There are echoes of similar tales and similar gods in other Celtic lands so the likelihood is that they shared similar legends localised to their own countries. The Irish version simply happens to be the one that has best survived into the present.

In the *Book of Invasions* we hear how the Tuatha landed on a mountain in Connaught in the west of Ireland one First of May (Beltaine) amid dark clouds that hid their arrival from the current inhabitants, the Fir Bolg. The Tuatha are described in this account as 'the most handsome and delightful company, the fairest of form, the most distinguished in their equipment and apparel, and their skill in music and playing; the most gifted in mind and temperament that ever came to Ireland . . . The Tuatha De excelled all the peoples of the world in their proficiency in every art.'

In the twelfth century *Book of the Dun Cow* the scribe notes that scholars could not say for certain where the Tuatha had come from but that it seemed 'likely to them that they came from heaven on account of their intelligence and for the excellence of their knowledge'. This opinion probably encouraged the common belief into modern times that they were fallen angels who were not quite bad enough to be consigned to hell; or else that they were angels who happened to have been stranded on the outside when the gates of heaven were slammed shut against Satan and his rebels, so had settled on earth.

An old rationalisation of the account of their arrival is that they did not in fact come in flying ships amid magical storms but that when the Tuatha landed on the coast in quite ordinary galleys, they then set fire to them in order to destroy the possibility of retreat; and it was under cover of this burning cloud that they marched inland and surprised the natives by appearing suddenly in their midst.

But whatever their ultimate origins and the manner of their coming, in the legends the Tuatha are described as having immediately come 'from the north', from four great cities – Falias, Gorias, Finias and Murias – where they had learned their arts and from which they had brought four great treasures which were later to shape the legendary history of both Ireland and Britain. These were the Stone of Destiny (Lia Fail) from Falias, the irresistible Sword of Nuada from Gorias, the Spear of Victory from Finias and a magic cauldron from Murias, from which no company ever left unsatisfied no matter how much they ate. This later became famous as the Cauldron of the Daghda.

Before entering the tale of the Tuatha's arrival in Ireland, let's consider a few of the dominant characters in the drama.

The People of the Goddess Dana

In Greek mythology the picture of the relationships between the various gods and goddesses and the Titans who ruled before them is often confused enough, despite their tales having been first extensively written down a couple of thousand years ago. Celtic mythology is even less clear and consistent, but again it is surprising just how much has survived after being filtered through primitive Christian scholarship. We still do get a broad picture of the general beliefs in other Celtic lands whose own legends almost died out with their druids.

One of the noticeable features of ancient Celtic society is the status of women, who are very much equal to their menfolk. In fact there are strong traces of a recently matriarchal society, with some descents being traced through the female rather than the male line. Some Romans commented on this at the time; also that Celtic women often fought in battle beside their men and when they did were as much to be feared. Boudicca was not a rare exception. Thus it is that the faerie people who invaded Ireland were named after their principal goddess rather than her consort.

Dana

Although she gave her name to the faerie folk of Ireland, the goddess Dana or Danu is a shadowy figure. What is certain about her is that she was worshipped by all the Celtic people from ancient times because variations of her name survive in all the countries they once ruled, especially in the names of rivers, the most famous of which is the Danube (Latin Danuvius).

It is likely that Dana is identical with the goddess Anu, Anna and even possibly Aine, said to be the patroness of Munster province in the south west of Ireland, where two prominent breast-shaped hills near Killarney are known as the Paps of Anu or Anann. Also she is probably identical with the Welsh goddess Don, who was also called there the mother of the gods. In later mythology she was displaced by, or possibly evolved into, Brigid, becoming the crone aspect or cailleach (which simply means 'old woman') of that triple goddess – maiden, mother, crone. As a crone or hag she was the ruler of all the harsh aspects of winter, the gales and tempests and freezing north wind.

In Scottish legends the fact that she is just one of three aspects of the same goddess became almost forgotten and as the Cailleach Bheur, or simply Dark Beira, she tries to keep Bride, goddess of spring, captive in order to prevent winter ever ending. Then when Bride inevitably escapes and marries the King of Summer, Beira makes a pilgrimage to the Fountain of Everlasting Youth and becomes young and beautiful again herself. At one time the tale was almost certainly slightly different and Beira herself became the Bride of Summer by drinking of the fountain, but their identity became blurred through the ages. Some echo does remain however in that she is often called Dark Beira (as opposed presumably to the Light one), and is credited with being mother of the gods and creator of all the major mountains and lakes of Scotland. The Cailleach Bheur is sometimes described as having just one eye and red teeth in a face of mackerel blue.

In some areas of Scotland and Ireland the first farmer in a district to bring in the harvest traditionally made a corn dolly representing the Cailleach Bheur, and the last farmer to bring in his harvest had to keep it for the winter as a forfeit. The belief that Beira and her servant hags were responsible for winter storms, especially at sea, probably helped the suspicion in the sixteenth and seventeenth century Scottish witch hunts that witches conjured storms to sink ships, many being strangled and burned at the stake after being convicted in law of having done so.

There is a curious survival of all this in the local legends of Leicester in England, an area not otherwise much known for its Celtic roots. There Black Annis, a blue-faced, one-eyed crone with iron claws was said to live in a cave in the Dane Hills on the edge of the city, from where she once preyed on passing humans (especially children) whose flesh she loved to eat, or lambs if she was out of luck. Nearby lived a giant called Bel who once boasted that he could reach Leicester in three leaps. So he mounted his sorrel mare at Mountsorrel and took one leap to Wanlip (best said with a Leicester accent), the next leap to Birstall where his mare's harness burst, and a final leap which killed them both, so he was buried at Belgrave, on the edge of the Dane Hills, having almost reached his target.

Bel

Bel (Belen, Belenus, Belinus, Belennos, Belenos and Bilé) is usually described as Dana's husband and is an even vaguer figure, probably because by the time legends came to be set down in writing he had long drifted into the mythological background. At one time he was one of the most widespread Celtic gods and his name has survived in many place names across southern and western Europe. Several Roman writers mention sanctuaries dedicated to Belenus in Gaul and northern Italy, while in Ireland Bel or Bilé is sometimes called 'The Father of Gods and Men.'

Bel means 'Shining One' and it is assumed that he was the early Celtic sun god later replaced by Lugh, just as Helios was displaced by Apollo in Greek mythology. Beltaine, the May Day festival that begins summer is still named after him. Bilé in Gaelic means 'sacred tree', meaning the oak, which was famously revered by the druids. Although in Ireland Dana was occasionally described as a daughter of the Daghda, more commonly she and Bel are said to be his parents, which seems more likely.

Bel was the god of agriculture, sheep and cattle; and of both death and rebirth, because another possible root of the syllable 'bel' means 'to die', which is possibly what prompted Caesar's comment that the Celts believed themselves descended from Dis Pater, or Pluto, the god of the underworld (*Gallic Wars VI; xviii*). He probably did not realise that the Celtic idea of Land of the Dead was very different from the gloomy Roman one, being a bright faeryland; though elsewhere he does remark on the Celts' remarkable fearlessness of death.

At the time of the Roman invasion of Britain the most powerful King in what is now East Anglia was Cunobelinus (Cunobel) whose name means 'Hound of Bel', suggesting that his cult was still strong at the time.

In Welsh mythology Beli and Don are the parents of Arianrhod and Gwydion.

Daghda

The Daghda, also known as 'the Good God' (because he was good at everything he did, rather than that he was especially benevolent), 'All-Father' or 'Red Man of All Knowledge', was sometime ruler of the Tuatha, a master of magic, a skilled craftsman and a fierce warrior. Like Bel before him he was the god of agriculture and husbandry, and also of treaties. Because of his enormous appetites he is often portrayed in an affectionately comical light, but this did nothing to diminish the love and respect he inspired. The son of Dana and Bel, he was the father of Brigid and Angus Og among many others, because among his other appetites he was rampantly sexual, and despite his unpromising appearance was rarely short of willing partners.

The Daghda's chief treasures were his cauldron which produced an inexhaustible supply of food, a golden harp with which he could conjure any mood and even command the weather, and an enormous club with one end of which he could kill nine enemies with a single blow, and with the other restore them to life. He also had two magical pigs which took turns to be roasted one day and restored to life the next.

Unlike most of the other Tuatha, the Daghda was not tall, graceful and beautiful. In the early accounts of the Second Battle of Moytura (Mag Tuired) he is described as a scruffy, ugly buffoon: 'his belly was the size of a house cauldron. He had a cape to the hollows of his elbows and a grey-brown tunic around him to the swelling of his rump. He trailed behind him a wheeled eating fork which was the work of eight men to move. His long penis was uncovered. He had two shoes of horsehide with the hair outside'.

In Roman mythology his nearest counterpart was Saturn. Not the dour, niggardly timekeeper people generally think of but the aspect of him that presided over the Saturnalia with which Romans celebrated the winter solstice, the master of revelry and excess at whose festival people rewarded themselves for all their laboured discipline over the year with a week or two of wild abandon. He and his counterparts in other pagan countries, including the Daghda, survive as a synthesis in the figure of Father Christmas who continues to rule indulgently over our excesses today.

More directly, the Daghda is often related to Cernunnos and his later form of Herne the Hunter though there is no direct evidence to show that they were identical. In Welsh mythology the Daghda is equated with Gwydion.

Morrigan

The Morrigan was a battle goddess and wife of the Daghda. Her name means 'Great Queen' or 'Phantom Queen'. As with Dana, Brigid and other Celtic goddesses she is sometimes referred to in the singular and sometimes as three sisters Morrigu, Badbh and either Macha or Nemain. Nemain inspires battle frenzy, which is the literal meaning of her name. Macha is a fury who loves to dance in blood and Morrigu is the leader of the three whose main function is to either inspire courage and battle frenzy in her chosen champions, or sap it in those she wishes to lose. She was especially helpful to the Tuatha before the Second Battle of Moytura, warning the Daghda where the Fomorians would land and promising to drain their King Inneach's courage and 'the blood from his heart'. She also told the Daghda to gather his poets and taught them spells to chant against the enemy.

It is possible that Badbh is merely their collective name, meaning as it does 'crow', especially the Royston or hooded crow which is the form they often took, especially on the battlefield, though they could as easily take the shape of beautiful women; but it may have been an alternative name for one of the three. Despite being war goddesses the Morrigan did not delight in indiscriminate slaughter just for the sake of it, but only when necessary to fend off threats to their chosen land or people. In Celtic lands it was long considered unlucky if a crow landed on your roof because it meant an imminent dispute.

In her aspect of Macha the Morrigan was the patron goddess of Ulster whose capital, Emain Macha, was named after her. Much later she fell in love with the Ulster hero Cuchulainn and when he rejected her advances she became his enemy, attacking him in the form of an eel when he was locked in combat at a ford, and driving a herd of cattle against him. But when he was then injured she took pity and in the form of an old woman nursed him back to health.

The *bean sidhe* or banshee is a close relation.

Lugh

Also called Lugh Lamfhada, meaning Lugh of the Long Arm, not for any physical reason but because of his skill at throwing the javelin by means of a sling. He was also called Samhildanach, Summer Who Possesses All the Arts. Although the Irish tales locate him specifically there, as with several other gods, he seems to have been revered by all the Celtic people and the Celtic place name Lugudunon meaning fortress of Lugh has survived in many places including Lyon, Laon, Leyden and Luguvalium in Roman Britain, now called Carlisle.

Julius Caesar noted that the Gauls worshipped a god he compared to Mercury, because like Lugh he was said to be the inventor of all the arts; but Lugh has also been compared to Apollo, being a sun god and also a late arrival in the pantheon. A great Celtic harvest festival at Lyon, almost certainly dedicated to Lugh, was forcibly suppressed by the Romans, who changed the name of the month to August in honour of Augustus Caesar. In Ireland the festival survived much longer as Lughnasadh on the first of August. Under Christianity it became Lammas, or Loaf Mass, at which the first bread of the season was baked. In Ireland the famous annual games at Telltown (Taillteann) in County Meath on 1 August were said to have been instituted by Lugh in honour of his foster mother Tailtiu.

As Caesar noted, Lugh was the inventor or patron of all the arts. Ball games, horse racing, acrobatics and other events that took place at festivals were also attributed to him. His Welsh equivalent was Lleu Llaw Gyffes (Lleu of the Steady Arm), but much less is said about him than in the Irish literature.

Brigid

Brigid or Brigit is another deity who was once celebrated across Europe under various names: Bride in Scotland, Brigantia in Britain, Berecynthia and Brigandu in France and Brigindu in Switzerland. The Brigantes tribe in Britain named themselves after her and traces of her name still cling to many places, especially hills and rivers.

In Irish legends Brigid was the daughter of the Daghda and the wife, at least for a time, of Bres of the Fomorians, one of several intermarriages by which the Tuatha tried to make peace with their rivals. With Bres she had three sons who were blacksmiths, Ruadan, Goibniu and Creidhne. When her eldest son Ruadan was treacherously murdered, keening was heard for the first time in Ireland as she gave voice to her grief.

Brigid was principally the goddess of poetry, healing and the blacksmith's craft, being associated with metaphorical and real flames – the fire of poetic inspiration, the hearth as representative of nurture and care, and the blazing flames of the forge where the blacksmith works his technological magic. She is often portrayed as a triple goddess, three sisters all called Brigid.

The pagan goddess's place was later taken by St Brigid, a real enough person in the sixth century who became one of the three patron saints of Ireland along with Patrick and Columba (Columcille). St Brigid was almost certainly seen by the Irish at the time as an incarnation of the goddess within the new religion, just as many kings, heroes and other saints were also considered incarnations of the Tuatha de Danann. It is also likely that St Brigid's church at Kildare (Church of the Oak) was formerly the pagan goddess's sanctuary. All men were excluded from it and nineteen nuns tended a sacred flame there that, apart from a brief occasion in the thirteenth century, was only finally extinguished by Henry VIII's dissolution of the monasteries.

Although a real person, legends of miracles quickly built up around this popular saint. She was said to have been born at sunrise on 1st February, the pagan goddess's feast day. Her house once burst into a pillar of flame which reached to heaven. A flame rose from her forehead when she took the nun's veil and she was famous for many miraculous cures of the sick and even the dead. One such story tells how two lepers once came to the sacred well at Kildare hoping to be cured. Brigid told one of them to wash the other, which he did and the disease peeled away from his skin. Then she told the cured one likewise to bathe his friend; but he shrank from touching the diseased flesh. So Brigid herself bathed the man and cured him.

Young Brigid was so beautiful that men were always chasing after her. She prayed to be released from this burden so that she could remain a virgin and was struck with smallpox that blighted half her face, which she considered a blessing.

Brigid's Night at the beginning of February is at exactly the opposite pole of the year from Lugh's feast at the start of August, and marks the secret rebirth of nature beneath the cold mantle of winter.

Ogma

Ogma (Oghma) is sometimes described as the brother of the Daghda but more often as the son of Brigid, and therefore his grandson. He was the champion of the Tuatha at the time of their arrival in Ireland and is often described as having a radiant countenance. Besides being their greatest warrior he was gifted with eloquence and is described in an early Irish text as 'a man most knowledgeable in speech and poetry'. In fact he is said to have won more battles with his tongue than with his weapons, and preferred such victories. Another name for him was Cermait which means 'honey-mouthed'.

Ogma was credited with the invention of the Irish ogham lettering used for inscriptions in wood or stone. In the form that has survived

ogham is based on the Latin alphabet and probably dates from the fourth century AD, but it is almost certainly a development of a much earlier magical script of the druids.

In Gaul he was known as Ogmios. The Roman writer Lucian described a picture of Ogmios he saw in Provence in the second century AD which showed an old, sunburnt warrior with club and bow, but also thin gold chains running from his mouth to the ears of a happy band of men following after him. A Gaulish friend explained that to the Celts the god of eloquence was not Mercury (Hermes) as it was for the Romans, but Hercules because he was as strong as he was eloquent.

Ogma is also credited with being a guide of souls to the otherworld (a function of the Greek Hermes) and a guarantor of contracts, probably because they are the kind of thing that would be carved in stone or wood with ogham.

No drawing like that referred to by Lucian has survived but Albrecht Durer made his own version with a more youthful Ogmios than that Lucian described leading souls to heaven.

Nuada was King of the Tuatha de Danann when they came to Ireland, but almost equal among the males was his brother Ogma, Manannan mac Lir who ruled the waves, Dian Cecht the great healer and Goibniu the blacksmith.

Ireland at the time was inhabited by a race called the Fir Bolg, which means Men of the Bag, who had come to Erin from the south. Their King was Eochaid, son of Erc. When news came to him at Tara that a new people had arrived and were camped at Mag Rein, he gathered his counsellors to decide what to do. Finally it was decided to send an envoy to see what the strangers wanted. They chose Streng, a great warrior, who set out for Mag Rein with his great shield and spears and sword.

When the Tuatha saw him coming they sent Bres, a champion of their own to meet him. The two met warily but when neither tried any treachery and they found they could understand each other's speech easily enough, they soon relaxed and began to compare weapons; and while Bres marvelled at the weight and bluntness of the Fir Bolg spears, Spreng marvelled at the slim sharpness of the Tuatha's. Then in a chivalrous spirit they exchanged weapons so that each side could measure the merits of the other's and Bres delivered his message, which was that if the Fir Bolg were prepared to surrender half of Ireland, the Tuatha would be content to settle there without war. Then the two envoys declared that they would be friends no matter what the outcome and parted.

Back at Tara, Streng passed on the message and showed the marvellously fashioned spear he had been given, recommending that against an enemy so well armed it might be wise to settle for the suggested truce. However, Eochaid and his counsellors decided that were they to give up half their land so easily it would not be long before the Tuatha would want it all, so they declared war.

At the First Battle of Moytura (Mag Tuireadh or Mag Tuired), so named after the plain near Cong in Connaught where it was fought, beginning one Midsummer Day, the Tuatha thoroughly defeated the Fir Bolg after great slaughter on both sides. The settlement was that the Fir Bolg were allowed to keep the province of Connaught while the Tuatha took possession of Tara, the seat even then of Ireland's High Kings, and the other four provinces. At Tara they placed the Lia Fail, their Stone of Destiny, which ever after would cry out when touched by a truly crowned High King. Opinion is divided over whether that stone is the one still to be found at Tara. Many believe it was carried off to Scotland by Kenneth MacAlpin to become the Stone of Scone in the ninth century, on which Scottish Kings were crowned until it was stolen by Edward I in 1296 and built into the English coronation throne. It was returned to Scotland in 1996 as part of the devolution measures leading to the re-establishment of a Scottish parliament.

However, back in Ireland after the First Battle of Moytura things did not go as well for the Tuatha after their victory over the Fir Bolg as might be imagined. Their King Nuada had lost a hand in the battle and although the healer Dian Cecht made him another out of silver that was every bit as good, it was the law that only a whole man could be King. So Nuada stepped down and the champion Bres the Beautiful became King in his place.

The Fir Bolg were not the only obstacles the Tuatha faced in taking possession of Ireland. There was another race, the Fomorians, to whom the Fir Bolg had been paying tribute. It appears that the Tuatha had made some kind of alliance with the Fomorians before invading Ireland because their champion and new King Bres was half Fomorian, the product of marriage between the Fomorian King Elatha and the Tuatha queen Eriu, who later gave her name to the island of Erin.

The Fomorians are a shadowy people, often described as monsters with one eye and one leg, but in other places they seem as beautiful and gifted in magic as the Tuatha themselves. Bres himself was so beautiful that any woman was proud to be compared with him, but his reign brought the Tuatha little joy. It is supposed that the Tuatha made him King in order to cement whatever agreement or alliance they had made with the Fomorians, but he proved a tyrant. He not only continued the tribute to the Fomorians but increased it. A third part of everything produced in Ireland, including their children, was shipped overseas to the Fomorians. The Daghda and Ogma were reduced to manual labour to pay their taxes and the whole island groaned under its burden of taxes.

The Tuatha longed for Nuada to be King again and luckily Dian Cecht's son Miach was an even better healer than his father. He recovered Nuada's lost hand, restored it to health and successfully grafted it back onto his arm. Then all the Tuatha gathered at Tara and restored him to the throne. Bres and his immediate followers left in disgrace and sailed off to the lands of the Fomorians over the ocean to seek their aid in recapturing the throne of Ireland by force.

The Coming of Lugh

A while after his restoration to the throne, Nuada of the Silver Hand (as he was still called) was holding a great feast at Tara when a young stranger arrived seeking admission so he could offer his services to the King.

'Who are you?' the gatekeepers asked.

'I am Lugh, the son of Cian mac Dian Cecht of the Tuatha de Danann, and Ethlinn, daughter of Balor of the Evil Eye, King of the Fomorians.'

'What are your skills?' they asked. 'For no-one enters Tara without some fresh art to offer.'

'I am a carpenter,' Lugh replied.

'We already have a carpenter,' the doorkeepers said.

'Then I am a smith,' Lugh said, only to get the same response.

So it went on. Lugh said he was a champion, a harper, a poet, a storyteller, a magician, a doctor and many other professions besides; to all of which he received the same answer.

Finally Lugh said: 'Then go and ask the King if he has any man that can do all these things; and if he has I will not ask again to enter.'

So the doorkeepers went to the King with this message and Nuada told them to test the stranger with the fidchell board. Fidchell was a chess-like game peculiar to the ancient Celts and held in very high reverence by them. It was only played by the nobility and druids and was often, in legend, used to test if heroes were of the high lineage they claimed. In *The Cattle Raid of Froech*, a tale set much later than this in the Heroic Age, the eponymous hero's set is described: 'beautiful his fidchell set: the board was of white gold, and the edges and corners were of gold, while the pieces were of gold and silver, and a candle of precious stone provided light.'

The game board was brought and Nuada's champion played against Lugh, but he won with a move no-one had ever seen before, and which became known from that day on as as 'Lugh's Enclosure'.

So Lugh was invited to sit in the Sage's Seat beside the King and demonstrate some of the many skills he had claimed at the door. First there was a giant stone which no-one but Ogma the champion could move. Ogma pushed it along the floor of the hall and out through the door, but Lugh easily pushed it back again, then carried it off and restored it to the much larger rock it had been taken from. Then on the harp he played an air that was so merry he had everyone laughing; then one so sweet they all cried; then one so restful that everyone in the court fell asleep and did not wake till the same time the next day. These and other demonstrations convinced Nuada that Lugh was as good as his claims, winning for himself the title Ildanach or Samildanach, which means Master of all Arts.

Mindful of the war that was inevitable with the Fomorians once they stopped paying tribute, Nuada saw that Lugh might be very useful to them. Surrendering his throne to Lugh for thirteen days he invited him to show them how with all his talents he thought the enemy could be beaten, and so wise was his council that it was decided to give him command of the Tuatha army when the time for battle came.

The King of the Fomorians was Balor of the Evil or Piercing Eye, so called because one of his eyes had the power of destroying anyone upon whom its gaze fell, and whole armies could be robbed of their strength merely by its glance. He had acquired this power in his youth when spying on his father's druids mixing a poisonous brew. Fumes from the potion had entered his left eye and given it the dreadful enchantment. From then on he kept that eye shut except when he wished to kill people, and so heavy was the eyelid that servants had to raise it for him with hooks.

That Lugh declares himself the grandson of the Fomorian King is also a parallel with the story of Zeus, who overthrew his father Cronos to take the throne of heaven. As with Cronos, Balor of the Evil eye had a warning of his nemesis. One of his druids foretold that his grandson would one day destroy him. At the time Balor had only one child, a daughter named Ethlinn (Ethniu or Eithne), so he shut her away in a tower on the Island of Glass out in the western ocean where he lived, believed to be Tory (Toraigh) Island off Donegal. Twelve women were set to tend and guard her, and keep her from all knowledge of men. She was not even told of their existence though sometimes she did spy them far off in passing ships on the ocean. When she questioned her women about them though, they would tell her nothing. There was also a man who came sometimes into her dreams, but of him she said nothing because she had secretly fallen in love with him.

Ethlinn grew very beautiful but her wicked father Balor lost no sleep over this because he was sure she was locked safe from temptation in her tower. He carried on as he had always done, wrecking and plundering passing ships and occasionally making raiding trips into Ireland. Now there were three brothers of the Tuatha at that time in Ireland, sons of the Daghda. They were Goibniu the smith, Samthainn and Cian and they lived together at Druim na Teine, the Ridge of Fire. Cian had a wonderful cow that was the envy of Ireland because it was never without milk, and that milk was the sweetest ever tasted. So many people tried to steal this cow that Cian always kept it in sight, so he had the cow with him when he and his brothers went to a forge to have new swords made. Leaving Samthainn outside to hold the cow, the other two went in to conduct their business.

Now Balor happened to be passing just then and he had long coveted this cow. Seeing his chance, he magically transformed himself into a young boy and approached Samthainn, saying he had just heard two men telling the smith to use the finest steel for their swords, but common iron for their brother's. Samthainn was furious. Asking the boy to hold the precious cow, he rushed into the forge and a furious row broke out. By the time they realised they had been tricked and rushed outside again, it was to see Balor far in the distance making off with their cow. They gave chase all the way to the seashore but were too late to stop the Fomorian loading the cow into his ship and sailing away.

Desolate, Cian consulted a druid who told him that as long as Balor

lived there was little chance of recovering the cow because he was sure to guard it as closely as Cian had, and because of his evil eye no-one could take it from him. Cian then consulted the druidess Birog of the Mountain and she said much the same, but said there might be a way if Cian was patient. She told him about the prophecy and of how Balor had locked his daughter away because of it. Moreover, Birog also knew that Ethlinn had been dreaming of none other than Cian himself and that if only they could somehow be alone together Cian could father on her the child who would be Balor's undoing.

Dressing Cian up in women's clothes and putting a 'glamour' on him so he looked like a woman to match the dress, Birog whistled up a wind and they put to sea, soon landing in the Isle of Glass by Ethlinn's tower. Knocking at the door, Birog told the women inside that she and the queen with her had been shipwrecked and asked for shelter within. They were admitted and Birog immediately cast a spell on the twelve women so they fell into a deep sleep. Then Cian, his disguise removed, went in to Ethlinn's chamber and she immediately recognised him from her dreams and welcomed him into her bed. The next day he and Birog sailed away again with none but Ethlinn in the tower being any the wiser.

Balor was furious when he learned his daughter was pregnant, and mystified too because no-one could tell him how it had happened. When the baby Lugh was born in due course, Balor had him sewn into a bag and thrown into the sea, but the wise-woman Birog was there waiting. She rescued the child and sailed back to Ireland with him, where Cian sent him to be fostered by Taillte (Tailltiu), daughter of the King of the Great Plain, in whose honour the Telltown games in Meath were later celebrated.

After presenting himself to the Tuatha and being accepted by them as their leader, if not yet their King, Lugh and the other faerie lords began preparations for the war that was coming. For a year Lugh, Nuada, Ogma, Goibniu, Dian Cecht and others held a secret conference so the Fomorians would not guess what they were about, before separating to make their preparations, Lugh going off to seek his foster brothers, the sons of Manannan mac Lir.

In the meantime the Tuatha continued to pay taxes to the Fomorians to allay any suspicions they might have until the day of reckoning. This happened at the great annual Beltaine (May Day) gathering on the Hill of Uisneach west of Tara, where representatives of all the people of Ireland gathered for games, settling disputes, forming alliances and meting out justice. This hill was anciently reckoned to be the geographical centre of the island and was marked by the Stone of Divisions or Cat Stone, which is also said to mark the burial spot of the goddess Eriu. Since the oppression by the Fomorians this was also the occasion they chose to come and collect their taxes from the people of Ireland. So confident were they of their strength that they only sent nine times nine of their number to do this, but until this day no Fir Bolg or Tuatha had dared question anything they said or did. The hill was even called Balor's Hill in those days.

However, on this particular May Day things went very differently. All the Tuatha and the remaining Fir Bolg were gathered on top of Uisneach when the Fomorians arrived, and a motley and frightening crew they were too – giants and trolls and monsters as well as fierce warriors – and their captains were Eine, Eathfaigh, Coron and Compar, who would kill a man as soon as look at him. But then from the opposite side in the east came riding a glittering host led by a young man who seemed to shine like the sun. It was Lugh of the Long Arm riding Manannan mac Lir's own horse, white Aonbharr of the One Mane 'swift as the naked cold wind of spring' upon whose back no rider was ever killed. And Lugh was wearing Manannan's own breastplate within which no man had ever been wounded; and the helmet he wore was set with jewels which shone as brightly as the light on his forehead; and Manannan's sword Freagarthach, the Answerer, was in his hand which so weakened any enemy against whom it was drawn that they grew as feeble as a woman in child-birth, and no-one wounded by it ever lived.

With Lugh came the sons of Manannan and the whole fighting host of the Land of Promise. They fell upon the Fomorians and slaughtered them all, save nine that they sent back to tell Balor that the days of his easy tribute from Ireland were ended. Then on both sides preparations began for war.

Fate of the Sons of Tuirenn

Now they had openly declared war, Lugh sent messengers all over Erin to gather all the warriors of the Tuatha ready for battle. One messenger was his own father Cian, son of Dian Cecht, the god of medicine. As Cian was crossing the Plain of Muirthemne between the Boyne and Dundalk, he saw three armed warriors approaching in the distance. As they came nearer he recognised them as the three sons of Tuirenn mac Ogma – Brian, Iuchar and Iucharbar. Now there was an old enmity between these three and Cian and his own two brothers.

Finding himself alone against these enemies, Cian decided to hide. Seeing a herd of pigs grazing nearby on the plain, he struck himself with his magic wand, changed into a pig himself and joined them. The three sons of Tuirenn were puzzled by the sudden disappearance of the warrior they had clearly seen coming towards them, but they soon guessed the truth, that some enemy of theirs was hiding among the pigs. So Brian, the leader of the three, struck the others with his own magic wand and turned them into two swift wolf hounds to sniff out the impostor. This they soon did and drove it out into the open where Brian gave chase and speared it.

The wounded pig fell, crying out in a human voice: 'That was an evil throw of yours, for I am no pig but Cian, son of Dian Cecht, so spare me!'

'If the life came back into you seven times I would take it again each time,' said Brian, who was in no mind to let his old enemy go with his life.

'Then let me at least change back into my own shape before you kill me,' said Cian.

'Gladly, for there is more honour in killing a man than a pig.'

So Cian changed back into his own form and laughed: 'Now that I am a man again you are obliged to spare me.'

'That we are not,' replied Brian, changing his brothers back into their own forms too.

'Then it will be the worst day's work of your lives,' said Cian. 'For if you had killed me as a pig you could have claimed it was a mistake and would only have had to pay the blood-fine of a pig. But if you murder me as a man your blood-fine will be more than ever was or will be again, and your very weapons will cry out to my son Lugh about such a crime.'

But the sons of Tuirenn would not listen and to avoid using weapons that might betray them they stoned Cian to death. Then they tried to bury him but six times the earth cast him out again in horror. Only the seventh time did he remain buried, and then they laid a mound of rocks over his grave to keep him there.

As time passed and Lugh heard no news of his father, he grew worried and finally set out with some followers on his trail. From where they had last parted he travelled in the direction Cian had taken and in time he too came to the Plain of Muirthemne. When he reached the place where his father had been killed and buried the rocks, the weapons that had killed him, cried out and told the tale of what had happened and who had done the deed. Lugh had his people dig up the cairn and wept over the cruelly smashed body of his father. Then he had it buried again and after carving a memorial stone in Ogham over the grave, he headed back to Tara, swearing his companions to secrecy until he had said what he wanted to say.

Arriving at the hall he found the sons of Tuirenn among the company there. When he was ready he took up the 'chief's chain' and shook it to call for silence, as was the custom when anyone wished to address the whole assembly.

'People of the goddess Dana' he called, 'tell me, what vengeance would you take upon those who have murdered your father?'

Everyone was astonished.

'Are you telling us,' asked the High King Nuada, 'that your father Cian has been murdered?'

'I am,' declared Lugh. 'And I am looking at his murderers right now, as they know even better than I.'

Nuada declared that he would be satisfied by nothing less than hewing his father's murderers limb from limb and everyone agreed, including the sons of Tuirenn.

'The very ones who did the deed say that,' cried Lugh. 'So let them not leave this hall till they have settled with me the blood-fine they shall pay.'

'If I had killed your father' said Nuada, 'I should think myself lucky if you were ready to accept a fine rather than my life.'

Now it was clear from the way his gaze fell upon them that Lugh's suspicions were on the sons of Tuirenn. Also the feud between themselves and the sons of Dian Cecht was famous, so they consulted in whispers. Iuchar and Iucharbar were in favour of confessing but Brian was afraid Lugh might withdraw his offer of a fine if they did. So he stood up and said that although they were not guilty, it was clear Lugh thought they were; so they would pay the same fine as if they had done it, just to keep the peace.

'Very well,' said Lugh, 'here is the fine I demand: three apples, a pig's skin, a spear, two horses and a chariot, seven pigs, a hound-whelp, a cooking-spit and three shouts on a hill. That is the fine. If you think it is too much I will remit some of it; but if you do not, then pay it.'

'If it were a hundred times that, we would not think it too much,' replied Brian. 'Indeed, it seems so little that I fear there must be some trick hidden in it.'

'I do not think it too little,' said Lugh. 'So give me your pledge before the People of the Goddess Dana that you will pay me faithfully, and I will give you my pledge that I will ask no more.'

So the sons of Tuirenn gave their pledge, then Lugh said: 'Now let me tell you the details of what you have pledged. The three apples are from the Garden of the Hesperides on the western edge of the world and you will know them by three signs: they are of the size of a baby's head, the colour of burnished gold and they taste of honey. A bite from one of these apples will cure any illness and moreover the apple will make itself whole again afterwards. Also, whatever you throw an apple at, it will return to your hand. By these signs will I know that they are the true apples and I will accept none other.

'The pig skin is that of Tuis, King of Greece. It cures any wound or illness if there is any life at all left in a person; and moreover any stream of water that flows through it is turned into wine for nine days. The spear is the poisoned spear of Pisar, King of Persia, which is so fiery that out of battle it must always be held under water lest it destroy the city in which it is kept. The two horses and chariot are those of Dobhar, the King of Sicily, which run equally well over land or sea. The seven pigs are the pigs of Easal, King of the Golden Pillars, which may be killed and eaten every night but are found alive and well again the next day. Moreover, anyone who eats the pigs cannot be harmed by any disease. The hound-whelp I require is that of the King of the Cold Country, which catches any wild beast she sets her eyes on and is more beautiful than the fiery wheels of the sun. The cooking-spit is one of those of the Women of Fianchuive, which is beneath the sea between Erin and Alba.

'You have also pledged to give three shouts upon a hill. The hill upon which they must be given is that of Miodhchaoin in the north of Lochlann (the Fomorians' homeland). Miodhchaoin and his sons permit no shouts on that hill upon pain of death. Besides this, it was Miodhchaoin who taught my father the use of arms so that even if I were to forgive you, he will not; so that even if you achieve all the others I think you are sure to fail in this adventure. Now you know the fine you have agreed to pay to me.'

The sons of Tuirenn were dismayed when they heard this and realised that they had indeed fallen into a trap. They took their problem to their father who advised that their case was hopeless unless Lugh or Manannan were willing to lend a hand. They were to go to Lugh and ask to borrow Aonbharr, Manannan's steed that he had borrowed for battle against the Fomorians. Almost certainly Lugh would refuse, saying that he could not lend something which had been lent to him. Then they were to ask him to lend them Manannan's magic coracle 'Wave Sweeper' which would sail wherever it was bid. This time Lugh would be forced to comply because he was under a geasa or taboo not to refuse two requests in a row. Then with Wave Sweeper they would at least be able to reach easily the many countries they needed to visit.

The sons of Tuirenn went to Lugh and things worked out just as their father had said; and truth to tell he was quite willing to help them up to a point, because although he wanted his father's murder avenged by their deaths, he was also thinking that if they won even a few of the prizes it would help in the war against the Fomorians. So he lent them Manannan's enchanted ship and they set off, bidding it first to sail to the Hesperides as Hercules once did in his famous Labours.

Well to cut short a story that has been told often enough at length elsewhere, the sons of Tuirenn succeeded beyond expectations because besides their cowardly killing of Cian they had never been lacking in wit, strength or valour. In fact they had been ranked among the foremost heroes of the Tuatha and they proved it on this great adventure that has often been likened to that of the Greek Argonauts. One by one they succeeded in winning the treasures.

When Lugh learned this by his magical arts he wanted to see them before they attempted the final task of the three shouts on the forbidden hill, the task which he was surest of all would kill them. So he cast a spell of forgetfulness and sent it to them on the wind so that they believed they had fulfilled the blood-fine. In good cheer they set sail for home. When they arrived at Tara, Lugh had absented himself so they handed over all the treasures they had won to Nuada of the Silver Hand and awaited Lugh's return.

When he did, he said: 'So did you give the three shouts upon Miodhchaoin's Hill?'

The hearts of Tuirenn's three sons sank as the spell of forgetfulness fell away and they remembered that the greatest task of all still lay ahead. They set sail and when they came to the shore of Lochlann below the Hill, Miodhchaoin was there waiting for them. Brian went to face him and they fought like two lions till finally Miodhchaoin fell dead. Then his three sons came out to avenge their father and they fought with the three sons of Tuirenn till they too fell dead, but not before they had inflicted such wounds on the brothers that 'birds might have flown through their bodies from one side to the other'.

Only Brian was left standing. With a mighty effort he raised his two brothers and they climbed the Hill to raise three feeble shouts. Then with the last of their strength they returned to their ship which carried them back to Ireland, which they reached on the point of death. Their father Tuirenn went to Lugh to ask the loan of the pig skin of the King of Greece to restore them, but Lugh refused, still wanting their deaths to avenge the cowardly killing of his father. So Tuirenn returned to his sons and when they died, so did he of a broken heart.

The Second Battle

Seven years were the Tuatha de Danann in preparation for war with the Fomorians but when the enemy finally landed a week before Samaine, the Tuatha were still not quite ready. So they sent the Dagdha to parley with the Fomorians and gain a little time. The Fomorians decided to have a little fun with the Good God. As he was famous for his love of porridge they prepared a great cauldron of it for him. Gallons and gallons of milk they poured into the cauldron, with oats and bacon in proportion. Then they added whole carcasses of goats, pigs and sheep and boiled it all for a while before pouring it into a hole in the ground. Bringing the Daghda there, they said: 'Now you must eat all this or we will be forced to kill you, because we cannot have you going back to your people saying we lack hospitality.'

However, they had reckoned without the Daghda's appetite which was legendary. He said cheerfully: 'If it tastes as good as it smells I will be delighted.' Then, pulling from his robes a spoon the size of a bathtub he proceeded to demolish the meal, even scraping the last traces from the bottom of the hole. Then he waddled unsteadily away to sleep it off, his stomach hanging between his knees like the belly of a whale.

With the time gained by the Daghda the Tuatha finished their preparations and the Second Battle of Moytura began. It developed gradually, as was often the way with battles in those days. First there were single combats and then small groups, and to begin with the Fomorians were confident that the Tuatha would soon yield and agree to pay them tribute again; but that was not how it went and finally the skirmishes escalated until one day the two sides drew up their whole ranks for a pitched battle.

All this time Lugh had been kept out of the conflict, guarded by nine warriors, because he was reckoned too precious to lose, but on this day he escaped his keepers and suddenly appeared before the Tuatha in his chariot, his head blazing like the sun and roused the battle spirits of his people, telling them it was better to die that day than submit again to the Fomorian yoke.

The Fomorians saw him too and Bres remarked to his druids: 'It seems wonderful to me that the sun rises today in the west rather than the east.'

'It would be better if that were so,' they replied, 'for what you see is the radiance of Lugh of the Long Arm.'

Then the battle was joined and the blood soon began to flow in rivers. Among those who died that day were Nuada of the Silver Hand, killed by Balor himself. Finally Lugh came face to face with Balor of the Evil Eye, his own grand-father. Faced with a shouted challenge from Lugh he called to his helpers: 'Now raise my eyelid that I may look upon this chatterer.'

But Lugh was ready for this and had earlier prepared a magic stone from the blood of toads, bears, lions and other exotic ingredients. As the servants struggled to raise the deadly eyelid, Lugh cast his stone and knocked Balor's poisonous eye clean out the back of his head, where its unshielded gaze wiped out a company of Fomorians. This turned the battle and inspired the Tuatha to ever greater feats till finally they drove the surviving Fomorians back into the sea.

As he was dying, Balor told Lugh that he regretted having made an enemy of him and said that if Lugh cut off his (Balor's) head and placed it on his own, he would receive all his knowledge and power. Suspecting a trick, Lugh cut it off and placed it on a large rock which instantly splintered into tiny pieces.

When the battle was over the Morrigu and Badb proclaimed victory from all the heights of Ireland, singing:

Peace climbs to the heavens
The heavens descend to earth
Earth lies under the heavens
Strength fills every person.

The old manuscripts say that more Fomorians died that day than there are stars in the sky or grains of sand on the shore, and that the burial mounds of the fallen at the site of the battle were at Carrowmore near Sligo, where they can still be seen today. The site is reckoned the finest and largest collection of prehistoric dolmens, stone circles and megaliths anywhere in Europe besides Carnac in Brittany. They almost certainly do commemorate some great clash of cultures that shaped the course of Irish history several thousand years ago, though no-one can say how closely it resembled the legends as they have come down to us.

With the death of Nuada, Lugh became High King and ruled for forty years. Some say he then died at Uisneach, the hill where the five provinces of Ireland meet, but if so it was not in the manner of mortal death because he often reappears later in Irish legends, not least in that of the birth of Cuchulainn, Ulster's champion, who was his son. He also later entertained Conn of the Hundred Battles and confirmed him in his High Kingship of Ireland. Probably the truth is that he withdrew from active day to day affairs in Ireland and retreated like Manannan to the Land of Promise beyond the ocean, from where he occasionally returned to play a part in the shaping of Ireland.

CHAPTER 2

Magical Realm

Tales of the Tuatha

Although later looked back on as a golden age, the reign of the Tuatha in Ireland was not without incident and drama because often they behaved very like the Gaels who succeeded them. A good example is the tale of how the Daghda was tricked out of his palace. Some say this happened after the Tuatha retreated into the faerie mounds of Ireland, but other chronologies place the incident within the period of their undisputed rule over the land. That is how it's presented here but purely for convenience; there is no way of telling for sure which chronology is correct.

When the Daghda followed Lugh as High King of the Tuatha, he built his palace or rath at Brugh na Boyne, now better known as Newgrange. There he kept his famous harp and the cauldron that was one of the four chief treasures of the Tuatha, and from which no man ever left hungry. Also his battle club which was so huge it needed to be carried around on a cart; the two pigs of which one was always roasted and ready to eat and the other running round the yard, and they miraculously changed places each day; and the ale vat that never ran dry.

Newgrange is believed by archaeologists to have been built around 3,000 BC by an unknown people. Irish legend never doubted who those people were though – the Tuatha – as shown by this verse from a poem in the fourteenth century *Book of Ballymote* that lists the faerie mounds of many of the most famous Tuatha – Lugh, Ogma, Etain, Boann and Angus:

Behold the sidhe before your eyes
It is manifest that it is a King's mansion
Which was built by the stout Daghda
It was a wonder, a court, a marvellous hill.

The Daghda had a beloved son called Angus Og, the Ever Young, who could sing and play the harp so beautifully that he could make his audience laugh, weep, fall in love or asleep as he chose; and his kisses turned into birds which flew around his head.

Angus had been conceived through an illicit affair between the Daghda and Boann (or Boinn) after whom the River Boyne is named. She was married at the time to Elcmar, a close neighbour of the Daghda's by the Boyne and when the Daghda took a fancy to her, she returned his feelings but was afraid of her husband's jealousy. Being High King at the time, the Daghda sent Elcmar off on an errand and then made the sun stand still for nine months, so Angus was conceived and born 'in a single day', and when Elcmar returned he was none the wiser about it.

Angus was called 'the Young' because his mother remarked at his birth that 'young is the son who was begotten at the beginning of a day and born before evening.' He was sent to be fostered by Midir, as was a common Celtic practice in later days. Most sons of the nobility were fostered by other parents, to forge bonds of alliance and also prevent too great a protectiveness towards sons who would almost certainly have to be warriors when they grew up.

Angus however was kept in ignorance of his true parents and believed he was Midir's son till one day in a quarrel during a hurling match (at which he was a great champion) a rival told him this was not so. Angus went and demanded the truth of Midir, who revealed who his true parents were and took him to the assembly at Uisneach to be presented to his father. The Daghda greeted and acknowledged him joyfully and explained the diplomatic reasons why Angus had not been told sooner.

Angus accepted all this happily enough but for one thing – he was the son of the Tuatha High King but had no palace of his own. The Daghda said he would willingly assign him one except that there were none free at the moment. So Angus decided he would have to win one for himself. His friend Manannan mac Lir suggested a ruse by which he might do so and, duly primed, Angus went to his father and asked the loan of his palace at Brugh na Boyne for a night and day. The Daghda agreed willingly enough, but when the time came to ask for the brugh back, Angus gleefully told him that he had unwittingly surrendered it for all time, because all time is made up of night and day.

The logic of this trick gets rather lost in translation because in the ancient Irish tongue there is no verbal distinction between 'a night' and 'night', the phrasing can mean either, depending on the context, so by lending his palace for 'night and day' the Daghda had given it to Angus for all time. Also forgotten is the delight the ancient Celts took in making someone promise more than they realised through such verbal trickery, and how binding such a promise was nevertheless.

The Daghda however realised immediately that he had been caught out, and gave way gracefully enough. Some old chronicles say that Manannan helped things along with a spell of compliance but it is equally likely that the Daghda, with his famous sense of humour, simply admired his son's trick enough to let him have the palace as a reward. Either way, he and his immediate retinue moved out, some say to Tara or Uisneach and others to a modest new rath nearer the Boyne that ever since has been called 'The Tomb of the Daghda'.

Another version of this tale has the Daghda advising Angus to use the same trick to obtain Newgrange from his stepfather Elcmar, but this seems less likely unless Elcmar had by this time accepted and forgiven his wife's infidelity.

The Daghda fades from prominence after his move from Newgrange, to be succeeded in due course by his eldest son Bodb the Red (Bodb Dearg).

The Dream of Angus Og

One night Angus Og dreamed that the most beautiful maid in Erin appeared at his bedside, but when he reached out to her she disappeared. The next night she appeared again, playing a harp so sweetly that she lulled him back to sleep. After that she came regularly and he fell ever more deeply in both love and despair, because he could only see her in his dreams. During the day he gave up eating and was listless and pining. This went on for a year and Angus wasted away, to the worry and wonder of his family because he told no-one the cause of his malaise.

The finest doctors among the Tuatha were called in but none could help until one guessed the cause, and that it could be fatal if no cure was found. Angus's mother Boann was sent for and finally he opened his heart to her. Boann then sent out messengers seeking the girl of Angus's dreams but after a year they returned with no news. Then Boann turned to the Daghda for help. He sent a message to his eldest son Bodb the Red at Sidhe Femaine (or Femuin) who undertook the search for the next year, at the end of which he had good news to report. A maiden answering Angus's description had been found in Connaught. She was Caer, daughter of Ethal Anbuail and was to be found at Dragon's Mouth Lake in Tipperary.

Angus was sent for and then he and Bodb and all their followers visited the lake where Angus recognised his dream-maiden immediately, with her silver necklace and gold chain, even though she was surrounded by thrice fifty other maidens or nymphs. Through the right channels of protocol Bodb then asked for the girl's hand in marriage to Angus, but her father Ethal bluntly refused. Bodb, the Daghda and their champions then stormed Ethal's rath (fortress) and put the request to him again at the point of a sword.

Ethal said that even now he could not consent to his daughter's marriage because the consent was not his to give. His daughter, he revealed, was a swan maiden. From one Samaine to the next she had the form of a maid, then for the following year she took the form of a swan, she and her thrice fifty maidens. Well, peace was made between them on hearing this and the Daghda sent words of advice to Angus Og on how to proceed.

The next Samaine Angus went to Dragon's Mouth Lake and there he found the waters covered with swans; but even so he picked out Caer as easily as he had spotted her among the maidens before. He called out to her and asked her to marry him. She replied that she would, but only if he did not ask her to put off her swan's form or change her ways. This he agreed to readily enough so she changed him into a swan too and after circling the lake three times they flew off to Brugh na Boyne where they sang so sweetly that all who heard them fell asleep for three days.

The Children of Lir

When Bodb the Red was chosen to succeed the Daghda as High King of the Tuatha, not all agreed, especially Lir, the father of Manannan, and Midir the Proud, because both felt the honour should have been theirs. Bodb was sad about this, especially about the rift with Lir who had once been his great friend. Not wanting to enforce his authority on Lir by war, Bodb sought more diplomatic ways of reconciliation. His chance with Lir came when Lir's beloved wife died. After a tactful interval Bodb offered one of his own three foster-daughters as a bride. Peace was made between them when Lir chose the eldest, Aebh and was very happy with her. She bore him a daughter Finola of the Fair Shoulder and a son called Aed (Hugh); then twin boys called Fiachra and Conn, but she died delivering them.

Then Lir married Bodb the Red's second foster daughter Aoife the Fair and they too were happy for a while; but Aoife was childless and soon began to grow jealous of Lir's four children by her sister, who were beloved by all the Tuatha and used to shine at their feasts and gatherings. Bodb would often visit Lir to admire them; and Lir would often take them to Tara where everyone made a great fuss of them. Lir would rise early each morning just to watch them play and Aoife felt they were stealing Lir's heart away from her.

When the fires of jealousy grew unbearable, she tried to persuade her servants to kill the children but they were so popular that no-one would touch them. So one day Aoife took the children to Lake Davra (Lough Derravaragh in Westmeath) for a swim and while they were in the water she magically transformed them into swans, perfect in every way save that they kept their voices and minds, not forgetting who they had been. Some say this was out of a lingering female pity, but others say it was only because her power did not reach that far.

Then Aoife told them that they were condemned to remain there as swans for three hundred years, then for three hundred years upon the Sea of Moyle between Ireland and Scotland, then for three hundred years on Erris Head in Mayo, after which the spell would be finally broken by the sound of a bell of the new religion that would have come into Ireland by then. Then she sang:

> *'Out on the lake with you, children of Lir!*
> *Cry with the water-fowl over the mere!*
> *Breed and seed of you ne'er shall I see;*
> *Woeful the tale to your friends shall be.'*

She rode home and told Lir with a great show of grief that the children had drowned while swimming. But Lir could not altogether believe this and rode to the lake to see for himself what had happened. At the lake he saw four swans swimming near the shore and talking in words he could understand. Seeing him, the swans flocked around Lir and Finola told him what had happened. They begged Lir to change them back but not even his magic could undo the spell.

Aoife was brought before her foster father Bodb for judgement and after hearing the whole tale he said to her: 'This treachery will prove worse for you than for them, Aoife, for they shall be released in time, but your punishment will last forever.' Then he struck her with his druid wand and she turned into a Demon of the Air, flying shrieking from the hall.

The Tuatha took turns from that day forward to visit the four swans that were the Children of Lir, and this was no mere duty because the sweetness of their singing was reward enough in itself. No such music, say the chroniclers, was ever heard in Ireland before. The sick and broken-hearted forgot their woes, the angry forgot their rage and the jealous their fears, and not just for the duration of a song. A mood of peace and gentleness spread out from Lake Davra across Erin in those days.

After the Sons of Mil came to the island and seized it from the Tuatha, they also used to visit the lake to marvel at the music of the swans. After three hundred years the Children of Lir were condemned by their curse to move to the lonely and wild Sea of Moyle, so they bade farewell and flew away, and the Milesians made it a law in Ireland that no man should harm a swan from that day for fear it might be them.

Only once in the next three hundred years did the Children of Lir see any friends, when the Sons of Bodb managed to find them and tell them all the news of home. Then at last they were free to fly to Erris Head, which was a bit less wild but almost as lonely.

During this last three hundred years St Patrick brought Christianity to Ireland and the Tuatha withdrew even further from the visible world of men, so when finally the Children of Lir were free to leave Erris and went flying to find the palaces of their friends, all they found was ruins. They did not know that the Tuatha lived on invisibly within the mounds and met no-one to tell them this. So in despair they returned to Erris and their only remaining friend, the Lonely Crane of Inniskea who to this day is said to guard the holy well on the tiny island of Innis Glora, off the coast of Mayo.

There they did not see anyone else till one day some monks landed on the island and built a church there. When their bell first rang out on the island the other swans were terrified but Finola recognised the sound as signalling the end of their enchantment. After instruction and telling their tale, the four swans were baptised and this returned to human form, breaking Aoife's spell at last; but then their age caught up with them and in a short while they withered and died and were buried on the island while their souls entered heaven.

CHAPTER 3

Triumph of the Humans

Arrival of the Sons of Mil

FROM OUR POINT OF VIEW one of the mysteries of the faerie retreat into their Otherworld is why? If they were so gifted, talented and skilled in the ways of magic, why did they lose their battles and have to concede the daylight world to humans?

The old manuscripts that chronicle this curious and supposedly historical event have little explanation to offer except that Mil and his people had druids whose magic could counter that of the Tuatha; also that they too were of divine descent, coming from the Otherworld. Beyond that it was simply accepted as a fact of history that the ancestors of the Gael defeated the gods and took over their land. Possibly there were reasons which seemed so self-evident at the time that there seemed no need to spell them out for the audience. Something like an explanation does come however in a much more recent body of myth by Tolkien in which one of the undercurrents of the main drama is that the age of Elves and magic is drawing to a close and the more prosaic age of Man is about to begin.

Much of Tolkien's inspiration for creating his Elvish language (and thence the *Lord of the Rings* as a peg to hang it on) came from seeing, as a child in Birmingham, England, railway trucks bound to or from nearby Wales and marked up in the Welsh language. Fascination with this strange and (to him at the time) incomprehensible script led to his interest in old languages and from there, he said, to the ideas that underlay them, especially mythology. Only then, apparently, when looking for digestible stories in which to use his invented languages and mythology as a background, did he find that he was also a master storyteller; though this might have been guessed from the crowds that flocked to his lectures in Oxford when he gave readings of ancient Anglo-Saxon poetry.

Although Tolkien drew on Anglo-Saxon and other mythologies for his *magnum opus* it is Celtic faerie lore that pervades it – the solemn and beautiful sadness of the elves leaving Middle Earth for their Otherworld across the sea to the West, and the love between humans and elves that often demands terribly final choices.

Some legends say that after their defeat of the Fomorians, the Tuatha ruled for four centuries before they were challenged by the Sons of Mil, the ancestors of the present day Gael in Ireland. After Lugh, the Daghda became High King for eighty years, then his eldest son Bodb the Red. He was followed by Ciarmat Honey-Mouth who was succeeded by his three sons Mac Cuill, Mac Cecht and Mac Greine who were ruling jointly when the Milesians arrived. Their names mean respectively son of the Hazel, the tree of inspiration; son of the ploughshare, the instrument for taming the land; and son of the sun, the source of the land's fertility.

The origins of the Sons of Mil as given in the *Book of Invasions* is generally accepted as a highly fanciful attempt by Christian scholars to tie them in with biblical and classical history, with only the faintest foundation in fact. It says they originated in Scythia, north east of the Black Sea and from there they gradually migrated down into Egypt and then westwards across the Mediterranean to Spain. Even this final destination is disputed, with suggestions that the scribes simply substituted 'Spain' for the mythical Otherworld of the Celts: Tir na nOg, Avalon, or the Summer Isles.

However, 'Spain' is where the story begins. Here their leader Bregon built a great watchtower from which one clear winter evening his son Ith saw an island far out over the sea that he had never noticed before. Curious, he set sail with thirty warriors and landed in the mouth of what is now called the Kenmare River in County Kerry. The country seemed deserted to them so they marched north till finally at Aileach near Derry they met the three current Kings of the Tuatha Mac Cuill, Mac Cecht and Mac Greine who were debating how to divide the country between them. They invited Ith to join their debate but were so alarmed by his enthusiastic praise of Ireland's blessings, its gentle climate and its richness in fruit, honey, grain and fish, that they feared his intentions, set a trap and killed him.

The survivors of Ith's company sailed back to Spain with his body and the grief and anger of his kindred was so great that Ith's nephew Mil (or Mile) determined to get revenge. With his eight sons, led by the eldest, Donn, and thirty-six other chiefs, each with their own shipload of warriors, they set sail and landed in Kerry on the first of May. The druid Amergin (Amairgen) was the first to set foot on Irish soil and burst into a prophetic chant very characteristic of the ancient Celts which was also a kind of charm for taking possession of the land:

'I am the wind that blows upon the sea; I am the ocean wave; I am the roar of the tides; I am the bull of seven battles; I am an eagle on a cliff I am a ray of the sun; I am the fairest of flowers; I am a bold wild boar; I am a salmon in the pool; I am a lake upon a plain; I am a cunning word; I am a giant sword-wielding champion; I am a god with a fiery head; In what direction shall we go? Shall we hold our council in the valley or on the mountain top? Where shall we make our home? What land is better than this isle of the setting sun? Where shall we walk to and fro in peace and safety? Who can find you clear fountains as I can? Who can call fish from the depths of the sea as I can? Who can call them to the shore as I can? Who can change the shape of the hills and headlands as I can? I am a bard who is called on by sailors to prophesy. Javelins shall fly to avenge our wrongs. I prophesy victory. I close my song by prophesying all other good things.'

The Milesians (as they came to be called) began their march on the capital at Tara. Along the way they met the goddess Banba, wife of Mac Cuill. She greeted Amergin with the words: 'If you have come to conquer Ireland, your cause is not just.'

'Certainly we have come to conquer,' Amergin replied honestly.

'Then grant me this,' said Banba, 'that if you succeed you will name the island after me.'

'Surely,' replied Amergin.

They continued and soon afterwards met another goddess called Fotla, the wife of Mac Cecht who made the same request, and was given the same reply.

Then at the Hill of Uisneach, at the heart of Ireland, they met a third goddess Eriu, the wife of Mac Greine.

Welcome warriors,' she greeted them. 'To you who have sailed from afar this island shall henceforth belong, and from the rising to the setting sun there is no fairer land; and your people will be the most perfect the world has seen.'

'That is a fair greeting and a good prophecy,' Amergin replied, thanking her.

But then Mil's eldest son Donn broke in rudely, saying to the Tuatha queen: 'But it will be no thanks to your prophecy. Whatever victory we win here will be due to our own might.'

'What I prophesy does not concern you,' Eriu rebuked him sharply, 'for neither you nor your descendants will live to enjoy this land.' Which proved to be perfectly true because he died soon after. Turning back to Amergin she too asked that Ireland might be named after her.

'It will be its principal name,' he assured her. And that indeed came about because of the three ancient names for Ireland, Erin (the Isle of Eriu) is the one that survives to this day.

This curious incident with the three goddesses of Ireland seems to show that they were turning their backs on the Tuatha in order to welcome the Sons of Mil, either because they were bowing to the inevitable or for some other reason that has not survived in the tale. Possibly they had grown impatient with their three husbands for their squabble over dividing the land; or possibly it was that Milesian bards introduced the episode later to justify their invasion and prove that the goddesses representing the land welcomed the newcomers from the beginning and approved their taking possession.

The Sons of Mil and their host arrived at Tara where they were met by Mac Cuill, Mac Cecht and Mac Greine, with a corresponding host of the Tuatha. They sat down to parley and the Tuatha complained that they had been caught off guard by the invasion. The Milesians admitted that it was not chivalrous to invade a country without warning, so the Tuatha then proposed that the Milesians should leave the island for three days to give them time either to prepare for war, or decide whether to surrender the land peacefully.

The Milesians were not happy with this suggestion, fearing the Tuatha would raise magical winds and storms to prevent them landing again (which indeed was exactly their plan). After some debate the three Kings of the Tuatha nominated their opponents' druid Amergin to come up with a fair solution, on pain of death should it be too obviously partial to his own side. Amergin proposed that the Milesians should indeed put out to sea again, but only for the distance of nine waves. Then if they managed to get back to land, possession of the island would pass to whoever won the ensuing battle, with a stipulation that the victors should be merciful and fair to the losers.

This judgement was accepted by both parties and the Milesians went back to their ships while the Tuatha drew up in battle formation on the shore. Then, just as the Sons of Mil had feared, a strong wind sprang up blowing from the land out to sea. The Milesians strained on their oars but could make no progress against it. Donn sent a man up the mast who reported that the air was quite still up there, so they knew it was a druidical wind. So Amergin cried out a spell of his own that invoked the powers of the island itself:

'I seek the land of Eriu
Coursed be the fruitful sea
Fruitful the ranked hills
Ranked the showery forest
Showery the river of cataracts
Of cataracts the lake of pools
Of pools the hill of a well
Of a well of a people of assemblies
Of assemblies of the Kings of Tara
Tara, hill of peoples
Peoples of the Sons of Mil
Of Mil of ships, of barques
The high ship Eriu
Eriu lofty and green
An incantation very cunning.'

This broke the power of the wind because, as we saw with the episode of the three goddesses, the island of Eriu wanted to receive the newcomers. But then Manannan mac Lir called up a tempest out of the ocean that scattered the Milesians' ships. Donn and three other sons of Mil drowned along with many of their followers. After a long struggle the survivors came ashore at last, then gathered their forces and marched on the Tuatha. Two great battles were fought, one in the Slieve Mish mountains on the Dingle Peninsula and the other at Telltown or Tailtiu in County Meath. The Tuatha lost both battles and their three Kings were killed by the three surviving Sons of Mil – the druid Amergin, Eremon and Eber.

Eremon and Eber then had an argument over who should rule, which they settled by dividing the land into northern and southern halves, Eremon taking the north and Eber the south. This only postponed the day of reckoning though because at the end of a year war broke out again. Eber died and Eremon became High King of all Ireland.

The Tuatha meanwhile divided, some sailing away westwards to the Land of the Young, Tir na nOg and some retreating into the parallel world whose gateways were the faerie mounds and hills, the sidhe (pronounced shee) from which they derived their later name: the People or Riders of the Sidhe, often abbreviated simply to the Sidhe, which could mean either the faeries or their mounds. Some say that what happened was that those Tuatha who died in the battle were buried in the faerie mounds, and those that survived sailed away; but if this is so having died made little difference to the Tuatha's activites. They carried on as busily as before only largely invisibly from the eyes of humans.

When it comes to exactly how the Tuatha remaining in Ireland divided and organised themselves we have several different accounts in the old manuscripts. Those used by Lady Gregory in her magnificent *Gods and Fighting Men* (1904) say that they asked Manannan mac Lir to decide things for them before his departure to the west, on account of his great age and wisdom. He portioned out the most beautiful hills and valleys for them to settle in and raised magical walls around these places so they were hidden from human eyes and only the Tuatha could come and go as they pleased.

This was done at the great Feast of Age that he hosted and where they drank the ale of Goibniu the Smith, that kept all who tasted it from sickness and death. At this feast too they decided to select for themselves a new King to replace the three killed by the Sons of Mil. The five candidates they chose were Bodb Dearg, eldest son of the Daghda, Ilbrech of Ess Ruadh, Lir of the Hill of the White Field on Slieve Fuad, Midir the Proud of Bri Leith and Angus Og.

A problem with this account is that it repeats a line of succession given elsewhere that ends in the rule of the three Tuatha Kings who have just been killed by the Sons of Mil. Yet other versions of the tale say that it was the Daghda who portioned out the faerie mounds at this point, that Angus Og had not yet been born and that his mischievous tricking of the Daghda out of his own palace at Brugh na Boyne took place after the Tuatha's retreat into the hills.

There is no definitive version of events and the confusion arises from different scholars trying to map out a chronology that was absent from the original tales they were transcribing, because they operated within the time scale of immortals, which is fluid and dreamy. What matters at points of historical confusion like this is the broad picture, which is that after their overthrow by the Sons of Mil the Tuatha continued to live a vibrant life of their own in their parallel world, but then increasingly withdrew from centre stage.

Yet other versions of their settlement with humans tell that it was neither the Daghda nor Manannan who decided events after their defeat but a previously obscure member of the Tuatha called Finvarra (Fionnbharr, Fin Bheara or Finbar, meaning 'bright hair'). Here we can cut right through the contradictions to their end, which is that whatever the ins and outs of it, the High King of the faeries who emerged from their new condition was Finvarra, who is said to still rule them today from the faerie hill of Knockma in Galway, just west of Tuam, with his wife Onagh. As High King he has taken over the Daghda's ancient duties of assisting the harvest and wellbeing of livestock, and is also sometimes spoken of as the King of the Dead. He brings great wealth to those he favours, in particular the family of the Kirwans of Castlehackett on the northern slopes of Knockma, who prospered for many years under his patronage and were especially successful in horse racing.

Despite his wife Onagh being more beautiful than any human female, Finvarra is famous for his many dalliances with mortal women, and after being seduced by him few have been able to settle for a mortal husband. He is also a great fidchell and chess player, and many men have lost heavily to him that way too.

PART 2

Retreat into the Hills

CHAPTER 4

Meetings & Exchanges

When the faeries retreated from our world into their parallel one it was far from the end of their interaction with humans. Celtic legends are full of tales of encounters and even exchanges, where sometimes humans swapped places with faeries in order to set one or other of their worlds to rights. It is a curiosity of human-faerie relations that while they can do many things in our world that seem magical, we have certain strengths in theirs that they lack, which is presumably how humans came to conquer them in the first place. The gateways between the two worlds were and still are in many cases well known – faerie mounds, holy wells, caves, fords and mountains where, especially at crucial turning points of the year, one could in the misty past easily wander into the faerie dimension, or meet them wandering in ours. Many such places are still honoured by pilgrims and many Celtic hills still have the reputation that if you survive a night at the top alone, you will return at dawn either mad or a poet, thanks to the approval or otherwise of the faeries.

This book has until now concentrated on Irish legends, but only because they best documented the very earliest times. Parallel tales must have once circulated in the other Celtic lands because whatever their own particular legends of how it came about, the very same relationship between humans and faeries existed. In Scotland this is perfectly understandable because Scottish lore is taken directly from Ireland due to migration; but it is less obvious in Wales because the Celts arrived there by a quite different route. Their languages were close enough for them to be able understand each other but the differences are also distinct enough to suggest a separate evolution for centuries before the two groups met again in the British Isles. The same goes for their legends. Although localised to their own countries, the legends of each Celtic group have broad similarities, though with many differences in detail that mirror the separate evolution of their languages.

In Wales the old pagan legends are much more fragmentary. There are recognisable parallels in the pantheon – Don and Danu, Manawydan and Manannan, Lleu and Lugh for example – but there is no equivalent legend of how humans drove the faeries underground or across the sea. The British Celts must have had such a legend though, to account for their same relationship with the faeries.

Once we come to the period following the faerie withdrawal though, we are on much firmer ground because the *Mabinogion* and other collections are full of magical tales of human-faerie interactions.

Pwyll, Lord of Dyfed

One of the most famous examples of a faerie exchange is the story in the Welsh *Mabinogion* of Pwyll, lord of the seven cantreds of Dyfed. One day as he was out hunting near Glyn Cych, between Cenarth and Llechry, he became separated from his companions while chasing his hounds. Pressing on through the woods, he heard the baying of another pack ahead. Then, bursting into a clearing he saw some marvellous shining white hounds with red ears bringing down a stag in the midst of the glade.

He should have known these were faerie hounds because this was well known to be the colouring of their dogs and cattle, but in the heat of the chase Pwyll thought little of it and drove them away so his own hounds could finish off the stag. Then another hunter came galloping into the clearing on a pale grey steed. He was dressed in green-grey, a favourite colour of the faeries, and had a hunting horn slung around his neck.

He was furious. 'How have I deserved this insult?' he cried. 'That you should chase off my dogs so yours can steal their prize? This theft will cost you more than a hundred stags.'

Pwyll, being an honourable and decent man, immediately regretted his haste and asked the stranger what he could do to make amends.

Perhaps not by accident, the stranger immediately came up with a very clear plan for how Pwyll could redeem himself. Introducing himself as Arawn, a King of Annwyn, the faerie Otherworld, he explained that he had feud with a rival King in Annwyn named Havgan, whom he was due to meet for a duel at a ford in exactly a year's time. What Arawn proposed was that Pwyll and he should swap places for a year, disguised by his magic so that not even their closest friends would be able to tell. Then once Pwyll had defeated Havgan, they would change places back again.

So Pwyll went to Arawn's palace in the Otherworld and so successful was his faerie disguise that not even Arawn's beautiful wife guessed what had happened, though she was very puzzled by her husband's sudden avoidance of bedtime intimacies. For a year Pwyll hunted and feasted and enjoyed the pleasures of Arawn's court that was 'of all the Courts upon the earth, the best supplied with food and drink, and vessels of gold and royal jewels.'

Then the day of the contest at the ford with Havgan dawned and the hosts on either side gathered to watch. First it was formally agreed, as was often the ancient Celtic custom, that none but the two Kings would fight, and that whoever won the contest would take possession of the whole realm of the other. Then mounting their horses the battle commenced. As luck (or some other enchantment) would have it, on their first clash Pwyll's lance shattered Havgan's shield and knocked him over his horse's crupper (as medieval tales were fond of saying) with a mortal wound.

Havgan then begged to be put out of his misery, but luckily Arawn had warned Pwyll against this when their agreement was first made. If he gave Havgan a second blow it was certain that he would only spring up again stronger than ever. So Pwyll refused and turned away, saying: 'Slay thee who will, I will not.'

So Havgan was carried off by some followers to die at his own pace. Pwyll then accepted the allegiance of his nobles, challenging and doing battle with any who refused to bend the knee. Within a day the two rival Kingdoms of Annwyn were united and then Pwyll left to meet Arawn at the appointed time and place. They exchanged appearances again as agreed, and when each returned to his own Kingdom he was more than happy with reports of their conduct over the past year; and Arawn's beautiful wife was as happy with her husband's suddenly renewed affections as he was to hear that she had been neglected for a year.

Thus great friendship sprang up between the two realms with many exchanges of goods and treasures that did much to ensure the prosperity of Dyfed in those days; and when Pwyll told the true story to his people they gave him the title Chief of Arawn as well as Prince of Dyfed.

Rhiannon and Pwyll

A while after his year in the Otherworld, Pwyll went to the Mound of Arberth near his palace at Narberth, during a feast with all his people. It was a peculiarity of this mound that whoever sat upon it would not leave without either battle or seeing a wonder. With so many friends at hand Pwyll was not much troubled by the prospect of battle, so he sat in the fateful place to see what would come. Soon he and his companions saw a beautiful lady in a dazzling golden robe riding towards them on a pure white horse. 'Do any of you recognise her?' Pwyll asked his fellows. None did, so he sent one of them to intercept her on foot to see who she was. No matter how fast he ran, though, he could not catch up as she rode at a seemingly casual pace past the mound and away into the distance.

The next day the same party again left the feast and went to the mound, this time taking with them the swiftest horse in the stable. Once again when Pwyll sat on the mound the shining lady and her mount appeared, coming along the road at a casual pace. A rider was sent to meet her but though he rode the horse half to death, he came no closer to catching her up than had the runner the day before.

On the third day Pwyll himself determined to try and catch the lady. They went to the mound again and when she appeared he mounted up and rode after her; but no matter how hard he spurred and lashed his horse the distance between them remained the same, even though she seemed but to be trotting along casually. Finally he called out desperately: 'Lady, in the name of whoever you love best, please wait.'

'Gladly,' she replied, reining in, 'and it would have been kinder on your horse to have asked sooner.'

She threw back her veil to face him and Pwyll thought he had never before seen any woman more beautiful. He asked where she had come from and where she was going.

'I journey on my own errand,' she replied, 'and glad I am to see you.'

'Why?' he asked, overcome with wonder.

'Because my purpose was to meet you.'

Again he asked why, and who she was.

'I am Rhiannon, the daughter of Heveydd Hen,' she replied and went on to explain that her people were trying to force her into marriage against her will but for love of Pwyll she would marry no-one but him, if he would have her. Well by now Pwyll was completely in love with her and so he happily agreed. Rhiannon said it could be so if only he promised to meet her a year from that day at her father's palace. Then she left and when Pwyll returned to his people he said nothing of what had passed between him and his newly promised bride.

A year later he gathered a hundred knights and led them to Heveydd Hen's palace where they found a great wedding feast prepared. Pwyll was seated in the place of honour with Rhiannon on one side and her father on the other, and the father indeed seemed happy that the wedding should go ahead. Then after the main course as they relaxed into the wine and entertainment a tall, auburn-haired youth clothed in satin entered the hall with a commanding air and walked straight up to Pwyll between the tables. Bowing courteously, he asked the happy bridegroom for a favour. Pwyll, flushed with wine and joy, grandly replied that if it lay within his power, he would give the stranger whatever he asked.

Rhiannon gave a sharp cry of dismay: 'Why did you say that?' she asked.

The stranger smiled: 'But he did say it, in front of the whole company.'

Pwyll was suddenly troubled at the turn of events. 'What is this favour you wish from me?' he asked. The stranger then asked for Rhiannon's hand in marriage, because he was none other than Gwawl, the one her family had tried to force her to marry before against her will. Pwyll was thrown into despair. In the circumstances he was honour-bound to fulfil his pledge, but how could he do so? Rhiannon however had a plan.

'Bestow me upon him,' she told Pwyll, 'but I will make sure that I never become his bride.'

So it was settled that a year from that day there would be another feast at which Rhiannon would become Gwawl's bride; and when they were alone Rhiannon explained to Pwyll the stratagem by which he could prevent it happening.

A year passed and Pwyll returned to Heveydd Hen's palace. In keeping with Rhiannon's plan, his hundred knights hid in the orchard outside and Pwyll went on in alone, disguised as a beggar and carrying a magic bag which she had given him. The power of this bag was that no matter how much was put into it, it could never be filled. The wedding feast of Gwawl and Rhiannon was in full swing when Pwyll entered. Approaching the groom, Pwyll asked for a favour.

'Anything within reason,' replied Gwawl, being more cautious than Pwyll himself had been a year before.

'All I ask,' said Pwyll, 'is that this bag of mine be filled with meat so that I shall not go hungry.'

'That is a reasonable enough request,' said Gwawl, and ordered his servants to fill the bag; but no matter how much meat they put into it, there still remained room for more.

'My soul,' exclaimed Gwawl, 'will your bag never be full?'

'Not until a great lord shall stamp down the food with both feet and declare: "Enough has been put herein",' said Pwyll.

At Rhiannon's urging Gwawl left his place and stepped with both feet into the bag. Whereupon Pwyll quickly tied it tight over his head and blew a horn to call his men. They rushed in before anyone could gather their wits and disarmed Gwawl's followers. Then they beat the bag until Gwawl cried for mercy.

He was released on condition that he renounced all claim to Rhiannon's hand, and swore not to seek revenge for the trick played upon him. Then Pwyll and his men took their places at the feast and, as the *Mabinogion* says: 'they ate, and feasted, and spent the night in mirth and tranquillity. And the time came that they should sleep, and Pwyll and Rhiannon went to their chamber.'

Thus Pwyll won for himself a faerie bride and in due course (though not without much further adventure) she bore him a son, Pryderi (Peredur) of the golden hair who came to rule not just the seven cantreds of Dyfed, but seven others as well, becoming one of the most noble Kings of Britain.

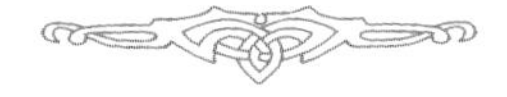

Rhiannon

Rhiannon was no ordinary Welsh faerie princess. Under various names (Epona, Edain) she was one of the most revered goddesses of the pagan Celts across Europe, and one of the few actively adopted by the Romans as Rigantona or Bubona after their conquest of Gaul, rather than just tolerated or assimilated with one of their own goddesses in their usual way. She is the only Celtic deity to whom they dedicated a feast on 18 December, though the Celts themselves had a second feast on 13 June, at the opposite pole of the year.

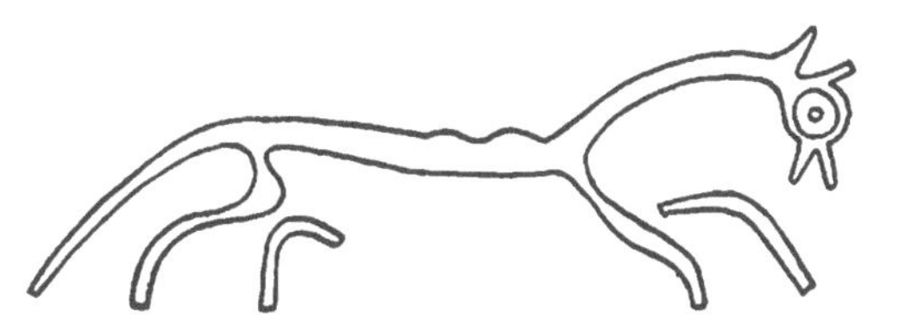

There are over 300 known shrines to Epona in France alone and the reason for this was that she was the goddess of horses, and this reflects the importance of that beast to both the Celts and Romans. In Britain the White Horse of Uffington and similar hill carvings of horses are assumed to have been dedicated to Epona and in the tale of Pwyll it is no coincidence that he first meets her riding a white horse.

Symbolically, Rhiannon was not just a horse goddess, she also represented the land and its fertility, so by uniting with Pwyll she was bestowing legitimacy on his rule, as was the case in Ireland when the three goddesses greeted and approved the Sons of Mil. Gerald of Wales recorded (with some distaste) the custom of some Irish Kings of symbolically marrying a horse which was then butchered and stewed and eaten at a feast presided over by the King. Behind the apparent barbarity of the custom, as Gerald perceived it, was the symbolic re-enactment of the King mystically marrying his realm and fertilising it with his seed.

Pwyll however seems to have barely appreciated the honour Rhiannon was doing by marrying him and leaving her own faerie world to live with him at Narberth, though it all started very promisingly. When he brought her back to his palace a great feast was held to which all the nobles of Pwyll's realm were invited. Rhiannon charmed them with her beauty and grace and the generosity with which she gave them rings, precious stones and jewellery, the customary means by which Celtic rulers secured the loyalty of their vassals and allies.

For two years Dyfed prospered under their joint rule but then discontent began to rumble because there was no sign of Rhiannon producing an heir. Some say this was because of the sorcery of her jilted suitor Gwawl. Whether or not this was so, the discontent gathered pace because Pwyll was not a young man and people wanted to see his dynasty safely established before some mischance carried him off. So his people came to Pwyll at Prescelly and urged him to take another wife, otherwise he might not long count on their loyalty.

Pwyll asked them to grant him another year, and if nothing had changed by then he would consider their demand. Luckily Rhiannon conceived soon afterwards and a son was born to her within the year. Six women were brought to watch over the mother and babe that night, but it so happened that they all fell asleep and when they woke at dawn the child had disappeared. In a panic and thinking they would be blamed and punished severely for this, the women concocted a dreadful plan to shift the blame onto Rhiannon herself.

A hound in the palace had recently given birth, so they killed some of the cubs, scattered their bones around Rhiannon and smeared blood over her face and hands. Then when Rhiannon awoke they told her that in the night she had killed and eaten her baby, lashing violently out at the women who had tried to stop her. And this was the tale they carried to Pwyll.

Shock spread throughout the land as news spread of the dreadful crime Rhiannon was supposed to have committed. The nobles came and urged Pwyll to put her away and take another wife, but he replied that the only reason he might have divorced her was if she had been unable to bear children, and she had proved otherwise. As for the killing, he would be satisfied if she did penance for it, because he was sure it had only happened in some fit of madness.

Rhiannon agreed to do penance because she had little choice but to believe the six women; and the penance she was given was that for seven years she would stand by the horse block that was at the palace gate in Narberth and tell her story to every stranger that passed. Also that she should offer to carry visitors into the palace on her back like a horse, if they would permit it, though few did. This is the way she passed the next year, and several more too.

Now on the night Rhiannon's child disappeared a strange adventure had befallen Teirnyon, the lord of Gwent Is Coed who had found a golden-haired newborn baby on his doorstep wrapped in a satin mantle. As he and his wife had no son they adopted him as their own, telling people she had given birth to him the normal way. The boy grew remarkably fast. By the end of his first year he was as big as any other boy of three; and by the end of the second he was as large as a child of six; and by the end of his fourth year he was big enough to ride a full grown horse.

Teirnyon and his wife took great delight in their precocious son, who was as charming as he was talented and handsome. But word reached them of Rhiannon's penance for killing her own child, and the more he heard, the more a suspicion of the truth formed in Teirnyon's mind. He made enquiries and learned that it had happened the very night they had found their own boy. Then, having once served with Pwyll, he noticed more and more the boy's resemblance to him. Finally he and his wife decided they could let Rhiannon suffer no more, so they rode to Pwyll's court at Narberth where they told the truth of their discovery of the boy and let everyone marvel for themselves at the likeness between him and Pwyll and Rhiannon.

No-one doubted that Rhiannon's lost son had been found, and that she had been the victim of a horribly cruel trick. When she heard this Rhiannon said: 'I declare to Heaven that if all this be true, there is indeed an end to my anxiety.' And as 'anxiety' is 'Pryderi' in Welsh that is what the boy was called from that day.

When Pwyll died, Pryderi became Lord of Dyfed in his place and in due course his mother Rhainnon married Manawyddan son of Llyr, the Welsh counterpart of Manannan mac Lir in Ireland.

The Wooing of Branwen

When Rhiannon married Manawyddan she moved to Harlech or, as it was then called, Branwen's Tower where they held court with the other children of Llyr, the giant Bran who was then King of Britain and his sister Branwen of the Fair Bosom, plus two half brothers of Manawyddan by a different father called Nissyen and Evnissyen. Nissyen was a lover of peace and was always called upon to settle arguments; but Evnissyen delighted in stirring up trouble.

As they sat on the cliff one day gazing out to sea they saw thirteen ships coming over from Ireland. The visitor turned out to be Matholwch, King of Ireland, who had come to ask Bran for his sister's hand in marriage. She happily consented to this and the wedding was celebrated at Aberffraw in Anglesey, where a great pavilion was erected because there was no house there, or indeed anywhere else, big enough to contain the giant Bran. All went well at the feast until Evnissyen, who had been away all this time, learned of the wedding. He was furious that they had not waited for his consent before going ahead; and out of spite he cut off the lips, ears, eyebrows, and tails of all the horses which Matholwch had brought over with him.

The Irish King was furious and war could have broken out but Bran made peace by replacing all the mutilated horses and giving Matholwch a staff of silver as tall as himself, a plate of gold as large as his face and a magic cauldron of the Tuatha which had been brought over years before from Ireland. Its property was that any dead man who was put into it came to life again, only without the gift of speech. Matholwch accepted these gifts gracefully and made peace again with the Children of Llyr before sailing home with his new bride.

Before the year was out Branwen bore a son, Gwern, and all was going happily until the next year when news came to Ireland of the insult that Matholwch had endured in Britain. All his kin thought he had been far too easily appeased and insisted that the King revenge himself upon Branwen. So she was banished to serve in the kitchen where every day the butcher boxed her ears. In order that this should not come to the notice of her family, all traffic between Ireland and Britain was banned, and thus Branwen was humiliated for three years. However she reared a tame starling and taught it to speak. Then she told it how to find Branwen's Tower in Harlech and attached a letter to its wing for her brother.

When Bran learned how his sister was being treated he raised an army to cross over to Ireland, leaving his son Caradawc and seven others in charge of Britain. Bran was too large for any ship to hold so he just waded across the Irish Sea at the head of his fleet. Some swineherds who had been tending their herds on the Irish shore ran to Matholwch with the news that a mountain and a strange forest were advancing across the sea towards Ireland. No-one could understand what they meant until Branwen said: 'It is the men of the Island of the Mighty (a bardic name for Britain), who are coming because they have heard of my ill-treatment. The forest is the masts of their ships and the mountain is my brother Bran.'

The men of Ireland were terrified and fled beyond the Shannon, destroying the bridge behind them; but Bran just lay down across the river and his army marched across his back. Matholwch now sued for peace, offering to hand the throne of Ireland to Gwern, his son by Branwen; to which Bran replied: 'Why should I not just take the Kingdom for myself?'

To pacify him, Matholwch offered to build a house so large that it would be the first that ever could hold Bran. He consented to this and the vast house was built, but on each of the hundred pillars of the house a bag was hung, and in each bag was an armed warrior ready to leap out when a signal was given at the feast. But when Evnissyen inspected the mansion and saw the bags he was suspicious. 'What is in this bag?' he asked one of the Irish.

'Just meal,' came the reply. So Evnissyen kneaded the bag as if it

had been meal, crushing the man within; and this he did to every one of the bags in turn.

Soon the two hosts met for the feast, the men of Ireland on one side of the long blazing hearth and the men of Britain on the other. They sat down and then Gwern was crowned King of Ireland in his father's place. The new King then went to meet his uncles from Britain, Bran and Manawyddan and Nissyen, who all greeted him kindly and it looked as though peace had been restored between the two islands. But when he came to Evnissyen, the mischief-maker seized him by the feet and threw him straight into the blazing fire.

Branwen tried to leap into the flames after him but was held back by Bran. Then battle broke out and never was such a din heard in any one house before. Day after day they fought and the battle began to turn against the men of Britain because every Irishman they killed was thrown into the cauldron and brought back to life again. Evnissyen, who by now regretted his rash misdeed, saw a way of making amends. Disguising himself as an Irishman, he lay on the floor as if dead and was thrown into the cauldron after the others. There he stretched himself and with a mighty effort burst both the cauldron and his own heart.

With the balance now restored, in the next battle the men of Britain killed all the fighting men of Ireland, but of their own number only seven remained, including Manawyddan, Taliesin the bard and Pryderi the son of Pwyll and Rhiannon.

Bran himself was dying in agony from a poisoned dart, so he ordered the surviving seven to cut off his head and bear it to the White Mount in London, where they were to bury it facing France. He also prophesied the course of this journey – that on the way they would feast for seven years in Harlech, with the birds of Rhiannon singing to them all the while and Bran's own head conversing with them as entertainingly as ever he had done in life; then they would be eighty years feasting in Gwales, the isle of Gresholm off the Pembrokeshire coast; then someone would open the door facing Cornwall and this would break the happy spell and signal the time to head for London.

So they beheaded Bran and set sail for Britain, landing at the mouth of the river Alaw in Anglesey. There grief finally overcame Branwen. Looking first back at Ireland and then at their own tiny remainder of the host that had set sail, she cried: 'Alas that I was ever born! The mighty of two islands have been destroyed because of me'. Then her heart broke and she died on the shore, being buried there at the spot known ever since as Ynys Branwen.

The seven continued towards Harlech and on the way heard that disaster had befallen Britain in their absence. A usurper named Caswallawn had destroyed the regents Bran had left to rule the country and his son Caradawc had killed himself in shame. Caswallawn had made himself King of all Britain in the place of Manawyddan, son of Llyr, its rightful heir now that Bran was dead. However, they continued as they had promised Bran, and the journey happened just as he had foretold. At Harlech they feasted happily for seven years to the music of the three birds of Rhiannon, beside which all other songs sounded like the croaking of crows. Then they feasted fourscore years on the Isle of Gwales, entertained all the while by the pleasant conversation of Bran's head.

Then someone opened the door facing Cornwall and the spell broke.

Despite eighty-seven years of merriment, grief finally overcame them and sorrow rushed in. The head fell silent and they raced to London to bury it in the White Mount, where the Tower of London now stands. There it sat guarding the country till King Arthur rashly dug it up, saying it was beneath his dignity to defend the land with anything but valour. In the Welsh triads this is called one of the 'Three Wicked Uncoverings of Britain' because of the disastrous invasions that followed Arthur's death.

Earlier we met several of the principal deities of the Tuatha in Ireland. This may be a good place to look in detail at another one who plays a great part in the later tales – Manannan mac Lir.

When in Ireland the Tuatha surrendered the everyday world to the Sons of Mil, some withdrew into the faerie mounds but Manannan mac Lir was among those who moved to the Land of Youth over the western ocean. Some say he died in battle with the Sons of Mil and was buried standing upright; Lake Orbson (now Lough Corrib) springing into being from the spot. Even if true, death for the Tuatha, as we have seen before, was not the same as for mortals, often involving no more than a temporary departure.

Possibly that is what happened to Manannan because, as with other Tuatha, despite his reported death in some legends he continued to visit the Celtic lands from time to time and play a major part in their affairs. In fact he became one of the most popular gods of all in pagan times and was almost certainly considered their High King at some point.

Sometimes, it is said, Manannan took the guise of a mortal to move and live among the Gaels undetected. It is rumoured that Culainn, the smith who gave his name to the famous Cuchulainn, the Hound of Ulster, may have been none other than Manannan in such disguise. Certainly Conchobar mac Nessa, the King of Ulster recruited his blacksmith from the Isle of Falga, another name for the Isle of Man, on the advice of a druid. Later Manannan is said to have often hunted with Finn and the Fianna (or Fenians) on the hill of Knockainey.

In the nineteenth century Lady Gregory collected some old tales of Manannan's wanderings in Ireland in disguise playing comical tricks on people, no doubt with some faerie trickster purpose of teaching them a lesson or two, though after centuries of retelling these lessons are often obscure. In one tale he visits the house of a great lord, appearing suddenly in the midst of a feast looking like a tramp fresh from sleeping in the bushes. He politely wishes the lord good health and the lord calls for his gatekeeper to ask why he had let this vagabond in. The gatekeeper said he had never seen the stranger before.

'Let him be,' Manannan told the lord, 'because it was as easy for me to enter this house without your gatekeeper noticing as it will be for me to leave again.'

The lord was impressed enough by this to let his scruffy visitor sit at the foot of the table and the feast continued, with all the best musicians of the land playing on their harps and lutes. This was interrupted after a while by the stranger exclaiming loudly: 'Upon my word, I never heard a clamour of hammers beating on iron that was so hard on the ears as this racket your musicians are making!'

With that he took a harp from one of them and began playing so beautifully that it would put to sleep a wounded man or a woman in labour. The lord of the feast declared: 'Since I first heard mention of the music of the Sidhe that is played within the hills I never heard music sweeter than yours.'

'One day I am sweet, the next I am sour,' replied his guest enigmatically.

Then the lord invited him to come and sit near the head of the table but Manannan replied: 'I would sooner be as I am, an ugly fool making entertainment for the high-born.' So then the lord, thinking his rags might be why the stranger was embarrassed to accept the honour, called a servant and had him take their guest a new striped shirt and coat, but Manannan refused these as well, saying: 'I have no mind to let the nobility boast of having made a gift of such finery to me.'

By now the company had guessed they were entertaining one of the faerie folk and the lord ordered men to be placed on guard within and without the gate to prevent him leaving.

'What are those men for?' the clownish guest asked.

'To keep you from leaving,' said the lord. 'We wish to make your acquaintance better.'

'By my word, it's not with you I'll be dining tomorrow,' said his guest.

'If you try to leave between now and morning I'll have you knocked to a round lump there on the ground!' warned the lord, who was not used to being contradicted.

But his guest rose and, playing on the harp again, strolled towards the gate calling playfully to the men guarding it: 'Here I am coming now, so watch closely or you'll miss me!'

A strange frenzy seized the guards and as they tried to draw their swords and raise their axes all they succeeded in doing was slashing each other until half of them lay dead on the ground.

The gatekeeper was still standing though, so Manannan said to him: 'Let's ask your lord for twenty cows and a hundred of land as a fee for bringing his people back to life.' So this he did and the lord, by now thoroughly frightened of his guest, eagerly granted his fee. Then Manannan gave the reward to the gatekeeper along with some herbs to rub in each of the dead ones' mouths to bring them back to life, and went on his way.

This was how Manannan was said to travel round Ireland, never stopping in one place for long and entertaining people with his playing of the harp. He often played tricks on people, but whenever someone died because of them, he brought them back to life again with the magic herbs from his bag. More than once his tricks landed him on a scaffold but afterwards he was always found alive and well again nearby.

Manannan is said in some accounts to have stopped visiting Ireland after being insulted by St Columba. Up till then he had been happy enough to coexist with the new religion and continue to protect Irishmen abroad. He also continued to help with the crops and harvesting, setting his faerie workers to tend and weed the crops while humans slept. However, one day St Columba broke his golden chalice and gave it to a servant to take it for repair. On the way the servant met a ragged stranger who asked what errand he was on. He showed the broken chalice to the stranger, who breathed on it and immediately made it whole again. Then he asked the servant to return to his master with it and tell him that Manannan, son of Lir, had mended it. In payment he wanted Columba to tell him if he could ever enter the paradise that Christians spoke of.

'Alas,' said the ungrateful saint when he heard the tale, 'there is no redemption for one who does such faerie work as this.'

When the servant told Manannan this he cursed himself for having continued to help the Christians of Ireland and took himself off to

Scotland and other countries like the Isle of Man where he was better appreciated, and where he made occasional appearances into quite modern times.

In the *Contemporary Review* of October 1902 in an article titled 'Sea Magic and Running Water' Fiona Macleod told of an old crofter, Murdo MacIan, in the Outer Hebrides who claimed to be often visited by a tall beautiful stranger with a white, blue-tinged crest on his head and a cold blue flame under his feet. This stranger told him many strange and wonderful things, including the time of the old shepherd's impending death. Usually he kept his hands hidden under his white cloak but once he had touched old Murdo, who had seen that his flesh was like water, with sea-weed floating among his bones, so that he knew he was talking to Manannan mac Lir.

Apart from being given to the Isle of Man, Manannan's name was also taken by a dynasty of its human Kings who called themselves Manannan mac Lir for at least four generations, leading to much confusion in later years between their doings and those of the god.

The Boyhood of Cuchulainn

As with Manannan, the god Lugh is reported to have died in some tales, yet continued to play an occasional active part in Irish affairs and his festival on 1 August continued to be celebrated long after the arrival of Christianity. Not the least of his interventions was his part in the birth of Cuchulainn, the supreme champion of the Red Branch warriors in the great cycle of tales that built up around their exploits in the service of King Conchobar mac Nessa of Ulster.

The story goes that one day Conchobar was gazing out from the ramparts of Emain Macha (Armagh) when he saw a large flock of strange birds attacking his crops. He ordered some men to go and chase them off but no matter what they did, the birds returned as soon as they left the fields. So Conchobar ordered his chariot and, accompanied by his sister Deichtine and several Red Branch champions in other chariots, he rode out and when the birds flew off he gave chase. All day they chased the flock of strange birds without ever quite catching them up and by nightfall they found themselves by the River Boyne. Snow began to fall and they crossed the river looking for shelter for the night.

Soon they found a grand house owned by a handsome couple who made them welcome. The whole company entered and were treated to

a feast that soon drove the chill from their bones. Then their hostess went into labour and Deichtine retired with her to help with the birth. She produced a son and at the same moment there was a commotion in the stables outside. When this was investigated they found that a mare had given birth to twin foals at exactly the same time.

When Conchobar and his companions woke the next morning they found themselves in the open beside Brugh na Boyne (Newgrange) and the house and everything else had vanished, all save the baby and the two foals. So they took them back to Emain Macha where Deichtine raised the child as her own. Soon afterwards however, he died. Deichtine was distraught, but that night she dreamed she was visited by their host from the Boyne. He told her that he was Lugh of the Tuatha de Danann and that he had sent the strange birds to draw her to him so that she would foster his child. Although it had died, it would soon be born again from her own womb. She would call the child Setanta and people would take him for the son of Sualtam, Deichtine's husband, but his true father would be Lugh. Some say Lugh then gave her a drink with some small creature in it, which is how she got pregnant; but whatever the case, soon after she grew heavy with a child and when she was delivered she called him Setanta as agreed and fostered him with her sister Finnchaem at Airgdech on the Muirthemne Plain.

When Setanta was six years old he asked his foster mother to send him to the school for boy warriors at Emain Macha. As described by Fergus mac Roy in *The Book of the Dun Cow*, one of the oldest collections of Irish lore from the twelfth century: 'Three fifties of boys play there. Conchobar enjoys his sovereignty thus: one third of the day watching the boys play, one third playing fidchell and one third drinking till he falls asleep.'

Finnchaem told him he was too young and anyway would have to wait till some passing warrior could escort him, because the journey was far too dangerous for a child. But Setanta set out anyway, taking his toy shield and spear, and a hurling stick and ball; and as he went he played a game, throwing his javelin ahead and then catching it before it hit the ground. When he arrived at Emain Macha he watched the boys for a while, some practising fighting and some playing hurley on the green before the castle. Then he joined in the game and was soon running rings round all the other boys. They grew angry not only at this but because he had not first thought to ask permission. They threw their hurling balls at him, but he fended these off easily with his shield. Then the boys all threw their sticks at him and now Setanta grew angry too; and as he grew angry a terrible change came over him as he went into the battle fury for which he later became famous. Known as his Warp-Spasm, the change made his hair stand up in spikes on his head and sparks flew from the tip of the spikes. One eye closed till it was smaller than the eye of a needle while the other grew as big as a dinner bowl. He grinned from ear to ear and opened his mouth so wide they could see down his gullet. Then he attacked and overthrew fifty of the boys before they could escape back into the castle. He chased the rest in to where the King was playing fidchell and overturned the game board in

his eagerness. Conchobar caught him by the arm and asked who he was and what was going on.

Soon calm was restored and peace made between Setanta and the boy troops. He was allowed to join them in their studies and exercises and soon excelled them all in everything they were taught. Also, because of his battle fury they took care not to rouse his anger again.

King Conchobar at that time had a great blacksmith called Culann (Culand) that he had invited over from the Isle of Man to improve the quality of smithcraft in his realm. One day Conchobar decided to visit his smith for a feast and set out from Emain Macha with fifty other chariots full of his warriors. As was his habit, he paused on the way to watch his boy warriors at play and receive their blessing. As usual, Setanta was winning at whatever game he happened to be playing, so Conchobar called him over and invited the boy to join them at Culann's feast, for he wanted to show off his new prodigy. Setanta said he was not finished playing yet but would follow along behind when he was done.

So the King and his men rode on to the blacksmith's hall where they were greeted with Culann's hospitality. When they were all indoors Culann asked his guest if all the company had all arrived and Conchobar, forgetting about Setanta, said yes. So Culann released his hound to guard the courtyard while they feasted.

Now this hound was famous throughout the land for his strength and fury. It took three chains to hold him, and three men on each chain; and when he was on guard nothing got past him and no-one dared try and steal Culann's cattle, so he slept very peacefully at night.

He and his guests settled in to the feast and the wine and mead was soon flowing. Then as it grew dark, along came Setanta playing his game of hitting his hurling-ball ahead, throwing his javelin after it and then catching them both before they hit the ground. When Culann's hound saw him, it howled and sprang into the attack. Those in the hall heard this and suddenly remembered the boy. They ran out to try and save him but were too late to do anything but watch as the hound leaped upon Setanta, who was still playing with his ball and javelin and seem unconcerned. But at the last moment he dropped his toys, grabbed the hound by the throat with one hand, and by the back with another and dashed it so hard against a pillar that the life went out of it.

Conchobar and his men were delighted and carried the boy into the feast in triumph, but Culann was less happy: 'While I'm pleased you survived my hound's attack,' he told the boy, 'who is now going to guard me as well as that faithful servant?'

Setanta immediately said that he would raise a whelp from the same mother as the hound to take its place, and that while it was growing he would stand guard over Culann's hall at night. So from that day Setanta became known as Cuchulainn, the Hound of Culann, and the smith and his possessions were as safe under his guard as they had ever been under that of the old hound.

One day when he was still only seven years old Cuchulainn overheard Cathbad the Druid say that any warrior that took up arms that day would become famous throughout Ireland and his deeds would live on for ten thousand years. So Cuchulainn went to King Conchobar and asked to be given arms because Cathbad had told him it was a propitious day. Now besides being the chief druid of Ulster, Cathbad was Conchobar's father through Queen Ness, so the King was not inclined to doubt his word. He presented Cuchulainn with a sword and shield but when the boy put them to the test they immediately broke. The same happened again and again till finally Conchobar gave the child his own weapons, which survived the test. As Cuchulainn was thanking and saluting the King, Cathbad the druid came in and asked what was going on.

'He has taken up arms this day on your advice,' Conchobar said.

'Woe to his mother and his mother's son,' said Cathbad, 'for any who take up arms today will achieve glory and fame but die young.'

'Did you not instruct him to do so?' Conchobar asked.

'Indeed not,' came the reply.

'Why did you lie to me, sprite?' the King asked the boy.

'I did not lie,' Cuchulainn replied. 'I heard him instructing his pupils this morning that whoever took arms today would achieve fame and glory, and if I live but a single day and do that I will be content.'

Soon afterwards Cuchulainn was again eavesdropping and heard one of Cathbad's pupils asking him what was special about this day. Cathbad replied that any champion who rode his first chariot that day would be remembered forever in Ireland. So the boy went to the King and asked to be given his first chariot. Twelve chariots were brought and each shattered under the child's driving, till finally Conchobar gave him his own chariot, which stood the test.

Then Cuchulainn set off with Ibar, the King's charioteer to seek adventure and bloody his weapons, as was the custom when a warrior was given his first chariot. They came to the fort of Nechta Scene and her three sons, who were famous warriors that hated all Ulstermen ever since one had killed their father. Ibar was afraid, being there in sight of the three sons of Nechta, but Cuchulainn stepped out of the chariot and lay calmly down under a blanket on the ground for a nap, telling Ibar to wake him if the champions came. Before long they did, armed to the teeth.

'Who is it that sleeps there?' they asked Ibar.

'A young boy on his first chariot ride,' he replied, quaking.

'Sad for him that he will not grow one day older,' said the sons of Nechta.

'Sad for you that this boy has come looking for a fight!' cried Cuchulainn, leaping up, and with three blows he laid them all dead and cut off their heads to hang on the front of his chariot.

On the way home they passed a herd of wild deer. 'Which would be better,' the boy asked Ibar, 'to bring one in alive or dead?'

'No warrior has yet brought in a wild deer alive,' he replied.

So Cuchulainn leaped off the chariot and chased the largest deer on foot till he caught it and soon tethered it to the back of the chariot.

A while later they passed a flock of swans. 'Do the warriors of Ulster bring these in alive or dead?' Cuchulainn asked Ibar.

'The best bring them in alive,' he replied.

Cuchulainn threw two stones. The first knocked eight of the swans unconscious and the second twelve. They gathered them in and tied them with long tethers to the chariot so they could still fly when they revived. Then they returned to Emain Macha

where the lookouts on the walls were terrified by the vision of a chariot with three severed heads on the front, a large deer with antlers like a tree following on behind and a flock of swans hovering above.

By now Cuchulainn was so inflamed by his exploits that the warp-spasm had taken possession of him and when the gatekeepers refused him entry for fear of his temper he raged up and down threatening to do battle with everyone there until finally the women of Emain Macha were sent out to him with their breasts bared. When the boy hid his face in embarrassment, the warriors leaped on him and threw him into a barrel of cold water they had prepared. This immediately burst in a cloud of steam. They put him into a second barrel which boiled over, then a third which finally cooled him and his body returned to normal. Then Mugain the queen put a cloak around Cuchulainn and sat him on the King's knee where everyone gazed in wonder at the seven-year-old boy who could do such great deeds.

CHAPTER 5

Faerie Romances

MIDIR (MIDHIR, MIDER) who features in the next tale, one of the most famous in ancient Irish literature, seems to have been a god of the underworld and was equated with Pluto by several Roman writers. Sometimes he is linked with the Isle of Falga or Man where he is supposed to have kept three wonderful cows and a magic cauldron; but more commonly his home was said to be the faerie mound of Bri Leith (Slieve Golry) near Ardagh in County Longford, Ireland.

Midir the Proud once had three magical cranes, talking birds that guarded his door discouraging visitors. When anyone came seeking hospitality the first would shout: 'Don't come! Don't come!' Then if they persisted, the next would shout: 'Go away! Go away!' And if they still did not take the hint the third would then shout: 'Go past the house! Go past the house!' The cranes were stolen in the end by a greedy poet called Aitherne. His cows and cauldron were also stolen from Midir eventually by the Red Branch heroes of Ulster.

Midir is generally considered a son of the Daghda and one of the most powerful of the Tuatha, helping the Morrigan drive the Fomorians out of Ireland after the Second Battle of Moytura. Along with Lir, the sea god, he was not happy when his father passed the High Kingship to Bodb Dearg and isolated himself in Mount Leinster in County Carlow, which is what earned him his nickname The Proud. Every year Bodb and his subject kings besieged him and many of the Tuatha died in the battles between them, but still Midir refused to send hostages in recognition of Bodb's sovereignty.

The Wooing of Etain

Around the beginning of the Christian era, according to the old chroniclers, Eochaid Airem was High King in Tara, Conchobar mac Nessa ruled Ulster, Maeve and Aillil ruled Connaught, Curoi was King of Munster and Mesgegra was King of Leinster. This was the Heroic Age of Ireland, some centuries after its conquest by the Sons of Mil.

Eochaid was a wise, brave and generous ruler but there was one thing that lacked in his life, and which weakened his people's support – he had no wife. Because of this the provincial kings' wives were reluctant to go to Tara, there being no queen to greet them there and preside over the festivals. The kings were then reluctant to go without their wives and they muttered: 'A king is no king without a queen.' So after a brave beginning Eochaid's rule began to falter.

He decided to find himself a wife and a hunt was made all across Ireland for a maiden fit to wed the High King. Finally messengers came to say that such a maid had been found and she was Etain, daughter of Etair, one of Conchobar's vassal lords in Ulster. So the High King set out to woo her. By chance as he approached her father's castle, he came upon Etain and her maids washing their hair at a sparkling spring and, as the old books say: 'Her eyes were hyacinth-blue, her lips scarlet as the rowan-berry, her shoulders round and white, her fingers were long and her nails smooth and pink. Her feet also were slim, and white as sea-foam. The radiance of the moon was in her face, pride in her brows and the light of wooing in her eyes. Of her it was said that there was no beauty among women compared with Etain's beauty, no sweetness compared with the sweetness of Etain.'

Eochaid immediately fell in love, and he was not alone in this because Etain charmed everyone she met and many men had already sought her hand in marriage; but she had refused them all because she had already fallen in love with Eochaid from afar at a young age, through hearing of his high deeds. So Eochaid bore her away to Tara to become his queen and it was not long before her charm and grace and beauty had transformed the place. Kings and queens and lords and ladies all flocked to the court once again and carried some of Etain's charm back home with them afterwards. Every man that spoke with Etain felt that he was High King for that moment; and every woman, from the highest to the lowest, soon forgot any jealousy in the delight of her company. She banished care and brought joy wherever she went, and the only the sorrow in her bright presence came sometimes in her songs and her playing of the harp, which stirred strange longings in the hearts of her listeners, and woke visions in their minds of some lost land of perfection, more fair than mortal words can tell. There seemed something of the faerie about Etain, and this was no mere illusion, as we shall see.

Etain loved her husband Eochaid as dearly as he loved her, so all seemed to be going very well in Tara till one day, when she was alone in her garden, a stranger appeared. He looked young and handsome, with golden hair and a crimson cloak and a crown of gold upon his head.

'Etain,' he said, 'we have missed you long enough. It's time for you to come home.'

'Who are you?' she asked. 'And what home is it you speak of, for my home is here?'

'I speak of the Land of Youth, which is your true home.'

Then the stranger sang her a song:

'O come with me, Etain, come away,
To that overseas land of mine!
Where music haunts the happy day,
And the rivers run with wine;
Where folk are careless, young, and gay,
And none says "mine" or "thine".

'Golden curls on the proud young head,
And pearls in the tender mouth;
Manhood, womanhood, white and red,
And love that grows not loath
When all the world's desires are dead,
And all the dreams of youth.

'Away from the cloud of Adam's sin!
Away from grief and care!
This flowery land you dwell within
Seems rude to us, and bare;
For the naked strand of the Happy Land
Is twenty times as fair.'

With this song many half-memories filled Etain's head, just as her own songs stirred strange visions in others. For a while the urge to follow this stranger filled her but then she shook herself and said: 'Who are you that you expect the wife of the High King to abandon everything on the strength of your word?'

'I am Midir the Proud of Bri Leith, a prince of the People of Dana,' he replied. Then he told her how they had been in love and married in the Land of Youth. This had stirred the jealousy of his former wife Fuamnach. One day when Midir was away she had changed Etain into a butterfly and then conjured a gale that had swept her away on the winds of the world. By chance after seven years she had happened to blow into the palace of Angus Og, Midir's kinsman, at Brugh na Boyne. Angus had recognised her despite the enchantment and built a crystal bower filled with flowers and herbs and honey where she could shelter till the spell could be unravelled. But before this happened, Fuamnach heard about Angus's guest and sent another druidic gale to blow her away.

Seven more years Etain had been blown this way and that by the winds of Erin till by chance she had been blown down the chimney of Lord Etair in his castle by the Bay of Cichmany in the country known as Echrad. The butterfly had fallen into the goblet of Etair's wife and been swallowed by her without noticing.

'In due course,' concluded Midir, 'you were born again in the guise of a mortal maid and daughter to Etair the Warrior; but you are no mortal, nor of mortal kin, for it is one thousand and twelve years from the time when you were first born in Faeryland till Etair's wife bore you as a human child on the face of the earth.'

Etain was bewildered by this tale because much of it rang true and she half-remembered, as from dreams, many of the things Midir told her. Midir himself tugged at her recognition and the faerie light that danced around his head and shoulders seemed to remind her of the other life he spoke of. But in the end she said: 'I cannot tell if what you say is true or not. All I know is that I was born in Dun Etair and am married to the High King of Ireland, and I will not break my vows to him.'

'But,' persisted Midir, 'if Eochaid consented to let you go, would you then return to my land and your true home?'

'Perhaps,' she replied uncertainly.

Midir took his leave and life carried on for a while as before for Etain and Eochaid. Then one summer morning Eochaid rose early to lean on the ramparts of Tara and gaze out over the fair, flowery plain of Bregia. After a while he became aware of a young stranger standing beside him, golden haired and crimson cloaked and magnificently armed like some great lord of the Gael. Eochaid greeted him courteously and asked his name and purpose there.

'My name is Midir of Bri Leith, whom some call the Proud. I have come to play fidchell with you, for you are famous for your skill in that game and I would like to test my own skill.'

Indeed Eochaid was considered the best fidchell player in Ireland so he was willing enough for a contest, only his game board was in his bedchamber and he did not wish to disturb his wife so early.

'No matter,' said Midir, and produced a board of his own that was the equal of any in Ireland; the board was of silver with jewels glittering in each corner, and the pieces were of gold set with gems. Then they settled to play, but first they fixed the stakes of the game, which were simply that whoever won could ask what he liked of the other.

They played and Midir lost the first game, for which Eochaid set him and his people to clear the plains around Tara of rocks and stones. They played again and once again Midir lost and was set to cut down the Forest of Breg. They played a third time and Midir lost yet again and this time his task was to build a causeway across the Lamrach Moor.

Then they played a fourth time, and this time Midir won, as most likely he could have done all along.

'So what demand would you make of me?' asked Eochaid.

'To hold Etain in my arms and obtain a kiss from her,' replied Midir.

The High King was silent and thoughtful at this request, guessing that there had been more to their contest all along than he had realised.

'Very well,' he said finally, 'come back a month from today and the stake which I have lost will be paid.'

So Midir left and Eochaid immediately summoned all his hosts and over the next month posted them in defensive rings around Tara while he locked himself and Etain in the heart of the stronghold. On the appointed day he sat at feast with his followers, confident in the knowledge that no host of the Tuatha had been seen on its way to Tara. Then suddenly Midir appeared in the midst of them in the full splendour of his faerie nature, sparkling jewels dancing on his robes as he moved. Silence filled the hall as the whole company gazed on him in awe. Eochaid rose and greeted him as calmly as possible.

'Now,' said Midir, 'I wish to claim the wager, which is Etain's whole self.'

'All I agreed was that you should take her in your arms and kiss her,' said Eochaid.

'But a kiss and an embrace is the whole woman,' said Midir. Then, holding his weapons in his left hand he put his right arm around Etain and as they kissed they rose up in the air and out through a roof window in the palace. The whole company rushed outside but all they saw was two swans circling high in the air over Tara before flying away to the south.

Thus Etain returned to her own people, but shortly afterwards she gave birth to a daughter by Eochaid and she gave the child to him in remembrance of the love she had once felt for him. This daughter was also called Etain, and in time she equalled her mother in beauty and charm, and became the wife and mother of kings.

Some say there was another ending to the story though; that Eochaid searched high and low across Ireland for news of Etain till finally a druid named Dalan learned by means of divining with charmed ogham yew wands that Midir had her hidden in his faerie mound at Bri Leith. Eochaid marched there with an army and began digging into the hill. In alarm Midir sent out fifty faerie maidens, each having the appearance of Etain; but Eochaid would not settle for anything less than Etain herself. So finally, to save his sidhe, Midir surrendered her and it is said she lived with the High King of Ireland until they both died. Midir did not forgive the affront though and wove a grim fate around Etain and Eochaid's descendants till finally their line died from the face of the earth.

The Curse of the Ulstermen

Another famous faerie coupling in Ireland that was to have devastating consequences for the province of Ulster is told in the preamble to the Homeric epic known as *The Cattle Raid of Cooley* (*Tain bo Cuailnge*).

In this we hear of a certain Ulster nobleman called Crunniuc, grandson of Curir Ulad, from whom Ulster and its people gained their Gaelic name Ulaid. Well, Crunniuc lived in a lonely place with his wife and many sons, and when his wife died it was lonelier still. Then one day a beautiful female came along and entered the house. With no explanation at all she set about the chores of the household as if she were long accustomed to them, and when the sons came home that evening it was to a feast such as they had not tasted in a long while. That night she shared Crunniuc's bed and from that day forward lived as his wife.

They had no idea where she had come from or why, but Crunniuc and his sons were happy enough with this arrangement because since her arrival they had never lacked for clothing and food and home comforts. More than that, among her many talents the lady could outrun all their fastest horses, and would round them up when they were feeling frisky and rebellious.

Then the day came for the great fair when all the people of Ulster gathered for celebration, catching up on all the news and settling debts. On the way to the fair Crunniuc's strange and wonderful wife warned him: 'Be careful today of boasting or loose talk, my husband, because if you don't it will end in tears.'

Crunniuc consented easily enough because he had no wish to risk the happiness that had come to him so unexpectedly. But towards the end of the day of celebration when the chariot races came, the warning was long forgotten. When the king's horses won and everyone was agreeing that nothing in the world could beat them, Crunniuc could not help but boast: 'But my wife can run faster than them any day.'

Word of this rash boast soon reached the king's ears and Crunniuc was brought before him to justify it or lose his head for his presumption. His wife was sent for and she came, but protesting that she was nine months pregnant and in no condition for racing. But the crowd was in the mood for entertainment and not to be swayed.

'A mother bore each one of you,' she cried. 'Have pity on me, only wait till I am delivered and then I will race any creature you wish.'

But the crowd only roared for the race to begin.

'Very well,' she said. 'But great evil will come upon all of Ulster because of this.'

'Who are you?' the king asked, wondering at her boldness.

'My name is Macha, daughter of Sainrith mac Imbaith,' she declared, 'and my name and that of my offspring shall forever be given to this place because of your demands.'

Then the king's chariot was brought and the race began, and to everyone's wonder Macha ran ahead of the king's horses right to the finishing line where she collapsed and immediately went into labour. And amid the screams of her birth-giving she cried that from that day forth all men listening would suffer the same pains as her whenever they were in the greatest danger.

Thus a great curse fell upon the men of Ulster and for nine generations whenever they were most threatened with destruction they became as weak and helpless as women in childbirth just as Macha had predicted. Macha herself gave birth to twins, a boy and a girl, and the place became known as Emain Macha – the Twins of Macha – which is the name of the royal mound outside Armagh to this day.

The Wooing of Emer

The one exception to this curse on the warriors of Ulster was young Cuchulainn because of his faerie parentage, being the son of Lugh. This was later to prove a greater blessing than any could imagine, but in the meantime as he grew into a still beardless youth the other Ulster warriors began to worry about him on two counts. The first was that when the battle frenzy was not upon him he was so beautiful, witty and charming that all women adored him, and the warriors feared for the virtue of their wives and daughters. The second count was that because he was destined to die young they were eager for him to marry and have a son to perpetuate his wondrous talents.

So Conchobar sent out messengers into all the provinces of Ireland looking for a suitable bride for Cuchulainn. They returned empty handed but meanwhile Cuchulainn himself had heard of a maid towards whom his heart leaned because she was said to possess the six gifts that would make her his equal in accomplishment – the gift of beauty, the gift of voice, the gift of sweet speech, the gift of needle-work, the gift of wisdom and the gift of chastity. She was Emer the daughter of Forgall the Wily, so with his charioteer Laeg, Cuchulainn rode in his finest clothes and jewels to where she lived and found her with a gathering of her sisters and foster sisters on the playing fields before the rath.

Hearing the two-horsed chariot approaching in the distance Emer sent one of her sisters to see who it was and she returned to report on Cuchulainn as (in the translation of the tale by Kuno Meyer): 'the fairest of the men of Erin. A beautiful purple five-folded tunic around him, a brooch of inlaid gold on his white breast at its opening, against which it heaves, full strokes beating. A shirt with a white hood, interwoven red with flaming gold. Seven red dragon-gems on the ground of either of his two eyes. Two blue-white blood-red cheeks that breathe sparks and flashes of fire. A ray of love burns in his look. Me thinks, a shower of pearls has been poured in his mouth. As black as the side of a black-bird each of his two eyebrows. A gold-hilted sword resting on his two thighs. A blood-red hand fitted spear with a sharp mettlesome blade on a shaft of wood is tied to the copper frame of the chariot. A purple shield with a rim of silver, with ornamental beasts of gold over his two shoulders.'

In this finery Cuchulainn arrived at where the maidens were and he found Emer every bit as beautiful and charming as the reports had told. For her part she found the same in him and soon they were engaged in a riddling contest of words through which they measured each other's wits and secretly declared their intentions without Laeg or the rest of the maidens guessing what they were about.

Finally when out of hearing of the rest, and finding nothing but delight in Emer, Cuchulainn asked why they should not become one, for he had never before met a maid who could equal him in the kind of riddling talk they had been having.

'One question,' she replied, 'have you a wife already, who would be jealous and seek to harm me?'

'Not so,' he replied.

'Another thing, I may not marry before my older sister Fial whom you can see over there. She is as talented as I am, why not marry her?'

'But it is not her I have fallen in love with,' replied Cuchulainn, 'nor have I ever accepted a woman that has known a man before me, and I have heard that she once slept with Carpre Niafer.'

Now his eyes fell on the mounds of her breasts within the neck of her smock and he said meaningfully: 'Fair is this plain, the plain of the noble yoke.'

She replied: 'No-one comes to this plain who has not slain a hundred men at each ford from Ailbine to the Boyne.'

'Fair is this plain, the plain of the noble yoke,' Cuchulainn repeated.

She replied: 'No-one comes to this plain who has not slain three times nine men with a single blow, and performed the salmon leap across three ramparts.'

'Fair is this plain, the plain of the noble yoke,' Cuchulainn repeated a third time.

She replied: 'No-one comes to this plain who does not fight without harm to himself from summer's end to the beginning of spring, from the beginning of spring to May Day, from May Day to the beginning of winter.'

'It is as good as done,' said Cuchulainn.

'It is offered, it is granted, it is taken, it is accepted,' replied Emer.

With this compact made, Cuchulainn and Laeg rode away back to Emain Macha, not realising the trouble they had stirred up behind. When Forgall the Wily heard about Cuchulainn's visit he was not pleased at all. No-one could tell him just what Emer and her suitor had spoken about but he guessed that she had fallen in love with him and where things were heading, and he vowed to do all he could to save Emer from 'the madman from Emain Macha'.

So Forgall visited Emain Macha in disguise and persuaded the king that Cuchulainn would become an even better warrior if he went to study at the school of Scathach the witch northwards over the sea on the Isle of Skye, which is named after her. His aim in doing this was partly just to get Cuchulainn out of the way so he could marry Emer off to someone else, but he was also hoping that the youth might not survive Scathach's famously rigorous training, and was planning a few other unpleasant traps for him too.

Before setting sail, Cuchulainn visited Emer again and she warned him of her father's deception, but this only inflamed their love for each other and after swearing to be faithful they parted. Cuchulainn then had many adventures both on his way to Skye and when he got there because it was no easy matter gain entry to Scathach's warrior school, and then he had to help in her war with Aoife, one of the fiercest female warriors in the world. But like a true hero he triumphed over every adversity, including some thrown his way by Forgall the Wily. Forgall also tried to marry Emer off to a powerful king in Cuchulainn's absence, but she shamed the king out of forcing her into marriage and kept her virtue for her true love.

After a year during which he fulfilled the third of his pledges to Emer, by fighting many battles without harm to himself, Cuchulainn returned to Erin a more formidable warrior than ever. After resting at Emain Macha to tell the tale of all his adventures abroad, he headed for Forgall's rath to see Emer, but could not get near it for the host of warriors defending the fortress against him. In the end he rode up to it on his chariot and 'jumped the hero's salmon-leap' across its three ramparts. Upon landing he three times felled a group of nine warriors with a single blow. Then Forgall, in fleeing from the raging Cuchulainn, fell to his death from a rampart. Then Cuchulainn caught up Emer and her favourite foster-sister and leaped out of the fortress again as he had entered.

On their way northwards to the Boyne Cuchulainn slew a hundred of Forgall's followers at each ford and thus by the time they reached Emain Macha he had fulfilled all the requirements she had asked of him. Then in Emain they were wed and, apart from the tricky dalliance we deal with next, were together until death.

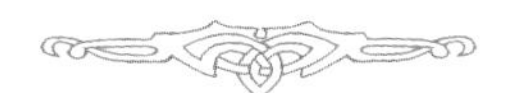

The Sick-Bed of Cuchulainn or: The Only Jealousy of Emer

A while after Cuchulainn and Emer's marriage it happened that Manannan mac Lir grew tired of his wife Fand and neglected her. She, feeling spurned, fell in love with Cuchulainn and with her sister Liban flew to Ulster in the form of two white birds linked by a golden chain to watch him out hunting with his companions. He, seeing the birds, decided to catch them for Emer and threw two stones at them, which missed, the first time he had ever missed such an easy target. So then he threw his javelin and injured the wing of one bird, but it still flew away with the other, helped by the golden chain.

Cuchulainn was mortified and went off on his own to calm his temper. He came in time to a standing stone and, feeling tired, lay down against it to rest. Soon he was asleep and in his dream two beautiful young women approached, one robed in green, the other in crimson. Each held a long slim whip and, smiling all the while, they took turns to lash the sleeping hero until he thought he would die. Then they left.

By now some of his friends had found Cuchulainn and saw him struggling in his sleep, but they did not dare wake him, recognising that he was in the grip of a vision. When he finally did surface they asked him what had happened, but he was unable to say a word and was so weak they had to carry him home where he took to his sickbed and did not speak to anyone for a year.

The following November Eve, when his closest friends were gathered around his bed, a stranger appeared suddenly in their midst and sang a message to Cuchulainn from Fand:

'A joyous day would it be
Were Cuchulainn to come to my land.
He would have gold and silver
And rivers of wine to his hand.

'Were he my friend now
Cuchulainn son of Sualtam,
Perhaps he could tell what he saw
In his sleep, apart from the host.

'There on the Plain of Muirthemne in the south
No evil will befall you this Samaine
I will send Liban to fetch you
Cuchulainn, sick as you are.'

Then the messenger disappeared as suddenly as he had come and at last Cuchulainn was able to speak and tell for the first time of his strange vision. He asked Conchobar's advice and was told that he must return to the place where it had happened and see what followed. So, having also recovered some strength, Cuchulainn rode with Laeg, his charioteer, to the standing stone on the Plain of Muirthemne where he had fallen ill and there he met the woman in the green cloak from his dream.

'Well met Cuchulainn,' she greeted him.

'It was not so well met for me this time last year,' he replied.

'But we did not come to harm you,' she replied. 'Rather to seek your friendship. I have come to tell you of Fand, daughter of Aed Abrat. Manannan mac Lir has left her and now she has given her love instead to you. I am Liban and I bear a message from my husband Labraid. He says that Fand can be yours in return for a day's battle against his enemies in the Plain of Delights.'

Cuchulainn said he was in no condition to fight anyone, but Liban told him that this would be no problem because they would first make him well again. Cuchulainn was cautious though. He was eager for a cure but wanted to know first what kind of country it was that he would be defending, so he sent his charioteer Laeg off with Liban to see how things stood. In a bronze boat they sailed away and when Laeg returned, he was so full of the wonders he had seen in Fand's fair country that Cuchulainn agreed to go.

After helping defeat Labraid's enemies, Cuchulainn settled to feasting and celebration, and in the midst of this became infatuated with Fand as she had hoped. But he could not completely forget his home and after a month he returned, with an arrangement for Fand to follow. Cuchulainn's wife Emer was furious when she learned he was in love with one of the Sidhe; and when she learned where they planned their tryst she gathered fifty women with knives and closed in on the place. Cuchulainn and Laeg were engrossed in playing fidchell and did not notice the danger, but Fand sensed it and raised the alarm. The three of them climbed into the chariot, though Cuchulainn was not seriously alarmed at the threat. There followed a touching scene in which he called Emer out into the open and asked why she threatened them with knives and spears.

'Why not, Cuchulainn, when you have shamed me before all the women of Ulster, and the women of all Erin?'

'Emer, why will you not let me meet this woman? She is pure and modest, fair and clever and worthy of a king. Beautiful she is on the waves of the great-tided sea, with her shapeliness and her beauty and her noble family, her abundance of horses and herds of cattle. Whatever you may promise, there is nothing under heaven that a husband could ask that she cannot provide.'

'Bur perhaps she is not really better than I,' replied Emer. 'What's new is bright, what's familiar is stale. The unknown is honoured while the known is neglected – until all is known. Husband, we lived together in happiness and harmony once, and we could do so again if only I still pleased you.'

Cuchulainn grew sad at this. 'But you do still please me,' he said, 'and you will please me as long as you live.'

'Leave me then,' said Fand, seeing Cuchulainn torn between herself and his wife and moved by pity for her.

'No, better leave me,' said Emer.

But, though she still loved Cuchulainn, it was Fand who gave up her claim on him, singing:

'I will continue my journey
Though I prefer my great adventure here
Whoever might come, however great his fame
I would prefer to remain with Cuchulainn.

'I would prefer to remain here
That I grant willingly
Than to go, however surprising it may seem,
To the sun-palace of Aed Abrat.

'Emer, the man is yours
And may you enjoy him, good woman.
What my hand cannot hold
I must still desire.'

Then Manannan mac Lir, who had heard rumours of what was going on and come to see what he could do, revealed himself to Fand's eyes alone. He then shook his cloak between Cuchulainn and Fand so that their paths would never cross again, then led her away kindly, for he regretted his neglect of her and wanted her to be his wife again, even knowing she that still loved the mortal Cuchulainn.

Cuchulainn was inconsolable at his loss of his faerie love and took himself off to Luachair (Luachra) to the south, where he lived alone in the mountains nursing his grief without food or water and sleeping in the open. Emer went to Conchobar for help and he sent his druids and bards to find Cuchulainn and subdue him with spells so he could be brought home. Then they gave him a potion that made him forget all about Fand and his time with her.

Then for Emer's jealousy and heartbreak they gave her a similar potion so that she forgot all about Cuchulainn's betrayal, and they went back to being the loving couple they had been before.

Deirdre of the Sorrows

The tale of Deirdre of the Sorrows or The Exile of the Sons of Usna (Usnech, Usnach or Uisliu) was part of the standard repertoire of every Irish bard as one of the Three Sorrowful Stories of Erin, along with the Fate of the Sons of Tuirenn and the Fate of the Children of Lir. So there are many versions of it on record from the very earliest days until the nineteenth century when folklorists heard it from the bards' successors, the peasant storytellers who kept alive the ancient legends. They vary much in their details and there is no definitive version, but here is one that comes close, taken mainly from the twelfth century *Book of Leinster* in Trinity College, Dublin, translated by Whitley Stokes.

King Conchobar mac Nessa of Ulster (Ulaid) was holding a feast one day at the home of Fedlimid, his bard, when a terrible screech was heard, coming from the womb of Fedlimid's wife, who was on the point of giving birth. Cathbad the druid was called on to explain it and he said:

'In the cradle of your womb there cried out
A maid with twisted golden hair
And beautiful grey-green eyes.
Foxglove her rosy cheeks,
The colour of snow her flawless teeth,
Brilliant her Parthian red lips.
A woman over whom will be great slaughter
Among the chariot-warriors of Ulaid.'

He said that she was to be called Deirdre and would grow up into the most beautiful woman in Ireland because she had faerie blood in her; but that this beauty would not only cause great bloodshed but imperil the whole kingdom of Ulster.

On hearing this, the Red Branch warriors (Ulster's champions) demanded that the baby be put to the sword but Conchobar refused. Instead he had the child taken to a remote and secret lodge where she was to be raised by foster parents and an old teacher, a druidess named Levarcham, with no other company but the birds and beasts of the hills until she was old enough to become his bride.

Despite her isolation and knowing that she was promised to the king, Deirdre as she grew into a young woman often felt the romantic yearnings of any young woman and felt little joy at the prospect of having to marry King Conchobar. One winter as they watched her foster father butchering a calf for the larder, she and her teacher saw a raven stooping to where blood had spilled on the snow. 'If there were a young man,' said Deirdre, 'with hair as black as that raven, skin as white as the snow and cheeks as red as the calf's blood, that is the man I could love.'

'Then luck and good fortune are with you,' replied Levarcham, 'for such a one lives not far off, Naoise (Noisiu), one of the three sons of Usna, nephews of King Conchobar.'

Then Deirdre would give her teacher no rest till she agreed to arrange a meeting with Naoise; and when this came about she immediately fell in love with him and begged him to rescue her from old King Conchobar. Naoise, just as immediately enchanted by her beauty, agreed and with the aid of his brothers Ardan and Ainle he fled with Deirdre to Scotland. There after various adventures that made them welcome there, they settled by Loch Etive.

King Conchobar was furious but kept this to himself and bided his time for revenge. Finally at a feast with the Red Branch warriors he asked if they had ever heard of a company to match their own in battle. They replied that they had not.

'But,' said Conchobar, 'we lack our full tally. The three sons of Usna could defend Ulster against any other province in Ireland on their own, but they languish across the sea in Alba for the sake of a woman. Gladly would I welcome them back!'

His warriors replied that this was just what they had long wanted themselves, only had been afraid to mention it because of Conchobar's anger with the brothers.

'Then I will send one of my three best champions to invite them back,' declared Conchobar. 'Either Conall the Victorious, Cuchulainn son of Sualtam or Fergus son of Roy, whichever of them loves me best.'

Then he spoke to the three in turn privately, asking them what they would do if the sons of Usna were killed while under their safe conduct on the way home. Conall and Cuchulainn both immediately said they would not rest until they had taken the heads of all those responsible; but Fergus said he would revenge the deed on anyone who was party to it, excepting only the king himself.

'Then it is you who shall go,' said Conchobar, and the next morning Fergus mac Roy set out for Scotland with his two sons Illann the Fair and Buinne the Ruthless Red. They were greeted warmly by Naoise and his brothers, who had long been feeling homesick and were delighted to hear that Conchobar had forgiven them for the loss of Deirdre and was inviting them back. She was much less happy though. Having faerie blood and 'second sight' she feared a trap and begged the brothers not to fall into it; but they trusted Fergus's assurances of safe conduct and when they prepared to set sail the next day, vowing not to eat till they were at Conchobar's own table, Deirdre chose to go with them rather than be parted from Naoise. As they left the shore, though, she sang her Lament to Alba that has lived on from that day to this:

'A joyous land is yon eastern land,
Alba with all its wonders.
I would not have come hither out of it,
Had I not come with Naoise.

'Glen Laid!
Often I slept there under the cliff;
Fish and venison and the fat of the badger
Was my portion in Glen Laid.

'Glen Masain!
Its garlic was tall, its branches white;
We slept a rocking sleep,
Over the grassy estuary of Masain.

'Glen Etive!
Where my first house I raised;
Beautiful its wood – upon rising
A cattle fold for the sun was Glen Etive.

'Beloved is Draigen,
Dear the white sand beneath its waves;
I would not have left it, left the east,
Had I not come with my beloved.'

They landed at the stronghold of Borrach, who had been primed on what to do by King Conchobar. As with many if not most ancient Celtic heroes Fergus mac Roy carried certain taboos or *geisa* that he must not break, one being that he could not refuse any invitation to a feast. So when he greeted them Borrach immediately invited the company to a welcoming feast. They politely refused, saying they had vowed not to eat till they reached Conchobar's palace at Emain Macha, all save Fergus whose geisa mattered more than this vow. Deirdre begged the others to wait in some safe place till the feast was over and they could all travel on together, for she still had a premonition of disaster ahead, especially without Fergus. But again they laughed at her fears and pressed on without Fergus.

When they arrived at Emain Macha they were given the Red Branch lodge to rest in and refresh themselves from the journey. Then Conchobar sent Deirdre's old teacher Levarcham to visit her and report back to him whether she was still as beautiful as before. She did this but lied, telling the king that Deirdre's hard life in the mountains of Alba had ruined her beauty. Conchobar had second thoughts about his planned revenge then, but later when he had been drinking awhile he sent a second messenger to check if Levarcham had been telling the truth. The man peered through a window (or some say a knot-hole in the wall) but Deirdre sensed this and told Naoise, who was playing fidchell at the time. He threw a game-piece that knocked out one of the spy's eyes; but when he reported to Conchobar he said Deirdre was so beautiful that he would gladly risk the other just to gaze on her beauty again.

Then Conchobar in fury ordered his men to set fire to the Red Branch lodge and kill everyone within, saving only Deirdre herself. A furious battle followed between the sons of Fergus and Usna and Conchobar's people. Many died, including Conchobar's son Fiacha and both sons of Fergus. Naoise, Ardan and Ainle held out till dawn however, killing many of their fellow Ulstermen and former friends. Then with first light they burst from the lodge with Deirdre in their midst and raced back north towards the coast. They might have escaped too if Cathbad had not cast a druid spell that to their eyes turned the plain into a raging sea. The phantom waves rose higher and higher till they had to throw away their arms and struggle against them. Naoise lifted Deirdre onto his shoulder and plunged on valiantly, but his mighty efforts were for nothing.

From the ramparts of Emain Macha, Conchobar and his remaining warriors watched the strange sight of three men trying to swim across dry land, and with little trouble they were caught from behind, bound and hauled before King Conchobar.

Conchobar had promised his druid Cathbad that he would be merciful, but again reneged on his word by condemning them to death. None of his Ulstermen would do the deed though, so he gave the task to a Norseman who bore an old grudge against Naoise. Each of the sons of Usna begged to be killed first so that he would not have to see his brothers die, and not even this melted Conchobar's cold heart. The only slight mercy they were given was to be permitted to kneel down side by side and have their three heads removed with a single blow by Naoise's own sword, which had been given him by Manannan mac Lir. Then Deirdre sang this lament by their graveside:

'Long the day without Usna's sons
Their company was never grave
King's sons ever keen to entertain
Three lions from the Hill of the Cave

'Three darlings of the maids of Alba
Three hawks of the Slieve Gullion
Sons of a king whom courage served
Whom warriors used to honour

'That I should remain after Naoise
Let no-one in Erin suppose
After Ardan and sweet Ainle
My time will not be long

'O man that digs their grave
And puts my darling from me
Make not the grave too narrow
For I shall soon join the noble ones.'

Some say that after singing this Deirdre immediately died of a broken heart and was buried with Naoise and his brothers. Others say that she survived and Conchobar forcibly took her for his bride, but that she was so joyless that after a year even he could take no more pleasure in possessing her. One day he asked who she most hated in the world and she replied that apart from Conchobar himself it was Eogan son of Durthacht, one of his followers that lusted after her. So Conchobar told her that for the next year she would be Eogan's wife. The next day they went to a fair in Emain Macha, Deirdre riding a chariot between Eogan and Conchobar, who jokingly remarked that she was like a ewe between two rams. As they rode past a large boulder Deirdre flung herself from the chariot and dashed out her brains against it.

Either way it was a hollow triumph for Conchobar because Deirdre cheated him by death. Also, when Fergus learned what had happened he slew another son of Conchobar along with many other warriors, then gathered all his own people and left Ulster to live with Queen Maeve and King Aillil in Connaught, where together they plotted Conchobar's downfall, something that very nearly happened in the famous Cattle Raid of Cooley.

CHAPTER 6

Faerie Gifts

Cattle Raid of Cooley

The ancient literature of Ireland is generally divided by scholars into four branches or cycles – the Mythological Cycle dealing with the arrival and rule of the Tuatha de Danann and subsequent overthrow by the Sons of Mil; the Ulster cycle mainly about the Red Branch warriors of Ulster and revolving around King Conchobar, his champion Cuchulainn and their enemies Maeve and Aillil of Connaught, supported by Fergus mac Roy. Third comes the Fenian or Ossianic Cycle revolving around the exploits of Erin's other greatest champion Finn Mac Cumhal (mac Cool) and his legendary band of warriors; and the Historical Cycle, a miscellany of texts relating to historical kings and queens of Ireland.

The divisions are not absolute. Figures from the Mythological Cycle play a large part in the Ulster Cycle, as we have seen with Macha's curse on the men of Ulster and Lugh's fathering of Cuchulainn; but the setting is after the withdrawal of the faeries into their mounds and more or less real humans are the main actors. Medieval scholars dated the events to around the time of Christ.

The Fenian Cycle is likewise dated to the third century AD in the reign of the High King Cormac mac Art, and is closer still to real history, though there remains a large magical component to the stories. The Historical Cycle covers events from then until the Viking raids of the eighth century.

The main event around which the Ulster Cycle tales revolve is the Cattle Raid of Cooley, in which Queen Maeve of Connaught, in alliance with the other provinces, makes war on King Conchobar mac Nessa of

Ulster. The ostensible cause of the war seems at first quite trivial, beginning with a bickering marital argument in bed between King Ailill and his wife Maeve over which of them was richer in their own right. One thing led to another, as happens in such disputes when neither will back down, and soon there was nothing for it but to tally up all their treasures and measure them against each other. They balanced perfectly except for one item: Ailill had in his herds a supernaturally magnificent white bull and Maeve had nothing to match it. At this proof that he was after all right, Maeve was as dashed as if she were the poorest woman in the land. She called her messenger Mac Roth and asked if he knew where she could find a bull equal to her husband's. Mac Roth indeed did know of such a bull, the Brown Bull of Cooley (Cuailnge) in Ulster, and it was Maeve's determination to possess that bull by hook or by crook that led to the great war in which the rest of Ireland laid siege to Ulster.

That at least is the superficial explanation, but reading between the lines to the shadows of historical events on which the saga was probably based, there must have been background reasons. The other provinces would not have rallied so easily to Maeve's cause just to win her private dispute with her husband; they must have wanted to go to war anyway and her rallying cry just provided an excuse.

On a more fantastic note, the two bulls were said to be the incarnations of two faerie pig-keepers in the service the Tuatha Bodb of Munster and Ochall Ochne of Connaught. The keepers had once been great friends, then rivals, then bitter enemies who had been feuding for generations in a variety of forms (birds, fish, dragons etc.) till finally in the form of maggots they were eaten by two cows and born into the world as the two supernaturally magnificent bulls of this tale. Prize bulls were considered astonishingly valuable in ancient Ireland and the crowning of a High King was always preceded by an elaborate Bull Feast.

However, within the legend Maeve's invasion of Ulster is where Cuchulainn comes fully into his own. As the only Ulster warrior not subject to Macha's curse in their hour of greatest need, it is left to him to defend the province single-handed, which he does in a variety of ingenious and heroic ways. The full story can be read in all its magnificent and savage glory in the masterly translation *The Tain* by Thomas Kinsella (Oxford University Press and Dolmen Press, Dublin, 1969).

Connla and the Faerie Maid

Just as the Ulster Cycle tales centre on the rulers Conchobar mac Nessa, Maeve and Ailill, those of the Fenian Cycle are presided over by Conn of the Hundred Battles, his sons Connla and Art, and Art's son Cormac. These tales are set two or three centuries after those of Cuchulainn and the emphasis is even more on mortals at the centre of the dramas, but there is still no shortage of magic and interaction with the faeries. Perhaps before coming to Cormac himself we should look at what became of his uncle Connla.

Connla of the Fiery Hair was walking with his father Conn of the Hundred Battles on the hill of Uisneach at the centre of Ireland when Connla noticed a maiden in a strangely-fashioned dress coming towards them. He greeted her and asked where she came from.

'From the Plains of the Ever-living,' she replied, 'where there is neither death nor sin. There it is always a feast day and in all our pleasure we have no strife. And because our homes are in the round green hills men call us the Hill Folk.'

Connla's father and their companions were astonished to hear Connla talking with the thin air, because although they could hear the faerie maid, only Connla could actually see her.

'Who are you talking to, son?' the High King asked.

The faerie maid replied for him: 'Connla speaks to a fair young maid for whom neither age nor death awaits. I love Connla and now call him away to Moy Mell, the Plain of Pleasure, where Boadag is King and where no sorrow or complaint has been heard in his reign. Come with me, Connla of the Fiery Hair, bright as the dawn with your tawny skin. A faerie crown awaits to grace your handsome head and royal form. Join me and your comeliness and youth will not fade till Judgement Day.'

Hearing this, the King called in alarm for his druid Coran to save his beloved son from enchantment. Coran cast his spells towards where the maiden's voice had seemed to come and she vanished from Connla's sight, but not before tossing him a little apple.

For the next month Connla would not eat or drink save to bite from that apple occasionally, and each time he did so, it grew whole again. All the while his longing for the faerie maid grew uncontrollably within him. Finally at the end of the month he saw her again. He and his father were on the Plain of Arcomin when once again he saw her coming towards him, saying: 'It truly is a glorious place that Connla holds among the short-lived mortals, awaiting their day of death. But now the

ever-living folk beg you to come to Moy Mell, for they have learned to love you, seeing you at home here with your dear ones.'

Hearing her voice, the King called once again for Coran the Druid, but the maid rebuked him for not letting Connla make up his own mind. So then Conn asked his son what he meant to do.

'It's a hard choice,' said Connla. 'I love my family and friends above all, and yet my heart longs for the maiden.'

When she heard this, she said: 'The ocean is less strong than the waves of your longing. Come with me, my love, in my crystal ship. Soon we can reach Boadag's realm and though the bright sun is sinking, we can reach it before dark.'

Then Connla of the Fiery Hair left his companions and ran down to her crystal ship which glided swiftly away towards the setting sun. The King and all his court watched sadly till their eyes could see it no longer, and so Connla with his faerie maid left his people and was not seen by them again. His brother Art took the crown in due course and is sometimes called 'the Lonely' because he continued to miss his brother so much, and after him his son Cormac took the throne.

Cormac the Magnificent in the Land of Promises

One day at dawn in May, Cormac mac Art, the High King, was sitting alone on Tara watching the sun rise when he saw approaching a grey-haired warrior with a branch of silver over his shoulder bearing three golden apples. This chimed so pleasantly that Cormac immediately felt his heart lift and all the cares of life fell from his shoulders. That indeed was the charm of the branch – that no pain or sorrow or grief could withstand its musical chime, and on hearing it people would drift into blissful slumber.

The stranger introduced himself as coming from a land where there is only truth and 'neither age nor decay nor gloom nor sadness nor envy nor jealousy nor hatred nor haughtiness.' Then he offered Cormac the branch as a gift if in return he would grant any three favours the stranger asked. Cormac agrees and receives the branch, whereupon the stranger instantly vanishes. Cormac returned to the palace on Tara and all his people marvelled at the wonderful branch; and when he shook it loudly for them, they all fell blissfully asleep till the next day. At the end of a year the grey-haired warrior appeared again as Cormac was gathered with his people and asked for his first boon.

'Of course, what do you wish?' asked Cormac.

'I will take your daughter Ailbe today,' the stranger replied; and as Cormac could not in honour refuse in front of all the company, having given his word, the grey-haired warrior then left taking his beloved daughter into the unknown. The court at Tara was in uproar with the women wailing and the men roaring in rage because the princess was as dear to them as to the High King himself. Finally Cormac shook the silver branch with its three golden apples and they were all calmed and fell asleep. And he continued to do this till they had forgotten their grief.

Then a month to the day later the stranger appeared again and it all went as before, only this time he left with Cormac's only son, Carpre.

This time the grief and anger were even greater but finally Cormac shook the silver branch and they were soothed as before.

Then the grey stranger came a third time. 'What do you wish today?' Cormac asked with grim foreboding.

'Your wife,' declared the stranger. 'Even Ethne the Longsided, daughter of Dunlang, King of Leinster.'

This time when he left with Cormac's own wife, he and his warriors rode after them but a great mist descended and soon Cormac found himself all alone on a great plain he did not recognise. There were palaces of bronze all around him and silver houses thatched with white feathers. Then in a grove he came upon a sparkling fountain overhung by nine purple hazels that dropped their nuts into the pool where five salmon fed on the nuts. Five streams tinkled melodiously from the pool and people gathered to drink from them. The most beautiful woman he has ever seen greets Cormac and leads him to the pool where first of all she bathes, then invites him to bathe too. Then she leads him to a feast where the grey-haired warrior-messenger who had stolen his family sings Cormac to sleep.

When he wakes, Cormac finds his wife and children by his side perfectly unharmed. Then Cormac is given a wonderfully fashioned cup of gold that he is told will break into three pieces if lies are spoken over it. The grey-haired one says to the High King of Ireland: 'Now take your family and take the cup so you can discern between truth and falsehood. And you will have the silver branch for music and delight. And on the day you die these gifts shall be taken from you. I am Mannanan mac Lir, King of the Land of Promise; and to see the Land of Promise was the reason I brought you here. The fountain which you saw with the five streams running from it is the Fountain of Knowledge, and the streams are the five senses through which knowledge is obtained. And no-one will have knowledge without a draught from the streams and the fountain; and those with many arts are those who have drunk from both.'

When Cormac wakes the next morning he finds himself back at Tara with his wife and son and daughter; and with his silver branch and cup, which became known as Cormac's Cup and which he used ever afterward to judge whether his people were telling the truth. Cormac in fact became famous for the wisdom of his judgements and laws, which is why he was called 'The Magnificent'. And when at last he died the faerie gifts mysteriously disappeared, just as Manannan had foretold.

Finn Mac Cumhal

Among the great achievements of the reign of Conn of the Hundred Battles was the establishment, or rather the revitalisation of the Fenians or Fianna Eireann with Finn mac Cumhal as their leader, which continued through to the reign of his grandson Cormac.

The Fenians were a unified and mobile fighting force ready to travel anywhere in Ireland to fight off invasions, mainly by the Fomorians who continued to attack Ireland occasionally from their island home across the northern sea known as Lochlann. During the six months of winter, the Fianna were quartered upon the population, but during the summer they foraged for themselves by hunting and fishing, living wild in the woods and on the open moors and by this means kept themselves hardened for battle.

Under Finn's leadership it was not easy to join the Fenians because besides proving themselves in battle, candidates had to establish that they were also men of culture and poetry. They also had to renounce their tribes, so that they would not get distracted by factional disputes or avenging wrongs done to their kin. They took other oaths too: never to refuse hospitality to anyone who asked; never to back down in battle; never to insult a woman and not to accept dowry with a wife. A candidate also had to pass a series of tests of courage, strength and endurance which grew ever more exaggerated in the legends till they reached a superhuman scale

The Fenians were established centuries before Cormac's time but had degenerated into two warring factions. In fact Finn's father Cumhal, who was the rightful leader of the Fenians, was killed in one such battle with a rival Goll of the Blows near Dublin while Finn was still in his mother Muirne's womb. For fear of her husband's enemies, known as the Clan Morna, she gave him to two female servants, a wise-woman and a druidess, to be raised secretly in the Slieve Bloom mountains.

Like Cuchulainn before him, the boy grew up to be an expert at hurling, swimming, running, and hunting, and he was as fair of face and form as one of the faerie folk, which was no accident because his mother is said to have been a sister or half-sister of the mighty Lugh. Under his foster mothers' tutelage he also learned the secrets of the druids and the history of his people and of his own right to the leadership of the Fenians.

The boy was at first called Deimne (or Demna) but because so many called him Deimne the Fair, Deimne Finn became his name, and later just Finn. Even as a boy he wandered widely on his own and his foster mothers did not discourage this, because the more he wandered the safer he was from his enemies. Once while wandering on the banks of the Boyne he met an old wise man called Finn the Seer who lived by a deep pond known as Fec's Pool near Slane in the hope of catching the Salmon of Knowledge said to inhabit it. This salmon was called Finntan in ancient times and was one of the Immortals, because it might be eaten and yet live again, and the first person who tasted of its flesh when it had been cooked would become the wisest of people. The old man had been there seven years in hope of catching this salmon because of another prophecy he had once heard that the prize would go to someone called Finn.

When the boy appeared, Finn the Seer engaged him as a servant and soon afterwards finally caught the fabled fish. He gave it to Deimne to cook, warning him severely not to eat any portion of it before his master. He did so but when he presented it he received a close, searching look from the old man, who saw a new light in the boy's eye and asked: 'Have you tasted it, as I forbad you to do?'

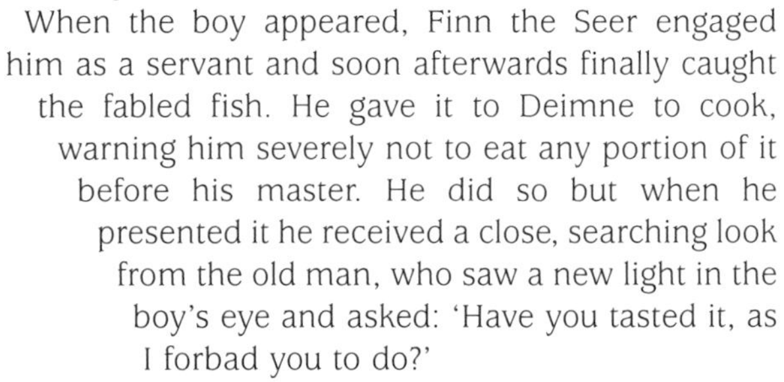

'No indeed,' replied the boy, 'but while I was cooking it a blister rose on the skin. I pressed down on it with my thumb and scalded it, so I put my thumb in my mouth to ease the pain.'

The old man was puzzled. 'You told me your name was Deimne,' he said, 'but have you any other?'

'I am also called Finn,' the boy replied.

'It is enough,' said his disappointed master. 'Eat the salmon yourself because it must be you that the prophecy spoke of.'

So Finn ate the salmon and ever after all he had to do was put his thumb in his mouth to receive foreknowledge and magic counsel.

Around this time Finn began gathering a group of like-minded youths around him and together they hunted in the wild places and practiced warfare. News of their exploits spread till it came to the ears of Goll of the Blows who had killed his father and now ruled what was left of the Fenians. He sent out spies, guessing who the golden boy might be. Finn's foster mothers told him he had to leave and live always on the move if he did not want to be caught. So this is what he and his followers did, and this was the beginning of their later custom of living wild for half the year.

When he felt ready to challenge his enemies, Finn went to the great annual assembly at Tara where Conn of the Hundred Battles was High King. It was an inviolable rule of this assembly that any noble could attend but that no quarrel could be aired and no weapon drawn, so that deadly enemies might find themselves sitting next to each other, but no voice would be raised.

Below the High King sat the provincial kings, then the clan chiefs and so on. Among the clan chiefs sat Goll, son of Morna, along with his brothers and other warriors of the Fianna who served the High King. There too sat a strange, fair youth that no-one had seen before. So calm and confident was his air that he caught Conn's eye. He had a servant take the youth a horn of wine and asked him to declare his name and lineage.

'I am Finn mac Cumhal,' he declared, rising to his feet.

A murmur spread through the hall, particularly among the Sons of Morna and the captains of the Fianna, who started and stared as if at a ghost.

'What do you seek here?' asked the King.

'To be your man and offer you my service in battle just as my father did,' declared Finn.

'Certainly,' said Conn, 'you are the son of a friend and a man of trust.'

So Finn knelt before the High King and put his hand in his and swore loyalty. Then Conn placed Finn in a seat of honour beside his own son Art and the feast continued with much speculation as to what might come of this event.

Now at that time Tara was plagued by an evil sprite who would sometimes come at night and do great mischief, attacking man, woman or beast, setting fire to buildings and any other trouble that caught its fancy. No-one could stop it because the goblin had a faerie harp which it played as it came and anyone who heard that music fell under its spell and could not move until it passed away. Conn had offered a great reward to anyone who could rid him of this menace and in this Finn saw a way by which he might gain his rightful inheritance without fighting the Sons of Morna. So he went to the High King and offered to rid him of the menace in return for being made captain of the Fianna as his father had been, and to this the High King readily agreed before the whole company.

Among Conn's people was a man named Fiacha who in his youth had been a trusted friend and follower of Finn's father. He came to Finn now and gave him an ancient enchanted spear with a head of dark bronze with glittering edges that was kept laced in a leather bag to contain its dark energy.

'By this you can overcome the goblin,' he said, and instructed Finn in how to employ the weapon, which could only be wielded by a great champion.

So Finn took the spear and patrolled the ramparts of Tara until one evening when the light had almost gone from the summer sky and mist blanketed the plains below Tara Hill, he heard far off in the distance the first notes of a faerie harp. As the old bards described it: 'Never was such music made by mortal hand, for it had in it sorrows that man has never felt, and joys for which man has no name, and it seemed as if a man listening to that music might burst from time into eternity and be as one of the Immortals for evermore.'

Finn listened, rapt in the music of the faerie harp, till he saw a shadowy and indistinct shape approaching rapidly and holding the instrument. With a mighty effort he fought off the bonds of lethargy, tore the cover from the enchanted spear-head and touched it to his brow. The demonic energy that had been forged into the bronze by ancient unearthly blacksmiths coursed through him igniting a battle-rage beyond anything he had known. Roaring his battle-cry he charged forward with the spear raised. The shadowy goblin turned and fled before him but Finn chased after it all the way to the faerie mound of Slieve Fuad in Armagh and there he drove the spear hard through its back.

Something like the shadow of a shadow fled into the mound, leaving a pale, sorrowful figure behind, whose head Finn took back to Tara; and from that day they were no more troubled by the goblin, whatever kind of being it was.

Then Conn of a Hundred Battles called the Fenians together, with Finn sat at his right hand, declaring to them: 'Here is your captain by birth-right and by sword-right. Let who will now obey him henceforward, and who will not, let him go in peace and serve Arthur of Britain or Arist of Alba, or whatsoever other King he chooses.'

Goll mac Morna, slayer of Finn's father Cumhal stepped forward first and bent his knee before Finn, swearing allegiance and loyalty; and after his example the rest followed suit. So from that day Finn Mac Cumhal became captain of the Fianna and it is said he ruled them for forty years until his death in battle with the Clan Urgrenn at Brea upon the Boyne. This was the golden age of the Fenians during which they fought many great battles in the defence of Ireland and killed many great monsters that threatened it; but it was also their last age because after Finn died they fell apart and were soon disbanded.

King Arthur

The parallel between King Cormac mac Art and his Fianna, and King Arthur and his Knights of the Round Table is no coincidence. They (or the real kings on whom their legends are based) would have been near contemporaries; and although Arthur was half Roman, or at least defending a half Romanised culture, when the Romans abandoned the British they fell back on Celtic patterns of behaviour which, even after four centuries within the embrace of the great empire, had far from been eradicated.

In Ireland the High King (Ard Ri) was not quite the supreme ruler he might seem from our perspective. Personally he ruled the smallest of the five provinces of Ireland, and could immediately call on fewer troops than any of his four nominally subject provincial kings. His role was to provide a centre around which the rest could rally when the security of Ireland as a whole was threatened. That was the function of the rigorously enforced truce at his great annual feasts. Rivals were required to come in peace so that when any national crisis threatened, such as invasion by the Danes, they could be called on in a similar spirit and made to pool their strength until that threat had been beaten off.

As far as one can tell through the fog of partial contemporary records and later fabulation, King Arthur's role was similar. He was not, at least at the start, supreme ruler of Britain but more like Finn mac Cumhal, the leader of a highly mobile cavalry force drawn from all the tribes of Britain that raced from one end of the island almost to the other engaging the invaders in a series of twelve successful battles culminating in that of Mount Badon or Mons Badonicus which broke the back of the invasions and ushered in a generation of relative calm, which probably even at the time seemed like a golden age compared with the chaos which had threatened. Possibly then he assumed a role equivalent to that of the Irish High King and remained a rallying point for preserving the integrity of the realm as a whole, without taking much active part in the detailed running of its constituent provinces.

That the realm did not last much beyond his death is the fundamental tragedy of Arthur's tale. He created a chimerical culture that fused the best of Roman and native British (i.e. Celtic) values, but it was too fragile to last beyond him. So the importance of Arthur to his countrymen at the time can hardly be exaggerated, even if the tales about him and his Knights of the Round Table most certainly have been ever since.

Despite the centuries of reworking and elaborating of the Arthur legend into the familiar shape we know today, largely carried out by medieval French poets and scholars, many genuinely Celtic elements survive at the kernel of the tale; for instance the gift of the sword Excalibur to him by the Lady of the Lake, who is a clear relation of the water-dwelling faeries of Ireland and Wales who by her gift signals the support of their British counterparts for his great undertaking. Sometimes this sword is confused with the Sword in the Stone but more commonly he receives it from a hand rising out of the water after his first sword breaks in battle with King Pellinore. Sometimes, confusingly, both swords have the same name and the John Boorman film *Excalibur*, 1981, reconciles this by having the broken sword re-forged by the Lady in the Lake. When he is dying Arthur famously asks Bedevere to cast it back into the waters, symbolising the end of his dream for the kingdom. Twice Bedevere pretends to do this because he cannot bring himself to waste so precious a weapon; and when Arthur asks him what happened and he says it just sank, Arthur knows he is lying. Then when at last Bedevere does throw the sword, a hand rises up out of the lake to catch it, and when he hears this Arthur is satisfied.

In drawing parallels between Irish and Arthurian motifs it is perhaps worth remembering the four great treasures the Tuatha brought with them to Ireland: the Stone of Destiny, the Irresistible Sword of Nuada, the Spear of Victory and the Cauldron of Plenty.

Under slight disguise these all feature in the Arthurian legend. The sword is of course Excalibur; the stone is the one from which he first drew the sword to claim the kingship; the spear is the one carried in procession with the Holy Grail, though it evolved over time into Longinus's lance which had pierced Christ's side; and the cauldron is the Holy Grail itself, which also feeds the lucky feasters at the Fisher King's table with whatever they most desire to satisfy body and soul.

The Fisher King and his elusive castle also fit the pattern of the Celtic faerie lord whose realm can only be reached through some portal into the Otherworld, so knights on the Grail Quest were not pointed in any specific geographical direction to find it, but had to follow the thread of the adventures that came their way in the hope of stumbling upon it. The castle is by its very nature not in this world but the parallel faerie one.

Other pointers to the genuinely Celtic foundation of Arthur's legend, besides the obviously druidic Merlin, show in the name of his witchy half sister Morgan le Fay (fay = faerie) and the arrival by boat of the queens to carry his dying body to Avalon for healing or burial. This is often identified with Glastonbury, which was indeed a holy island at the time, but Avalon was also one of the names given by the Irish to the fabulous faerie island far to the west of them.

Incidentally, another real candidate for being the British Avalon is the archipelago of the Scilly Isles off Cornwall, which have the largest concentration of ancient burial mounds in Britain. Many are now underwater because the existing islands are just the remnants of a much larger one which sank, possibly in Roman times. Even so, there are more rich burials than could be accounted for by even the original island, suggesting that royalty were shipped over there from the mainland. The Scillies have also been suggested among other places as the location of the lost kingdom of Lyonesse.

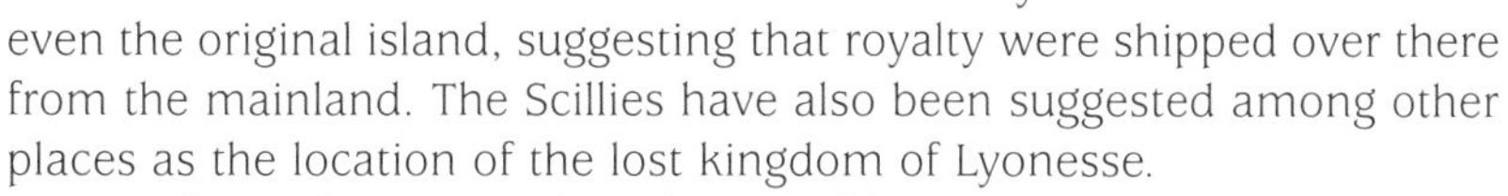

Geoffrey of Monmouth in his twelfth century *Life of Merlin* (*Vita Merlini*; 47-50) is tantalisingly vague about the placing of Avalon, (or Avalach which means 'The Island of Apples'), merely listing it among the Islands of Britain, but has some interesting details:

'The island of apples which men call "The Fortunate Isle" gets its name from the fact that it produces all things for itself; the fields there have no need of the ploughs of the farmers and all cultivation is lacking except what nature provides. Of its own accord it produces grain and grapes, and apple trees grow in its woods from the close-clipped grass. The ground of its own accord produces everything instead of merely grass, and people live there a hundred years or more. There nine sisters rule by a pleasing set of laws those who come to them from our country. She who is first of them is more skilled in the healing art, and excels her sisters in the beauty of her person. Morgen is her name, and she has learned what useful properties all the herbs contain, so that she can cure sick bodies. She also knows an art by which to change her shape, and to cleave the air on new wings like Daedalus; when she wishes she is at Brest, Chartres, or Pavia, and when she will she slips down from the air onto your shores. And men say that she has taught mathematics to her sisters, Moronoe, Mazoe, Gliten, Glitonea, Gliton, Tyronoe, Thitis; Thitis best known for her cither. Thither after the battle of Camlan we took the wounded Arthur, guided by Barinthus to whom the waters and the stars of heaven were well known. With him steering the ship we arrived there with the prince, and Morgen received us with fitting honour, and in her chamber she placed the King on a golden bed and with her own hand she uncovered his honourable wound and gazed at it for a long time. At length she said that health could be restored to him if he stayed with her for a long time and made use of her healing art. Rejoicing, therefore, we entrusted the King to her and returning spread our sails to the favouring winds.'

Culhwch and Olwen

Although the Arthur legend was largely elaborated in France and elsewhere in continental Europe, one of the earliest romances to feature him, several of his closest knights (Kay, Bedevere and Gawain) and Guinevere is that of Culhwch and Olwen, found in the fourteenth century *Red Book of Hergest*, but written some three hundred years earlier, and included by Lady Charlotte Guest in her translation of the *Mabinogion*.

The tale of the romance between Culhwch and Olwen is basically a vehicle for a much longer epic series of adventures for King Arthur and his knights, but if these are mostly extracted it stands up well enough on its own and is one of the most famous tales in the Welsh bardic repertoire. Its virtue for the old storytellers was probably that it could be expanded or shrunk to almost any size to suit the requirements of their immediate audience.

In the tale, the hero Culhwch's mother dies soon after giving birth to him. When his father, King Kilydd eventually marries again, his new wife tries to force Culhwch to marry her own daughter, probably to avoid having to give her a dowry. When he refuses she puts a curse on him that if he marries at all it can only be to Olwen, daughter of Ysbaddaden Pencawr, which means Hawthorn, King of the Giants. At the mention of her name Culhwch immediately falls in love with the maid, even though he has not met or even seen her.

Now not only was Ysbaddaden a giant of uncertain temper, but he was fiercely protective of his daughter and every man who had sought her hand so far had died. So it seemed likely that Culhwch would either stay a bachelor or die trying to win her hand. When he went to his father for advice, Kilydd suggested he seek the aid of his cousin King Arthur.

Culhwch travelled to Celliwig (meaning 'Forest Grove', possibly Callington or Kelly Rounds, a hill fort in the Cornish parish of Egloshayle) in Cornwall where Arthur was sitting with his court. There after some initial misunderstanding, the King readily agreed to help his young cousin with the quest. They set out with a great company of heroes and as they neared Ysbaddaden's castle they met a shepherd Custennin and his wife, who happened to be Culhwch's aunt, the sister of his mother. This pair were in the giant's service but had no great love for him. They tried to dissuade Culhwch from his quest but when he refused, agreed to help him. His aunt arranged a meeting with Olwen and Culhwch found her every bit as enchanting as he could have hoped:

'The maiden was clothed in a robe of flame-coloured silk, and about her neck was a collar of ruddy gold, on which were precious emeralds and rubies. More yellow was her head than the flower of the broom, and her skin was whiter than the foam of the wave, and fairer were her hands and her fingers than the blossoms of the wood anemone amidst the spray of the meadow fountain. The eye of the trained hawk, the glance of the three-mewed falcon was not brighter than hers. Her bosom was more snowy than the breast of the white swan, her cheek was redder than the reddest roses. Whoso beheld her was filled with love. Four white trefoils sprung up wherever she trod. And therefore was she called Olwen.'

Olwen was also smitten by Culhwch but said she could not marry without her father's permission, and that he would never give because it had been foretold that he would die the day she wed. The only hope, she said, was if he were to ask her father what he must do to win her hand, and then agree to whatever Ysbaddaden demanded, however impossible it seemed.

Armed with this encouragement and warning they proceeded to the castle and boldly asked for Olwen's hand in marriage. Ysbaddaden called for some servants to lift up his eyebrows, which had fallen down over his eyes, and examined his prospective son-in-law briefly before telling them to come back the next day. Then as they left he threw a poisoned spear at their backs. Bedevere caught it and threw it back, catching the giant's knee. He cursed that he would have to walk with a limp now but they left without further trouble.

The next day they returned and again demanded Olwen's hand in marriage for Culhwch. This time the giant said he would have to first consult with her grandparents, and as they left he threw another poisoned spear. Menw son of Gwaedd caught it, threw it back and caught him full in the chest. The giant cursed that now he would be short of breath when climbing mountains, but they left without further trouble.

On the third day Ysbaddaden again called for his servants to raise his eyebrows so he could the better see his future son-in-law, and he warned them not to shoot at him again. But as soon as he could, the giant again threw a poisoned spear. This time Culhwch himself caught and threw it back, right through one eye and out the back of his head. Ysbaddaden cursed that now his eye would water in the wind and he would suffer headaches.

On the fourth day Culhwch and his friends came again and warned the giant not to try any more tricks. Chastened by his failure to hurt them before, Ysbaddaden gave up trying to harm his visitors and reluctantly agreed that Culhwch could have his daughter for a bride, but only on certain conditions. He then went on to name a list of impossible tasks and treasures they would have to achieve, including the Thirteen Treasures of Britain amongst others, all of which had to be acquired in certain ways that made them even harder. However, forewarned by Olwen, Culhwch's only response to each of the escalating demands was a calm, 'It will be easy for me to compass this, although you may not think it.'

Finally Ysbaddaden ran out of demands (or possibly ideas) and Culhwch set off with Arthur and his warriors to achieve them. Then begins what to its authors was the main point of the tale, which is a string of wonderful and magical adventures for Arthur and his knights in which against all odds they succeed in each of the tasks in turn. Much of the narrative has been lost in the surviving manuscripts but the full version must have rivalled the Continental Arthurian epics in both scope and length, though with a distinctly more purely Celtic flavour very similar to that of the Irish heroic tales.

However, as far as the tale of Culhwch and Olwen goes, all that matters is that eventually they arrive at the final task, which is to obtain the comb, razor and scissors that lie between the ears of Twrch Trwyth, the most terrible of wild boars. These were needed, the giant had said, because they were the only barber's tools strong enough to tame his locks and make him presentable for the wedding. Twrch Trwyth had once been a human King but for his sins had been cursed into his present form as a monstrous boar with poisoned bristles. How the instruments came to be lodged between his ears is never explained, but currently he was living in Ireland with his seven younger pigs. So Arthur and his men crossed over the sea, made a truce with the Irish and enlisted many of them in support of the quest. They tracked down the beast and for the first day the Irish attacked him and his seven pigs, but to no avail. Then Arthur's men attacked him on the second day but still without success. Then Arthur himself fought the beasts for nine days and nights, but without killing even the smallest of them.

Then a truce was called and a messenger sent to tell Trwyth that all Arthur wanted was the comb, razor and scissors and that if he surrendered these he would be left in peace. Twrch Trwyth's response was to swim across the Irish Sea into south Wales with his piglets and begin devastating the country there. Arthur and his men followed in the ship Prydwen and the chase that followed gave the name to many places in Wales that survive to this day, each recalling an episode in the great hunt. Many of Arthur's men died, as did the younger pigs one by one till finally Twrch Trwyth was cornered in the Severn Estuary. Here he was driven into the water and surrounded, and two of the treasures were snatched from between his ears before he broke free and escaped. Then his hunters followed the beast into Cornwall and snatched the third treasure before chasing Trwyth into the sea, after which he was never heard of again.

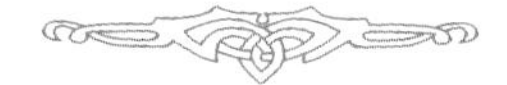

Finally they gathered all the treasure they had won and Arthur and Culhwch and as many as wished to go with them returned to Ysbaddaden's castle where they spread it all before him. He knew he was beaten. Kaw of North Britain then shaved the giant with the magic instruments they had won at such cost from the enchanted boar.

'Are you shaved, man?' Culhwch asked him.

'I am shaved,' replied the giant.

'Is your daughter mine now?'

'She is,' the giant replied, 'but for that you need not thank me but Arthur, who has accomplished this for you.' Which was true enough because Culhwch had not played any major part in the adventures. 'By my free will,' continued the giant, 'you would never have had her, for with her I lose my life.'

Which was also true, because they shortly removed his head from his shoulders and raised it on a stake above the citadel. Then they took possession of his castle and its treasures and that night Olwen became Culhwch's bride, and she continued to be his wife as long as she lived. Then the host of Arthur dispersed, each man to his own country.

PART 3

Parallel Worlds

CHAPTER 7

Christianity & the Faeries

CHRISTIANITY AS IT SPREAD ACROSS EUROPE always had to accommodate itself to some extent with paganism, usually by giving saints the same attributes as the old gods and displacing their temples with churches. This happened in Ireland after its conversion by St Patrick as much as anywhere, but somehow a different relationship and attitude towards the old gods developed there. They were demonised much less than usual and their continuing parallel existence as faeries was far more accepted than in most of continental Europe and what was soon to become England.

Much of this must have stemmed from the character of St Patrick himself who was determined enough in his challenges to the authority and religion of the druids, but charitable in victory. In fact druids were among his prime targets for conversion and he seems to have been able first to challenge them on their own terms in contests of magic and then persuade them with argument that the doctrines he taught were superior.

The background of his mission to Ireland is fascinating. In his own all too brief and modest *Confession* Patrick tells how he was born in Britain at Bannavem Taburniae, which was probably near the mouth of the Severn River, the son of a Christian deacon and grandson of a priest (celibacy not then being a necessary part of priesthood). Then at the age of sixteen he was captured along with several thousand others by Irish raiders and taken back as a slave. For the next six years he tended the herds of a minor noble named Miliuc or Milcho on Mt Slemish in County Antrim. By his own admission Patrick had not been a religious youth but now he took to praying and at the end of the six years his prayers were answered by a voice which told him in his sleep that it was time to leave, and that a ship would be waiting for him some two hundred miles away. Following his vision, Patrick ran away and did indeed find a waiting ship, probably around Wexford, which took him to France, from where he eventually found his way back to his family in Britain.

Patrick had not been home long though when he had another vision in his sleep of a messenger from Ireland who gave him a letter calling him back there. Similar visions followed and thus he found his vocation; but it was many years before he could follow it because he had first to train as a deacon and priest in France and Italy; then finally he was consecrated bishop in Auxerre and sent as an official missionary to the Irish from the Pope in Rome.

What exactly his methods were it is hard to say for certain because he frustratingly says nothing at all about them in his own brief writings. Many wonder tales were later written about his contests with the druids, but it is hard to separate fiction from fact in them. All that is certain is that he was utterly fearless, but also modest, loving and tolerant towards those he did not manage to convert.

His mission began around 433 AD close to where he had been held captive, at Saul (sabhall, meaning a barn) in County Down. There he converted the local chieftain Dichu who gave him a barn to be the first church in Ireland. He then tried and failed to convert his old master Miliuc before branching out across the rest of the country, beginning at Slane, ten miles from Tara. Here legend says he lit a fire in challenge to the pagan one then being lit on Tara for one of the great annual festivals (either Beltane or Samaine). This led to a wonderworking contest with the High King's druids that ended in Patrick converting two of them to his cause and even, some say, the High King Laoghaire (Leary) himself; though others say Laoghaire merely tolerated Patrick's activities and had a resolutely pagan burial himself when he died, planted upright in full armour in the ramparts of Tara facing south towards his old enemies in Leinster. From Tara Patrick went on to convert many other nobles and druids, some of whom became priests to help spread the word.

A charming account by the seventh century chronicler Muirchu tells how Patrick converted Laoghaire's two daughters Eithne and Fedelm:

'But St Patrick [and his people] then came, before sunrise, to the well which is called Clebach, on the eastern side of Crochan, and they seated themselves near the well. And behold the two daughters of King Laoghaire, Eithne the Fair and Fedelm the Ruddy came in the morning to the well to bathe, as women are wont to do; and they found the holy assembly of bishops and priests at the well.

'And the maidens said to them: "Who are you, and whence do you come?"

And Patrick said to them: "It were better for you to confess our True God than to enquire about our race."

'The maiden said: "Who is God? And where is God? And of whom is God? And where is His dwelling? Has your God sons and daughters, gold and silver? Is He everliving? Is He beautiful? Did many foster His Son? Are His daughters dear and lovely to the men of the world? Is He in the heaven or on earth? In the sea? In the rivers? In mountains? Make Him known to us. How is He to be seen? How is He to be loved? How is He to be found? Is it in youth? Is it in old age that He is to be found?"

'But St Patrick, filled with the Holy Ghost, answered and said: "Our God is the God of all men; the God of heaven and earth, of the sea and rivers; the God of the sun, the moon, and the stars; He has a dwelling in heaven and earth, and the sea and all therein; He gives breath to all; He gives life to all; He is over all; He has a Son co-eternal and co-equal with Himself; the Son is not younger than the Father; and the Father is not older than the Son; and the Holy Ghost breathes into them; the Father and the Son and the Holy Ghost are undivided; but I wish to unite you to the Heavenly King, as you are daughters of an earthly King, by believing."

'And the maidens, as if with one voice and with one heart, said: "Teach us most exactly how we may believe in the Heavenly King; show us how we may behold Him face to face, and we will do whatever you shall say to us."

'And they were baptised and clothed with a white garment on their head. And they besought that they might behold the face of Christ. And the Saint said to them: "You cannot see the face of Christ unless you taste death, and unless you receive the Sacrifice."

'And they answered: "Give us the Sacrifice, so that we may be able to behold the Son, our Spouse."'

Muirchu's version of this story then ends rather bizarrely with the two maids promptly dying after receiving Communion and going to meet their maker, but other records suggest they lived on in this world for at least a while longer, and their conversion is a historical enough event.

One aspect of the old faith that Patrick had no tolerance for, however, was of course the druidic practice of human sacrifice. It's impossible to know how prevalent this was in Ireland in his day and little mention of it is made in the old legends, despite the bloodthirsty nature of much of their narrative; but it must have been going on to some extent. Continental writers often remarked on the practice among Celts on the European mainland. Caesar commented distastefully that druidic temples, usually oak grottos, were often decorated with the bloody heads and limbs of sacrificial victims; though he was being a bit pious because it was only a century or so since the Romans had abandoned similar practices, and the legendary excesses of their public games still continued. Also Caesar quite routinely had captives tortured to death for information.

Pliny in his *Natural History* mentions the sacrifice of bulls in an observation on the druids' use of mistletoe, but it is likely that human victims often filled the same role: 'Having made preparation for sacrifice and a banquet beneath the trees, they bring thither two white bulls . . . Clad in a white robe, the priest (druid) ascends the tree and cuts the mistletoe with a golden sickle, and it is received by another in a white cloak. They then kill the victims, praying that the god will render this gift of his propitious to those to whom he has granted it.'

Caesar also mentions another method of druidic human sacrifice – the wicker man, which has become famous since the cult 1973 British movie of the same name. This involved building a large wickerwork effigy of a human which was filled with human victims and set alight. Preferred victims were criminals and enemies, but if none were available, innocent victims were supposedly chosen to placate the gods.

There is no mention of this kind of activity in the Irish chronicles but there are rumours of blood sacrifices, including human ones, to certain stones in Ireland which Patrick dismissed as 'idols'. The chief of these was Crom Cruach (Cenn Crúaic or Bloody Head) mentioned in the sixth century *Dinnshenchas* which stood on the plain of Mag Sleacht (now Moysleet) in County Cavan. This large stone, also called the King Idol of Ireland, was said to be covered in gold and surrounded by a ring of twelve smaller stones, often assumed to represent the signs of the zodiac. Sacrifices were made to it on either (or both) Lughnasadh at the start of August and Samaine at the start of November.

The cult of this stone was said to have been initiated by Tigernmas, the thirteenth King of the Milesians and its worship was dangerous even to initiates because Tigernmas and three quarters of his followers are said to have perished one Samaine night when presumably Crom was not satisfied with their offerings. In contrast to the other festivals aimed at promoting the land's fertility in Ireland, those at Crom Cruach and similar sites seem to have been more aimed at pacifying an inherently malign force rather than attracting the notice of a benevolent one.

However, the stone was no match for St Patrick who cursed it, whereupon it fell over and the twelve stones around it were buried up to their heads. Many other such stones, presumably less evil ones, were Christianised by being carved into crosses and it is quite likely that some of the finest of these high crosses, for which Ireland is famous, were once pagan 'idols'. There is no suggestion though that the stones were connected in any way with the other pagan gods of Ireland, the Tuatha who became the faeries.

In the wake of Patrick's conversion of Ireland another big change was the ending of the druidic convention that all ancient legend and lore should be carried purely in the memory, because of the Christian enthusiasm for books. This, combined with Celtic Christianity's remarkable tolerance of its own pagan past, probably helped by the recruitment of druids to the new priesthood, led to a mass of bardic tales being set in writing over the next few centuries which otherwise would have vanished completely. Much more material certainly did disappear, but it is still a remarkable literary treasure trove and a window into a unique ancient mindset. A whole new cycle of wonder tales also sprang into being, centred on Patrick, Brigid and Columba (or Columcille), who are all said to be buried in the same grave at Downpatrick. In these tales the faeries continue to behave much as they had done before, though their powers are no match for those of the saints. For instance:

In the time of St Patrick some faerie maids, Slad and Mumain, grand-daughters of the Daghda, fell in love with young Aedh, grandson of the King of Leinster. One day as he was playing hurley with his friends near the faerie mound of Liamhain Softsmock, they appeared clad in beautiful green mantles and enticed him and his fifty companions away into their bright underground palace. There they held them for three years until by chance the exit from the mound was left unguarded and they managed to escape. Having heard of Patrick's power over the faeries, Aedh sought out the saint and placed himself under his protection.

Dressing him up as a minstrel, Patrick took the prince on as a companion and in due course they came to the court of Leinster, still in mourning for its lost prince, where Patrick told the prince: 'Doff now for once and all your dark, capacious minstrel's hood and claim the spear of your father!'

Thus Aedh was restored to his inheritance and his overjoyed father Eochaid Lethderg declared: 'Holy Patrick, since you have taken my son under your protection, surely the Tuatha de Danann will no longer have power over him?'

'Surely not,' Patrick replied, 'and that death which the King of Heaven and earth has ordained is the one which he will have.' Meaning that the immortality which the faeries bestowed on those they adopted had been revoked, and Aedh was once again mortal and thus able to enter the Christian heaven rather than the pagan paradise of the faeries that was destined to vanish on the Judgement Day (*Silva Gadelica* [ii; 204-20]).

Not all humans were so keen to regain their mortality. There is a contrasting tale from around the same time of Laoghaire (Leary), heir to the throne of Connaught who, with fifty companions, willingly entered the faerie otherworld through a mound and enjoyed life there so much that after a year of it he decided to stay. Nevertheless, he regretted abandoning his family and people without explanation so he resolved to visit his old home to make his farewells. The faerie Fiachna explained to him how this could be done. He would lend Laoghaire and those of his companions that also wanted to stay some faerie horses for the journey, only they must not dismount or touch any person in the mortal world or else they would be condemned to stay there.

So at the great annual gathering of Connaught, Laoghaire and his friends suddenly appeared on horseback. His father Crimthann ran in joy to greet him, but Laoghaire cried: 'Keep back! It is only to bid you farewell that we have come.'

'Don't leave us!' his father cried. 'All Connaught's royal power is yours, its silver and gold, its horses and bridles, the choice of its fairest women. All of it can be yours, only leave us not!'

But Laoghaire turned away and returned to the otherworld where it is said he rules jointly with Fiachna to this day.

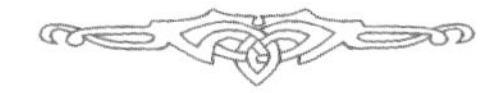

According to legend St Patrick's rescue of the prince Aedh was just one of many encounters he had with the Tuatha de Danann and the tone of them all is the same – their reality is accepted but their magic is inferior to his, just as the immortality the faeries offer is considered inferior to that of the Christian heaven.

In a thirteenth century manuscript known as *The Colloquy with the Ancients* (*Acallam na Senorach*) Patrick also meets some of the Fianna or Fenians from two or three centuries before, magically preserved beyond their natural span through having visited faeryland and then returned home to find that centuries have passed, a common penalty for visitors to the Otherworld, and also that people have shrunk during their absence, so that the Fenians seem like giants. These ancients, including Finn mac Cumhal's friend Caoilte, appear after Patrick says mass at the mound of Drumderg where Finn once lived: 'The clerics saw Caoilte and his band draw near them; and fear fell on them before the tall men with their huge wolf-dogs that accompanied them, for they were not people of one epoch or of one time with the clergy.'

Patrick as ever is totally unafraid of these pagan giants from the past but initially wary of talking too much to them, until his guardian angel appears to him in a dream to say that it is acceptable to God that he does so, and that his priests should write down what they have to say; which would seem to be how many of the tales of the Fianna come to have survived to this day. It all ends with Patrick baptising the old warriors, driving away a cloud of pagan demons that accompanied them and freeing their souls for the Christian heaven.

While Patrick and the Fenian Caoilte were talking, a lady appeared, wearing a 'mantle of green, a smock of soft silk being next her skin, and on her forehead a glittering disc of yellow gold.'

When Patrick asked who she was and where she came from, she replied that her name was Scothniamh or Flower-lustre, daughter of Bodhb Dearg and grand-daughter of the Daghda; and she came from the Cave of Cruachan. When Caoilte then asked why she had come, she replied: 'To ask of you the wedding-gift you once promised me.'

It turned out that back in the days of Finn mac Cumhal they had been lovers and, as they began to reminisce, Patrick broke in, saying:

'It's a wonder to see you two, she so young and lovely but you, Caoilte, a withered ancient, bent in the back and dingily grown grey.'

'It's no wonder at all,' Caoilte replied, 'for she is of the Tuatha de Danann, who are unfading and whose duration is perennial, whereas I am of the Sons of Mil, who are perishable and fade away.'

Soon afterwards, while still with Caoilte who joined him for a while, St Patrick met another faerie from Bodbh Dearg's sidhe. One Samaine Eve, according to legend, they were resting from their journey on a grassy mound when they were approached by a minstrel with a green cloak with a silver brooch, a tunic of yellow silk and a beautiful harp slung over his back. The stranger introduced himself as Cascorach, son of Cainchinn, a bard of the Tuatha de Danann, a position he aspired to himself. He said that he had come to hear tales of the Fenians from Caoilte to broaden his repertoire. Then to demonstrate his talents he began to play his harp for them and although he claimed to be just a student his music was so beautiful that soon most of the company was charmed into sleep.

Patrick himself was enchanted by the music but with a slight reservation, saying: 'Fine indeed it is, but for the twang of the faerie spell that infests it; apart from which nothing could more closely resemble the harmonies of Heaven.'

Although not present at the first meeting with Patrick, one of Caoilte's Fenian companions who also returned to Ireland at this time was Ossian (Oisin), Finn mac Cumhal's own son. He had married a faerie princess called Naimh and gone to live with her in the Land of the Young. They were very happy there and had two sons and a daughter, but eventually homesickness took hold of Ossian and he longed to see the green hills of Ireland again, and to hear news of Finn and the others. Naimh agreed to this, but sorrowfully because she feared she would never see him again. She gave him a white horse and warned him not to get down from it or set foot on Irish soil, or he would never be able to return to Tir na nOg.

Ossian returned to Ireland but found it strangely changed, the people diminished in stature and when he asked for news of his father Finn and the Fenians, they told him they had only heard of them in old tales from long ago. There are two versions of what happened next. One says that Ossian came across a group of these puny new humans trying to right a fallen stone, the other that he came upon a stone water trough where he and the Fenians used to refresh themselves and wanted to do this again. Either way, he dismounted, forgetting the warning, and as soon as his foot touched the ground the three hundred years he had been away caught up with him. Instantly he became a grey and shrivelled old man and his white faerie horse bolted and ran away, leaving him stranded.

In this condition he also sought out St Patrick, who attempted to convert him but Ossian put up a stubborn defence of his old pagan beliefs and the glories of the Fenian way of life and refused to succumb, saying that he would prefer to join Finn and the rest in Hell, if that indeed was where they were, than to join Patrick in his Christian Heaven. Although he failed to convert him, Patrick seems generous enough to have allowed their arguments to be set down in writing.

The Tuatha or Sidhe not only survived the arrival of Christianity in Ireland but continued to romance and have children with mortals, if one is to believe the legends. One of these was Mongan mac Fiachna, a historical Ulster King believed to have died around 624 AD. Here is one version of how he was conceived:

Manannan mac Lir had not visited Ireland for a long while, though he knew well enough what was going on there. So when he saw the country in fresh need of a hero he decided it was time pay a visit and help things along. Calling for his chariot, he rode out of the Land of Promise eastwards across the sea towards Erin, his chariot wheeling over the heaving sea as if it were a plain of grass.

Meanwhile Ulster's King Fiachna had been called across the sea to Scotland to the aid of his friend Aedan mac Gabran who was facing a Saxon army led by a giant that no-one could withstand. His wife, fair Caintigern, was left behind at Rathmore in Moylinny and it was here that Manannan came in the guise of a common mortal. He courteously explained to Caintigern that he would like to father a son upon her. She replied (probably less courteously) that nothing in the world would induce her to shame her husband that way.

'Not even if it would save his life?' asked Manannan.

He explained the situation, that Fiachna was going to face the Saxon's giant the next day and was certain to die unless some other champion killed him first. He offered to be that champion if only

Caintigern would sleep with him that night. Since she loved her husband, what choice did she have? The story does not tell of her feelings about the matter, but whatever they were, Caintigern submitted to the stranger's will and as he left with the dawn he let her know who he was, saying:

'I take my leave,
The pale pure morning draws near:
Manannan son of Lir
Is the name of him who came to thee.'

True to his word, Manannan appeared on the battlefield that same morning in Scotland and introduced himself to Fiachna, saying that his wife had sent him to face the giant in his place. Which he did, and when the Saxons saw their champion destroyed, their spirit broke and they were completely routed by Fiachna and Aedan's armies.

When Fiachna returned home to Rathmore he thanked his wife for the champion she had so fortunately sent, and even after hearing the price that she had paid, his gratitude was undimmed. And when after nine months she gave birth to her son Mongan, Fiachna accepted it as his own.

Other versions of the story say that what happened was that Manannan went to Fiachna first and offered to turn the battle if he was permitted to sleep one night with Caintigern, which he then did under faerie disguise as her husband, just as Uther Pendragon did when fathering Arthur upon Ygerne. Either way, Mongan was accepted by Fiachna as his heir and called his son, even though the parents knew his real father was Manannan mac Lir. More than this, though, Mongan was also the reincarnation of Finn mac Cunhal, with full recall of his former life. This was something he tried to keep secret but it came out through a foolish wager described in *The Book of the Dun Cow*.

One day when Mongan was King of Ulster he got into an argument with his bard Forgall, who was forever pestering other men's wives but was a great poet with a repertoire of tales that could last from Halloween to Mayday without repetition. So he was well rewarded by Mongan despite the jealous troubles he often caused.

Their argument was over where an old Irish King had died at the hands of the Fenian Caoilte, at a date which the *Irish Annals of the Four Masters* put as 285 AD. Forgall claimed it had been at Duffry in Leinster, while Mongan knew it had been on the River Larne in Antrim. He would not say why he was so certain however, and Forgall was so sure of himself that soon he was threatening the King with satires that would blight the crops and make him a laughing stock across Ireland unless he gave way: 'The poet said he would satirise him with his lampoons, and he would satirise his father and his mother and his grandfather, and he would sing spells upon their waters, so that fish should not be caught in their river-mouths. He would sing upon their woods, so that they should not give fruit, upon their plains, so that they should be barren for ever of any produce.'

This was no empty threat in those days when poetry was much mightier than it is now, so Mongan bargained with his poet and the wager they finally settled on was this – that if Mongan could not prove his case in three days Forgall could sleep with his wife Breothigern. She was furious and full of tears at this bargain but Mongan comforted her, saying that there was no chance she would have to go through with it, because proof was on its way.

On the third day Forgall came to demand his forfeit but Mongan persuaded him to wait till evening. Then night fell and Forgall came again to claim his prize; but as he was doing so it was announced that a cloaked stranger was approaching Rathmore bearing a mighty but headless spear-shaft. With this pole the stranger vaulted the three ramparts and strode into the palace till he stood between Mongan and Forgall.

'What is the matter here?' he asked.

'I and the poet yonder,' said King Mongan, 'have made a wager about the death of Fothad Airgdech. He says it was at Duffry in Leinster; I said that was false.'

The strange warrior declared that of course the poet was wrong. Then, addressing Mongan, he said: 'And it shall be proved, because I was there with you, with Finn.'

'Hush,' said Mongan, 'this secret should not be revealed.'

The visitor, it seemed was none other than Caoilte himself, the Fenian who had delivered the death blow and who had returned from the Land of the Dead to prove the truth of the matter. He then went on to describe the battle:

'We were with Finn,' said he. 'We came from Scotland and met with Fothad Airgdech yonder on the Lame River. There we fought a battle. I made a cast at him, so that the spear passed through him and went into the earth beyond him and left its iron head in the ground. Here is the shaft of that spear. The bare stone from which I made that cast will be found, and the iron head will be found in the earth, and the tomb of Fothad Airgdech will be found a little to the east of it. A stone chest is about him there in the earth. There, upon the chest, are his two bracelets of silver, and his two arm-rings, and his neck-torque of silver. And by his tomb there is a stone pillar. And on the end of the pillar that is in the earth there is an inscription in ogham which says: "Here lies Eochaid Airgdech. Caoilte slew me in an encounter against Finn".'

Caoilte then led them to the place he was talking of and everything was found just as he had described it. So Forgall lost his wager and it became known that Mongan was the reincarnation of the legendary Finn Mac Cumhal, though he did not like to speak of it. It is said his wife was often jealous of the long lost lovers he sometimes called to in his sleep.

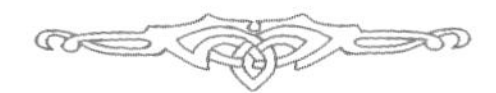

Aine

Another faerie romance well into Christian times that gave birth to a historical person is told in the tale of Maurice, Earl of Desmond, who lived near Lough Gur, fifteen miles south-east of Limerick, in the fourteenth century. Lough Gur is a magical place with the finest stone circle in Ireland nearby and castles, raths and floating islands testifying to its mostly happy occupation for several thousand years.

The goddess Aine is its patron and queen of the faeries of South Munster. Some have speculated that she is none other than the original goddess Dana herself, but much more commonly she is considered a daughter of Manannan mac Lir, which seems more likely. She was famous for her gifts of poetry and music to mortal men, to whom she often also gave her love and so became known as the Sweetheart of the Sidhe, Leanan Sidhe (Leanhaun Sidhe). A peril of this was that they often went mad and died young for love of her, but few thought this a harsh price to pay for her inspiration and the acclaim it brought them. She was also a great healer, and herbalists credit her with many of their cures.

While Leanan Sidhe was originally a nickname for just Aine herself, the term later came to be applied to the whole class of faeries who inspire mortal poets and musicians, with varying degrees of approval depending on the outcome of individual cases, because they are still inclined to go mad and die young. In the Isle of Man and Scotland it became the term for a whole class of vampiric faeries who deliberately set out to seduce would-be poets in order to destroy them (as opposed to benign inspiration simply proving too much for the poor mortal to cope with).

Aine's home was (and apparently still is) in the hill of Knockainey three miles away from Lough Gur, where on St John's Eve (Midsummer) all the people of the region would until about a century ago dance and light bonfires in her honour, afterwards making processions through the fields with straw torches to call down her blessing upon the crops and herds. Sometimes Aine herself appeared to a lucky few, usually maidens, and sometimes she let them look through her ring and see the rest of the faerie folk dancing beside them on the hill.

She lives three miles away but often enough visits Lough Gur to bathe and it was here, by the Camog stream that feeds into it that the Earl of Desmond came upon her one day long ago, combing her golden hair in the bright sun. He immediately fell in love and, guessing she was an immortal, stole her faerie cloak so she would have to do whatever he asked. Then of course he demanded that she sleep with him, which she did willingly enough because he was a handsome and charming man.

In due course she presented him with an enchanted son Gearoid Iarla, or Gerald, along with the condition or *geasa* that the Earl must never show surprise at anything the boy did, otherwise he would leave. Well, because he was half-faerie the boy was a magician and full of surprises, so this was not an easy thing to do; but the Earl managed for many years to keep a straight face whatever Gerald did.

Then finally one night at the feast, to show off to a fair maid, Gerald conjured himself completely into a bottle and then out again. The Earl's jaw dropped with amazement, along with the rest of the company, so this time it showed. Immediately Gerald left the feast and went down to Lough Gur where he changed into the form of a goose and swam out to the large island there, after which he was rarely seen again. The island is still called Garrett Island in his honour and whenever a goose and a swan are seen swimming together on the lake they are said to be Desmond and his mother Aine.

Gerald, the second Earl of Desmond is said to have disappeared in 1398. Also known as Gerald the Bard for his witty Gaelic verses, he is said to live in the lough still, appearing to locals in the moonlight once every seven years riding a white horse with silver shoes at the head of a faerie cavalcade. It is said that when the silver horseshoes wear out the spell will be broken and he will return to the world to lead his people once again in their darkest hour. Occasionally also his underwater palace has been glimpsed beneath the waves.

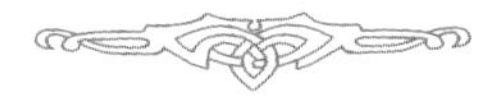

The Earl of Desmond was taking a greater chance than he knew in trying to force himself on Aine, or maybe just lucky that she was found him attractive. At another time she was raped because of her beauty by Aillil Olom, a King of Munster. During the rape she bit off his ear, which led to him being thereafter called 'Aillil Bare-Ear', but that was just the start of her revenge. Afterwards she made an enchanted hollow yew tree by a river near where he lived. In it she put a little man playing the sweetest music on a harp and when Aillil's son and his foster brother came by and heard the music they were delighted and each wanted the little harper and his tree for himself. They quarrelled and fought over it, then went to Aillil for a judgement over who should have it. He gave it to his own son and the bitterness this caused led in the fullness of time, years later, to the Battle of Mag Mucruimhe where Aillil and his seven sons all died.

In Brittany much the same beliefs about faeries prevailed as in other Celtic lands and lingered as long, much longer than in the rest of France. Their faeries were (and possibly still are) notoriously unpredictable. Although usually referred to as 'the gentlefolk', 'the good people' or 'the fair-folk' this was as elsewhere more a precaution against angering them than a description of their natural temperament. They could be charming, helpful, kind and generous, but they were equally likely to destroy human life on a whim.

This is shown in a charming tale from Brittany which must date from before the French Revolution, but was still being told by peasant storytellers at the end of the nineteenth century, when it was collected by the folklorist and poet Goulven le Scour of Carnac.

It seems that in the village of Kastel-Laer, near Finistere, there were once two neighbours and rivals Paol and Lon. Paol was a rogue who grew rich mainly through cheating everyone he had dealings with. Lon by contrast was honest but lame and weak and barely able to get enough work to keep body and soul together. Often he was reduced to begging.

One day Paol announced that he had seen enough of the backward provinces and was off to Paris to live the high life. To everyone's surprise

Lon declared that he would do the same, and they would see who came out of it better. The wager was joined and the two heroes set off. Paol strode off confidently and by one means or another reached Paris within three weeks, where he was soon happily employed as a thief and confidence trickster. Poor Lon limped along much more slowly, having to rely on the kindness of strangers and sleep where he could, often in the hedges when there was no barn or stable to be had. Finally he reached the great forest at Versailles near Paris and, having no other shelter, climbed into the hollow of an old oak by a pretty fountain that caught his eye.

He settled down to sleep on his leafy mattress but was woken at midnight by the clamour of a hundred faeries dancing under the moonlight in the clearing beyond the fountain. These were corrigans (or korrigans), the mischievous breed of faerie common in Brittany. As Lon peeped out both in wonder and fear, he overheard one of them boasting to the rest that he had cast an enchantment on the King's daughter that no mortal could break without knowing that all it needed was a few drops of water from this fountain in their faerie clearing.

Well, Lon managed to pass the night undetected in his hollow oak and the next morning before continuing on his way he filled his bottle at the fountain. Arriving in Paris, he heard the news that the King's daughter was seriously ill and that all the best doctors in France had been summoned to try and cure her.

So Lon presented himself at the palace, demanding an audience with the King. Looking like the beggar that he often was, it was no easy

matter but such was his insistence and so great were the fears for the princess that eventually it came about that Lon, freshly scrubbed and dressed in borrowed garments, was ushered into the presence of the wasting princess. No sooner had she drained the contents of his bottle than her malaise fell away and she rose from her sickbed as fresh as if it had been but a bad dream.

To celebrate her recovery, the King ordered a procession through all the grand avenues of Paris, in which Lon and the princess sat side by side in the golden state carriage. As word spread that she had been cured by a beggar, vast crowds turned out to line the streets; among them Paol, his old rival from home. When he saw Lon riding up there beside the princess he almost died of apoplexy.

At the end of the day Paol sought out his old neighbour at the hotel where he had been installed and asked how his dramatic change of fortunes had come about. Lon, honest and open as ever, told quite simply the tale of events and even described where he had chanced upon the faerie fountain. Paol raced off to the place that very night. Arriving just before midnight, he hid himself in the hollow tree to see what wonders he too might learn that might work to his profit. Just after midnight the corrigans arrived again with a great racket, only this time it was not a happy noise at all because they were furious about the princess's rescue from their spell.

'Someone must have overheard our plans,' cried their leader. 'And they must have been hiding in that old hollow oak. Let's destroy it so it can't happen again.'

And without more ado they blasted the old oak with elvish fire till it was burned to the ground with Paol inside. Lon on the other hand was given a pension by the King and was able to retire in comfort for the rest of his life, during which he acquired a great reputation for kindness to the poor and unfortunate.

CHAPTER 8

The Faerie Clans

ONE PROBLEM WITH DESCRIBING 'FAERIES' (however one spells the word) is that the term covers a much wider range of beings than, say, the word 'human'. In the Celtic lands formerly pagan gods became the Riders of the Sidhe, or Daoine Sidhe. These are the faeries we have mostly considered so far, but there are many other types which we shall look at in some detail next.

In the *Book of Invasions* the Tuatha society is described as consisting of 'gods and non-gods'. This has sometimes been interpreted as meaning that they fell somewhere between being gods and humans; but a much more likely reading is that their society was divided, as was ancient Celtic society, between nobles – warriors and their wives, druids and bards – and the rest who were basically servants dependant on the whims of their masters.

So far the faeries we have considered have mostly belonged to their aristocracy, but the others are just as interesting and have probably been much more commonly met in everyday life. In alchemy where, as with the faerie-faith, all kinds of pagan ideas lived on under a thin disguise, invisible beings were usually divided into four groups – Angels (equivalent to the Tuatha and the classical pagan gods), Demons (corresponding to the fallen Angels and inherently malign to humans), Elementals (sub-human nature spirits) and the Dead.

The third class of Elementals is further subdivided into four classes according to the four philosophical elements. These correspond to most

faerie groups below the level of the Tuatha. Although many people through the ages have suggested that these are just the dwindled remnants of the original proud and tall faerie folk, the earliest authorities suggest they are in fact quite separate in origin and come to be bracketed with the other faeries purely because like them they are mostly invisible. Broadly speaking, Earth sprites are gnomes, leprechauns, pixies, knockers, corrigans and other Little People who live in rocks, caves or underground. Air sprites are sylphs, flower faeries and most of the other faeries which people have seen through the ages. Water faeries include undines, mermaids, merrows and the like, including the Blue Men of Scottish lore. Fire sprites in alchemy were called salamanders and seem not to have any clear equivalent in Celtic mythology, unless one considers the dwarves who worked iron and grudgingly shared their secrets with human blacksmiths.

The dead were considered a separate class by the alchemists but folklorists have often found ideas of the faeries and the dead intermingled. When in the early twentieth century W.Y. Evans-Wentz was interviewing peasants for his monumental *Fairy Faith in the Celtic Countries* he found many witnesses who claimed to have seen familiar faces of the dead among faerie troops, and in some places like Brittany and Scotland he was told quite bluntly that faeries simply were the dead; while in Cornwall he found a quite common notion that piskies were the souls of the un-baptised dead. This was a minority opinion, that faeries were simply a kind of ghost, but there is some association between the two that possibly goes back to the days of ancestor worship.

According to Julius Caesar and others the pagan Celts were great believers in reincarnation ('In particular the Druids wish to teach this idea, that souls do not die but pass from one body to another.' *Gallic Wars* vi, 14) so it is quite likely that at one time they imagined that the dead joined the faeries for a time before being born again, but that the faeries themselves, being immortal, were a quite separate race. However, there is no one authoritative voice on the matter. Many different explanations for the origins of faeries have existed side by side and often in apparent contradiction – that they are fallen angels, the dwindled remnants of the ancient inhabitants of the land, the ghosts of the dead, or else the most common view that they are the inhabitants of a parallel universe partially overlapping our own.

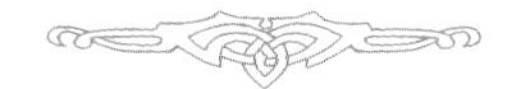

According to many authorities such as Robert Kirk, whose story we will come to later, there are broadly speaking five classes of Celtic faerie; and although their size and appearance is very elastic, they can roughly be arranged in accordance with the size and appearance they most commonly present to witnesses.

First come the Tuatha or Sidhe and their equivalents who are usually taller, wiser and more talented than humans.

Second come the Good People, often as tall as humans and also young and beautiful, but more frivolous than the Tuatha. They are said to direct the magnetic currents of the earth.

Third come the Little People who vary greatly in size but usually look tiny, young and beautiful and often dance in the air.

Fourth, and a little smaller, come leprechauns, brownies, Cornish piskies and Breton corrigans. They are often full of mischief and what people usually think of as gnomes (as in garden gnomes) really belong to this class of sprite.

Fifth, and smallest in stature, are gnomes – gloomy, thick-set earth spirits usually about two feet in height.

In practice though, these groups are usually conflated so that basically we have tall faeries, small faeries and solitary faeries like the leprechaun. Sometimes the division is simpler still and the faeries of all sizes are just divided between the more common trooping faeries of all sizes who seem to mingle quite freely (as in the many wonderful illustrations to Shakespeare's *Midsummer Night's Dream*), and the solitary ones like the Irish leprechaun and its kindred in other lands. As these form a quite distinct and popular class we are going to consider them next.

Leprechauns

Leprechauns are probably the most famous of the Irish faerie folk, apart possibly from the banshee. Though closely related to Scottish brownies, Welsh bwca, Breton corrigans and even the German kobolds, they have developed in folklore a quite distinct character. They are small people, witnesses usually describing them as between one and a half and three feet tall. Their main occupation is as shoemakers and tailors to the other faeries and they are usually discovered sitting cross-legged in a hedgerow with a leather apron tapping away at a tiny and beautiful faerie shoe. In fact the tapping is often what gives them away. Some Irish families have handed down such beautiful little shoes through the generations as heirlooms, along with the tale of how their ancestor managed to acquire it.

W.B. Yeats and others, including Lady Gregory, believed the name leprechaun is derived from the Gaelic *leith broghan* meaning 'the shoe maker', or even 'the one-shoe maker' because the leprechaun is almost always seen working on just the one shoe. Among other suggestions is that the word is derived from *luacharman*, the Irish for 'pygmy'. Whatever the truth, the term 'leprechaun' strictly applies only to the solitary Little People of Leinster Province around Dublin. Elsewhere in Ireland they used to be called by other names. In Munster Province they were luricaunes or cluricaunes, in Tipperary lurigadaunes and in Kildare luriceen. In Ulster they are or used to be called loghery-men or luchrymen; but the name leprechaun has generally come to cover them all.

An alternative explanation for its shoe-making was given to folklorist D.R. McAnally at the end of the nineteenth century by a peasant in Kerry, which was that the only time a leprechaun can be caught is when he happens to be mending his shoes, because the rest of the time he moves about so fast there is no chance; and his speed is why he wears out his shoes so quickly and is so often to be found mending them. However, much of what McAnally has to say about the leprechaun seems to belong more to the phouka that we'll deal with next. The more usual explanation is that leprechauns are shoe-makers to the rest of the Little People; they are working class faeries.

Leprechauns are mostly solitary and mostly male but there are tales of them being seen in company with others and although they seem determined bachelors it is assumed that they must occasionally have romantic liaisons for their line to continue; unless they are just the anti-social dropouts from the more sociable phouka that we'll consider next, who do have friends and wives. Leprechaun dress is usually old fash-ioned and threadbare, mainly in shades of green and brown that blend in with the hedgerows they frequent, but with occasional patches of red or even blue. Despite their look of poverty they usually have a crock of gold buried somewhere nearby, because they are great misers and, being faeries, know where treasure is hidden. Being misers they do not part with their gold easily. To get the secret of it out of them (according to folklore) you have to catch the leprechaun and hold on tightly, not taking your eyes off it for a moment and only then will he grudgingly lead you to it in return for his freedom, or grant three other wishes. Not taking your eyes off the sprite, even to blink, is essential and is the most common way by which leprechauns escape in the tales. They trick their captors into looking elsewhere for a moment, and when they look back all they are holding is the stump of a bush.

Another famous trick was that played on, among others, Oliver Thomas Fitzpatrick, a young farmer of Morristown Lattin in Kildare. One day during the harvest he was out in the fields binding up the oats when he heard a tapping like that of a stonechat, only it did not sound quite right to him for that time of year. So he very quietly went to investigate and what should he find in the bushes but a tiny man with an old fashioned cocked hat on his head and a leather apron, sitting cross-legged and tapping away at the heel of a tiny shoe. Now Tom knew all about leprechauns so he pounced and caught him tight. Gluing his eyes on the little fellow, he threatened him with all kinds of terrible things if he did not show Thomas where his gold was buried. Well the leprechaun seemed quite frightened. 'Very well,' said he, 'come along with me a couple of fields and I'll show you a crock of gold.'

So they went, Tom holding fast to the leprechaun and not taking his eyes off him though they had to cross hedges and ditches and a bog along the way, the leprechaun mischievously taking them the most difficult way possible. Finally they came to a large twenty-acre field full of ragwort or bolyawn. The leprechaun pointed to a tall plant in the middle of the field and said: 'There, dig under that bolyawn and you'll find a crock chock full of golden guineas.'

Now Tom had no spade with him and thought to run home and fetch one, but so he would know that particular ragwort again he took off one of his red garters and tied it around the stem.

'I suppose,' the leprechaun said quite civilly, 'that you've no more need of me?'

'No, you can go now if you like. God speed and good luck.'

'Well goodbye to you, Thomas Fitzpatrick, and much good may you do with what you'll get.'

Tom ran home as fast as he could, and then back again with the spade; but when he got to the field what did he find but a red garter identical to his own tied to every ragwort there.

The belief in Ireland that if you can catch and hold onto a leprechaun it will grant three wishes is very ancient. There is an eleventh century tale about Fergus mac Leite, a famous Ulster King who ruled just before Conchobar mac Nessa a thousand or so years before the story was written down.

One day Fergus fell asleep on the seashore and woke to find himself being carried away by a group of leprechauns. He struggled free and managed to catch three of them – one in each hand and a third pinned to his chest. 'Life for life!' they cried, an old bargaining formula to ransom one's freedom from a captor. So Fergus agreed to free the leprechauns if first they granted him three wishes. This they agreed to, if the wishes lay within their power. So first Fergus asked for the secret of how to travel underwater and was given a cloak which enabled him to do this (or some say it was certain herbs which he stuffed in his nose and ears when he wanted to go underwater). No mentioned is made of the other two wishes, the point of the story mainly being to explain how he acquired this useful talent. This story is believed to be among Jonathan Swift's inspirations for Gulliver's Travels.

From ancient times right into the beginning of the twentieth century this belief prevailed, and many tales of leprechauns being caught and forced to grant wishes in return for their freedom. Usually they managed to trick their way out of it but this did nothing to dampen people's eagerness to meet a leprechaun. When W.Y. Evans-Wentz was travelling Ireland in the early 1900s he was impressed by the commotion he found in Mullingar over a leprechaun that had been spotted by dozens of people. Half the parish were out looking for it and a rumour spread that it had been caught and locked in the town jail. But when the scholar asked an old local if this might be true, the man laughed and said of course not, for didn't everyone know that Leprechauns were a kind of faerie and could not be confined in any jail?

Leprechauns were once commonly believed to travel around in the form of 'dust devils' or mini whirlwinds and when people saw these they would often doff their hats with a polite greeting. Braver souls would throw a stone or branch at it because this made the leprechaun drop whatever it was carrying, including gold, but this could also anger the sprite and bring bad luck later.

Lady Wilde in her *Ancient Legends of Ireland* had this to say about leprechauns:

'The Leprechauns are merry, industrious, tricksy little sprites, who do all the shoemaker's work and the tailor's and the cobbler's for the fairy gentry, and are often seen at sunset under the hedge singing and stitching. They know all the secrets of hidden treasure, and if they take a fancy to a person will guide him to the spot in the fairy rath where the pot of gold lies buried. It is believed that a family now living near Castlerea came by their riches in a strange way, all through the good offices of a friendly Leprechaun. And the legend has been handed down through many generations as an established fact.'

She then told the tale of the ancestor who had made the family's fortune. It seems he was a poor boy who scraped a living by selling turf from his cart. He was a strange boy too, quiet and moody and unsociable, and people often said he was a changeling. He was also a great one for reading and had read all about leprechauns, so as he went about his business he always listened out for the tapping of a leprechaun's little hammer and kept his eye on the hedgerows.

Finally one evening as the sun was setting he came upon one working away under a dock leaf, dressed all in green and with a cocked hat on his head. So the boy jumped down from his cart and caught the little fellow by the neck.

'Now you won't stir from this,' he cried, 'till you tell me where to find some hidden gold.'

'Easy now,' said the leprechaun, 'don't hurt me and I'll tell you all about it. Mind you, I could easily hurt you if I wished, but we are cousins once removed, so I'll be good and show you where there's some gold. Come with me to the old fort of Lipenshaw where it lies. But hurry, because when the last red glow of the sun vanishes, so will the gold, and you will never find it again.'

So, still holding tight to the leprechaun, the boy climbed back in the cart and drove as fast as he could to the old fort. They went in through a door in the stone wall and true enough the whole ground was covered in gold pieces, and there were vessels of gold and silver lying scattered around.

'Now take what you want,' said the leprechaun, 'but hurry, because if that door shuts you will never leave this place alive.'

So the boy filled his arms with gold and silver and went out and flung them into his cart. He was just on his way back for more when the door swung closed with a clap like thunder and the place became dark as night, the leprechaun and remaining treasure both disappearing. So he drove home at once with the treasure he had and the next day went to Dublin and put it all in a bank, and when it was valued and counted up he found himself as rich as a lord.

Then as Lady Wilde concludes: 'So he ordered a fine house to be built with spacious gardens, and he had servants and carriages and books to his heart's content. And he gathered all the wise men round him to give him the learning of a gentleman; and he became a great and powerful man in the country, where his memory is still held in high honour, and his descendants are living to this day rich and prosperous; for their wealth has never decreased though they have ever given largely to the poor, and are noted above all things for the friendly heart and the liberal hand.'

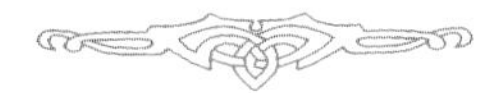

Phouka

A close cousin of the leprechaun but with rather different social habits is the phouka or pooka as described in the nineteenth century tales collected by Lady Wilde and W.B. Yates. The name they give this creature is slightly confusing because it has also been applied to a much wilder, almost demonic trouble-making sprite that often takes animal form for its pranks, but it was the name they found used in several different parts of Ireland. We'll come back to the pooka again later in its more evil form, but for now we'll consider just one of many examples in folklore of his tamer, helpful side.

'The Phouka,' Lady Wilde wrote in *Ancient Legends of Ireland*, 'is a friendly being, and often helps the farmer at his work if he is treated well and kindly.'

She illustrated this with the tale of a miller's son named Phadrig who was out in the fields minding cattle one day when a strange wind passed by, raising a swift-moving cloud of dust. Guessing what it might be, he ran after it shouting: 'Phouka, Phouka! Show yourself, and I'll give you my big coat to keep you warm.' In the next field he ran into an angry bullock, but calmed it down by throwing his coat over its head. It then told him (because it was of course the phouka in disguise) to go to the mill that night when the moon rose and he would find good luck.

Phadrig went to the mill that night and found nothing but sacks of corn ready for grinding and the miller's men all lying asleep. Soon he fell asleep too, but when he woke at dawn he found that all the corn had been ground, though the men were still snoring. This happened three nights in a row with no clue as to who was doing the labour. On the fourth night Phadrig hid himself in a big old chest, determined to stay awake and watch what happened through the keyhole. At midnight he saw six little men come in, each carrying a sack of corn. The seventh was an ancient little fellow in rags who ordered the rest about till soon the corn was all ground to flour.

The next night the miller himself hid in the trunk to watch this wonder. He was so delighted that he sacked all his men the next day and was soon growing rich on the wages he no longer had to pay them.

This went on happily for a while and Phadrig often used to hide in the trunk to watch the phouka and his little fellows at work. Then at last he began to feel a bit sorry for the old boy who, for all his labours, was still clothed in rags while Phadrig and his dad were piling up the money. So Phadrig had a little suit made of the finest wool and silk and laid it out on the floor one night at the spot where the old phouka always stood to direct operations. Then he crept into the chest to see what followed.

'What's this?' cried the phouka when he saw the clothes. 'Are these for me? I shall be made into a fine gentleman.'

So he put the suit on and strolled up and down admiring himself. Then he remembered the milling and was about to start ordering the rest about when suddenly he stopped and cried: 'No! No more hard work for me. Fine gentlemen like meself don't grind corn. I'll go out and see a bit of the world and show off my fine clothes.' And he kicked his old rags away into a corner and left.

So no corn was ground that night, or ever again by him and his band of little helpers, who all ran off. Phadrig never saw his helpful friend again but things were not so bad. The miller sold the mill and with all the money they now had they lived the life of leisured gentlemen. Phadrig became a great scholar and in time married a wife so beautiful people said she must be a faerie princess.

But a strange thing happened at the wedding. When they stood to toast the bride's health, Phadrig found by his hand a golden cup filled with wine. No-one could say where it had come from, but Phadrig guessed it was the phouka's gift. So he toasted his bride with it, and it must have brought luck for they were happy and prosperous ever after;

and the cup was still in the keeping of their descendants to the day Lady Wilde heard the tale.

The word phouka or pooka is related to the Welsh bwca and the English Puck, immortalised by Shakespeare and celebrated in Rudyard Kipling's *Puck of Pook's Hill*.

Ganconer

The ganconer (gancanach or gean-canach meaning 'love-talker') is an amorous and lazy cousin of the leprechaun who is never seen doing any kind of work at all but used to be famous for seducing shepherdesses and milkmaids and then, having had his wicked way with them, disappearing. This usually left them broken-hearted because after having made love to a faerie they could no longer settle for mere mortals. The ganconer was always smartly dressed and charming, and famous for his old-fashioned clay pipe or dudeen. When these were found near an old rath or ruin people would until about a century ago call them 'ganconer's pipes' and many of them were far too small, apparently, to have been used by humans.

Brownies

Brownies or brunaidhe are closely related to the Irish phouka (as described above) and are native to Scotland and northern England where it was once believed that almost every household, especially in the countryside, had one. Dobby the house elf in the Harry Potter tales is more or less one of them.

Brownies are generally described as being about half a yard tall, with brown, wizened faces and long, shaggy hair that grows all over their bodies so abundantly that they often don't trouble themselves with clothes at all. When they do, their garments are usually brown and very ragged but it was considered a mistake to pity them on this account. If presented with a bright new set of clothes a brownie will generally take umbrage and leave the household, just like Lady Wilde's phouka.

The explanations for this behaviour vary but it is such a consistent feature of brownie tales that it seems an integral part of their behaviour. Sometimes it is said to be vanity, that they suddenly get ideas above their station; but more commonly they are said to be insulted in some obscure way by such gifts. All they require in payment for finishing off all the little household chores left undone by their hosts is a modest portion of food and drink left discreetly by the kitchen hearth. Even here too much open generosity will drive them away. Brownies are said to be particularly fond of honey, cream and fresh baked cakes, if left out seemingly by accident, but are content with simpler fare such as bread and milk, according to the family's circumstances. In the days when most households brewed their own beer, they would be sure to pour a little malt from each batch into the hollow of a stone known as the Browney's Stane, so he would guard the brew and hurry it along. If this was forgotten, the chances were that the beer would go sour.

Apart from doing all the odd unfinished jobs around a house or farm, rounding up stray hens, finishing off the threshing and disturbing the sleep of lazy servants, a contented brownie brings good luck to a household. Often the brownie would move with its adopted family to a new place, riding in a milk churn or linen chest and then running on ahead at the end to make the new home welcoming.

If offended though they could easily ruin a family because a brownie can easily turn into a boggart or bogle, who do nothing but smash things and make trouble, behaviour which these days is usually attributed to poltergeists which are possibly the same thing under a different name. When they can find no congenial human house to live in, brownies are said to inhabit caves, hollow trees or river banks.

As with leprechauns, one rarely hears or reads about female brownies, but at least one was long famous in Scotland. Hairy Meg (Meg Mullach) and her partner Brownie-Clod were long resident in Tullochgorm Castle, owned by the Grants of Strathspey. Meg was a famous housekeeper who kept the castle spotless and could conjure any dish a guest asked for as if by magic. She was also a great fortune teller, and a talented chess player. When her lord was playing she used to stand behind his chair and silently steer him to victory.

Somehow Meg fell out with the Grants, probably for the usual reason of being overly appreciated, and moved away. Thereafter she travelled around Scotland not usually stopping long in any place, apart from a while at the mill in Fincastle in Perthshire. Her temper became dangerous though and she seems in the end to have turned into a boggart.

Another famous brownie was that which attached itself to the family of Maxwell, laird of Dalswinton in Dumfries in the late seventeenth century. In particular it attached herself to his daughter who was reckoned the prettiest girl in the River Nith valley. The brownie attended to her every need and when she married it was the brownie who dressed her for the occasion and, as Thomas Keightley expresses it (*The Fairy Mythology*, 1870) also undressed her for the bridal bed. When later the girl went into labour and a servant was dispatched for the midwife, the brownie was so furious at his tardiness at going about it that he wrapped one of his lady's furs around him took the servant's horse and rode out into the stormy December night himself, charging through the foaming waves of the Nith. When he got to the midwife's he pulled her up on the horse behind and terrified her by riding wildly back and plunging again into the river.

'Don't ride by the old pool,' she screamed, 'lest we meet with the brownie!'

'Fear not,' he replied, 'you've already met all the brownies you will.'

They arrived and he set her down safely on the hall steps before returning to the stables. There he found the servant whose job he had just done still only pulling on his boots. Removing the bridle, the brownie then chased the servant severely round the stable with it to teach him a lesson.

Sadly the brownie's loyalty was poorly returned by his master. This being the time of the Reformation, Laird Maxwell let himself be persuaded by a zealous minister that his brownie needed a good Christian baptism. The minister hid himself in the barn and when the brownie came to start his night's work, he jumped out, dashed holy water in the brownie's face and began the prayer. The brownie screamed in horror and fled, never to be seen in Dalswinton again.

In *Popular Tales of the West Highlands* (1890, Vol II; ch XXX) by J. F. Campbell we hear the tale of Callum Mor MacIntosh, who had a small farm in Lochaber around the time of the Highland clearances. Callum had a brownie (or bauchan) living with him with whom he was sometimes at war and sometimes quite friendly. One day for instance the brownie jumped out on Callum as he was coming home from Fort William market. They had a fierce scuffle but in the end Callum fought him off and carried on home. Later he found that he had lost a charmed handkerchief that was among his most treasured possessions. He and his wife searched high and low for it, till Callum remembered his fight and guessed the brownie had stolen it, for it had been blessed by the local priest and for that reason the creature hated it. He went searching and soon found the brownie rubbing the handkerchief hard on a flat stone.

'It's as well you found me so soon, Callum,' said the brownie, 'For if I'd rubbed a hole into this kerchief first it would've been the death of you, and no doctor or power on earth could have saved you. And you'll still have to fight me for it.'

'Fair enough,' replied Callum, so they fell to fighting again and Callum won his handkerchief back.

Soon after when Callum and his wife were snowed in and unable to get to a birch tree he had felled for the stove, he heard a loud thud outside on the front door and found the brownie had dragged the tree there for them. Then later when they moved to another farm nearby, Callum forgot to take a hogshead that they used for tanning hides. He was worried about it being stolen but the next morning he found it by their new front door, having been dragged five miles across the rocky hillsides. Years later people would show this hogshead to visitors as proof of the tale, pointing out the rugged course of its journey.

Later still when Callum was forced to leave his home and sail to America, he was kept in quarantine a while in New York. Finally he was put in a boat and taken to the mainland. When he leaped ashore, the first from that boat, he found the brownie there waiting for him in the form of a goat. 'Ha, Callum!' he said, 'I'm here before you.'

Callum was probably not best pleased at this but the rumour came back to Lochaber that in fact the brownie proved a great help in clearing his new lands for cultivation, and that he left off teasing and provoking Callum until he was comfortably on the way to prosperity.

Bwca

In Wales the faeries generally are called the Tylwyth Teg meaning the Fair People. This is a general term covering a wide range of them but on the whole it refers to the Little People rather than the type of faeries Pwyll and others met in the *Mabinogion*.

The Welsh counterpart of the brownie is the bwca, who is almost identical but more particular about neatness and will not help around the house at all if he considers it too untidy in the first place. Bwca need to be treated with the utmost respect because like brownies if they take offence they become regular demons, throwing things around the house at night, spoiling the milk and the baking, and ruining the beer. There is no end to the mischief of an offended bwca in fact, and they are as dreadful enemies as they are good friends. The only solution for those who have fallen out with their bwca is (or was in the old days) to call in someone who knew how to drive them away.

Piskies

Cornish piskies (pixies, pigsies) are close to leprechauns, phoukas and brownies in many ways, though with a slimmer and pointier appearance. Also the term seems to cover both solitary and trooping faeries, like the term 'corrigan' in Brittany. Under slightly different names, belief in piskies was strong in parts of the English West Country until about a century ago.

According to witnesses piskies usually have pointed ears, chins and noses. Often they look cross-eyed, but this is quite probably just their way of being rude to humans. There are various accounts of their origins, as with the Sidhe in Ireland. Some say they are the old pagan gods whose size has diminished in proportion to people's belief in them, so that most are now only about a foot tall and some no larger than ants. For this reason it is often considered unlucky in Cornwall to harm ants, in case they are 'meryons', or dwindled faeries. Some say they are the souls of the un-baptised dead who are neither good enough for Heaven nor bad enough for Hell. As the same is said about other Cornish sprites like knockers and spriggans, one suspects this suggestion for their origins was pinned to them by a Church reluctant to acknowledge the existence of spiritual beings that were neither angels nor devils.

In mischievous mode piskies delight in leading people astray and into bogs. Being 'piskie-led' or 'piskie-mazed' was once considered a very real peril on the moors of south-west Britain and many is the tale of hapless humans who only just escaped with their lives; and some that did not, though it is generally agreed that only bad people need fear being led seriously astray. Often at night people will be led by a mischievous light or Will o' the Wisp until they are hopelessly lost. But also sometimes in broad daylight they find themselves going round and round the same field, unable to reach the path home even though it is clearly in sight the whole time. Then they know that a piskie is misguiding their feet.

The cure is to sit down and turn your stockings

inside out, or sometimes just turning out your pockets will do the trick. If these fail, turn all your clothes inside out and the confusion will pass. There was a famous case of this in the parish of Costenton, or Constantine, collected by Robert Hunt about a hundred years ago. Not knowing the cure, the poor woman could only call out till someone heard her and came to the rescue.

There are many tales too of children being led astray, but this is usually a mark of favour. They are later found unharmed with wonderful stories to tell and are noticeably lucky in later life.

Piskies also love to steal horses and ride them round in circles, which creates fairy rings or 'gallitraps' of darker grass. Often when passing one of these places people will hear faint sounds of revelry. If they then step into the ring with both feet, they will become the piskies' prisoner. But if they put just one foot in, they can often see them without being caught.

Piskies generally live in caves, groves of trees or simply the meadows, but they have been known to adopt a family and move in with them. Then they help with housework, threshing and spinning and doing other such chores. Like brownies they appreciate being repaid with tactful gifts, but are generally insulted by gifts of clothing and will move out. Bowls of fresh water or milk should be left out for them as reward, and bread or cakes.

Like the cluricaunes of south-west Ireland, piskies were once fond of raiding the wine cellars of human gentry. From Luxulyan in Cornwall, in the bad old days when a thief was likely to end up on the gallows, comes the tale of John Sturtridge. One Christmas he was celebrating with other tin-miners, or 'streamers' in an inn called The Rising Sun above a moor called the Couse where they worked. They were in fact celebrating the original discovery of tin there by a man called Picrous, a festival which was honoured until quite recently and which at the time of this tale was still taken very seriously.

Well, John Sturtridge did his share of celebrating and then headed off rather unsteadily into the night for home. All went well till near Tregarden Down he came upon a group of piskies partying under a huge granite boulder. They shouted and laughed at him so John hurried on, a bit frightened. Soon he was totally lost, and soon after that he found himself back at the boulder. This time the piskies cried: 'Ho! and away for Par Beach!' And for some strange reason John found himself shouting this too. In a twinkling he found himself on sandy Par Beach with the piskies, and this time they let him join in their dancing and singing. Then soon the cry went up: 'Ho! and away for Squire Tremayne's cellar!' and they were all whisked away to Heligan (now famous for its Lost Gardens) and into the Squire's cellars there, which were full of beer and wine and brandy and all other liquors one can think of. Now the party really began and if the truth be told, poor old John Sturtridge supped a lot more than was good for him; and when the cry went up again: 'Ho! and away for Par Beach!' he was too slow to join in and was left behind.

So morning found him still there in the cellar among the spoils of the celebration feeling very much the worse for wear. Strangely enough, the butler would not believe his tale, and the Squire was even less sympathetic. John Sturtridge was thrown into jail, then tried and convicted of burglary. Finally one morning he was led out to the gallows where a crowd had gathered for his hanging. Well, poor John was just preparing to meet his Maker when there was a disturbance in the crowd and a little old woman forced her way to the front. In a shrill voice which he recognized, she cried: 'Ho! and away for France!' And in a flash they both disappeared, leaving the Squire furious.

On the whole the Church in Cornwall and Devon was quite tolerant of piskies, if only because of its flock's stubborn refusal to stop believing in them. But a few hundred years ago a certain Abbot of Tavistock decided to make war on them, banning the wearing of piskie charms, visiting piskie rings and the traditional leaving out offerings of food and drink for them. An immediate consequence was that the monks in the abbey dairy found that their butter would no longer set. Then when travelling on Dartmoor they were constantly piskie-led and unable to reach their destinations. Then all the trout vanished from the abbey streams because the piskies made them invisible, so there was nothing for the traditional fish meal on a Friday, which was a blow to the

Abbey's pride because its dinners were famous and it was a common local custom to describe a large person as being 'as fat as a Tavistock Abbot'.

Just as famous was the Abbey's cider, which was said to be the best in Devon, and even more famous than that was a unique liqueur the monks distilled from heather, whose secret recipe was only ever known to two monks at a time. This was the Abbot's favourite tipple but so determined was he in his war on the piskies that he took a vow in the chapter house before all his people that not another drop of heather liqueur would pass his lips until the piskies had been driven from all the land under his jurisdiction.

The story goes that when the piskies learned of this they devised a plan for the Abbot's undoing. One of them sneaked into the Abbey and changed the Abbot's cup of water into heather liqueur. As it had now been some time since he had last tasted it, the Abbot was transported with delight. Eager for more he went down to the cellars, dismissed the cellarer and had another cup of liqueur, then another and another because once he started he just could not stop. Finally he slumped sleepily to the floor, but then the piskies came and started tormenting him – pulling his ears and tweaking his nose and prodding his fat stomach. Drunkenly he chased them off and went back to sleep but soon they woke him again the same way and this was repeated many times till finally the Abbot was in such a rage that he stormed around the cellar cursing and swearing at them so loudly that the monks came to see what was happening – to find their master raving like a lunatic against invisible enemies and reeking of the drink he had sworn not to touch.

The disgrace that followed this episode would have broken a lesser man because the Abbot became the laughing stock of the county, but he was made of sterner stuff. After celebrating a High Mass he and all his monks made a solemn exorcism of the whole Abbey with bell, book and candle, sprinkling holy water into every corner. Then they made a tour of the Abbey grounds doing likewise. Then they made a tour of all the bounds of the Abbey lands, finally erecting a large granite cross at the boundary on the track to nearby Buckfast Abbey. Known as the Piskies' Cross it still stands there today on Whitchurch Common amid a golf course.

This seems to have done the trick because from that day no piskie was ever seen on Tavistock Abbey lands again. The fish returned to the streams and the butter set again as it had before. Life returned to normal, except that there were no more faeries; and apparently this continued long after the Abbey itself was destroyed by Henry VIII, no doubt to the piskies' glee.

Knockers

The other famous faerie folk of Cornwall, dating from when mining flourished there, are the knockers. These are generally helpful mine sprites and tin miners often used to hear them at work. Sceptics might say they were only hearing echoes of their own digging, but tin miners often swore to hearing them already at work when they first arrived on a shift, and carrying on after they left. They have also often been heard tapping away in long abandoned mines.

Knockers are naturally attracted to rich seams and following the sound of their little picks has led to many a rich strike. They also warn against cave-ins and floods by hammering wildly, or by throwing obstacles in the way of human miners at the entrance to a dangerous shaft. So in the old days gold and tin miners took care to keep in with them, leaving little gifts of food and drink and taking care not to whistle or swear when underground. Laughter and singing was permitted, however, so a happy mine was often a prosperous one.

Knockers were far more often heard than seen but there are a few sightings on record. In William Bottrell's *Traditions and Hearthside Stories of West Cornwall* (1870) a certain Captain Mathy describes how when following a tapping noise one day underground, he broke into a hollow in the rock where:

'When I rubbed my eyes and looked sharper into the inner end there I spied three of the knackers. They were no bigger, either one of them, than a good sixpenny doll; yet in their faces, dress, and movements, they had the look of hearty old tinners. I took the most notice of the one in the middle. He was settan down on a stone, his jacket off and his shirt-sleeves rolled up. Between his knees he held a little anvil, no more than an inch square, yet as complete as any you ever seed in a smith's shop. In his left hand he held a boryer, about the size of a darning needle, which he was sharpan for one of the knackers, and the other was waitan his turn to have the pick he held in his hand new cossened, or steeled.'

When he turned away for a moment to get his candle for a better look they scurried away. Another case is that of an old miner called

Trenwith and his son who lived near Bosprenis. One midsummer night they went to spy on a mine where the knockers were particularly active. At around midnight they saw a company of the Little People bringing out their rich ore into the open and by some means or other managed to negotiate a deal with them. The knockers would let them mine the rich seam they had found in return for a tenth share of the best ore, all properly 'dressed' and ready for smelting.

As a result of this deal old Trenwith and his son grew quite rich, but after the old man died the son tried to cheat the knockers by giving them short measures. As a result the lode failed, as did the son's luck generally. He took to drink, squandering their modest fortune until he died penniless.

In Wales knockers are known as coblynau and seem as close in general character and habits as the Welsh themselves are to the Cornish. Such mine sprites are known throughout Europe. In Scotland they are called 'black dwarves', in Austria 'shaft dwarves' and in Germany 'mountain monks.' Their size varies from a few inches to three feet or so.

Spriggans

The third most common type of faerie in Cornwall and Devon is the spriggan that guards buried treasure. Spriggans are standing stone sprites said to have come over from Brittany where they are known as korreds. In fact they are said to have brought over the megaliths and set them up in Cornwall in the first place. Some say spriggans are the dwindled ghosts of giants. They generally look small, even tiny, but can quickly swell up to enormous size, especially when defending their treasure. In appearance they are dour or fierce and often dreadfully ugly. They have a lot in common with Scottish boggarts except they usually content themselves with frightening people and robbing them, not actually harming them, though they have sometimes been blamed for blighted crops and bad weather.

As with piskies, a good defence against spriggans is turning one's clothes, or even just a pocket, inside out. Someone who put this to the test was the old widow of Trencrom Hill, an ancient hillfort overlooking St Michael's Mount in Cornwall. For some reason the local spriggans chose her cottage as their meeting place and most nights they gathered there to divide their spoils, while the old woman hid under her blankets and pretended not to hear them. At the end they always left her a coin for payment, so in fact she did not do so badly out of it for a miner's widow, but she wasn't happy and hatched a brave plan to get rid of them and make herself rich at the same time.

One night when they fell to bickering over a particularly spectacular pile of treasure, she contrived to turn her shift inside out under the bedclothes, then leaped out of bed and placed her hand on the treasure, crying: 'You shan't have any of it at all!'

The spriggans scattered in amazement and terror at the charm, leaving their treasure behind, but one of them struck her in passing and although she was indeed very rich from that day forward, and moved to St Ives to live like a gentlewoman, whenever she put on a nightshift again she suffered agonies.

At Carnac in Brittany the astonishing array of over 4,000 standing stones is said to be the work of corrigans (korrigans) who still dance among the stones at night. It is dangerous to spy on them though because they like to catch passers-by and make them dance till dawn, leaving them exhausted and with barely a breath left in their bodies.

If such visitors please them, though, the corrigans have been known to reward them by granting wishes. There is a famous tale of two brave tailors, Peric and Jean, who once dared each other to join the corrigans' dance. They drew lots to see who should go first and it fell to Peric, a humpbacked fellow with bright red hair. So the next night when they saw the corrigans dancing, Peric went up to them and asked if he could join in. They received him gladly and they were all soon dancing around to a song whose only words were 'Monday, Tuesday, Wednesday.'

Tiring of this monotony after a while, Peric added in a pause 'and Thursday and Friday.'

The corrigans were delighted by this extension to their song and offered a reward, asking him to choose between beauty, rank or riches. Peric laughed and said all he would like was for them to straighten his back and change the colour of his hair. So they tossed him into the air and passed him around their company like that till finally he landed back on his feet with a straight back and a fine head of black hair.

Scary Faeries

In Scotland they used to say of the faeries that there was the Seelie Court and the Unseelie Court; which was a way of saying there are good faeries and bad ones. In the Seelie Court are most of those we've considered so far, which are broadly speaking the 'good' faeries, although that does not mean that they are never dangerous to humans. Faeries have their own morality. For a start they are not prudish and many like to flit around perfectly naked, which in Scotland in the old days made them very suspect indeed, but to some faeries is just natural. However, there are some faeries who are purely malevolent, like the redcaps, who belong to the Unseelie Court and who deliberately set out to harm people just for the sake of it, or maybe from some kind of ancient jealousy or grievance.

The first scary faerie here though is alarming enough but not particularly malevolent at all. The banshee is only scary because she is the harbinger of grief; there is no question of her being the cause of it.

Banshee

Banshee (bean sidhe) literally means simply 'faerie female', just as 'fir sidhe' means 'faerie male' in Gaelic, but it has come to mean a quite specific type of faerie female, which is one that has adopted a family of ancient origin and screams when one of them is about to die. The traditional Irish keening at funerals was said by W.B. Yeats to be an imitation of this sound. Originally banshees did this for just five leading Irish clans: the O'Neills, the O'Briens, the O'Connors, the O'Gradys and the Kavanaghs, but there are tales of them having adopted many other families. Usually the banshee is solitary but occasionally there are three and there is a possibility that banshees are a survival of the ancient Tuatha triple war goddess, the Morrigan. As

with other triple goddesses the banshee can appear as a maiden, mother or crone, and she is related to the fabled ghostly washerwoman who, especially in Scotland but also in Ireland, washes in a pool or river the clothes of those who are about to die, keening all the while.

Thomas Crofton Croker, renowned nineteenth century collector of Irish folk tales, came upon a remarkable eyewitness account of a banshee from the previous century that was attached to the MacCarthy family of Spring House, Co. Tipperary, the diminished remnant of once powerful clan that included the Princes of Carbery in Cork. In 1749 young Charles MacCarthy inherited their modest estate at the age of twenty-one due to the early death of his father. He quickly fell into debauchery and excess, and after three years of this had so weakened his constitution that he caught some pneumonia-like infection that brought him to the brink of death. In fact his doctor pronounced him dead and the mourning had begun when in the middle of the following night Charles suddenly sat up and told of a startling vision in which he had stood before God's judgement throne, and as harsh but well earned punishment was being spelled out for his dissipations, his patron saint had spoken up and pleaded mercy for him. As a result, said young Charles, he had been given a second chance – a three-year extension of life in which to prove himself worthy of heaven. Having said this he relapsed into illness but from that point there was a steady improvement until he regained his full health.

Many people were inclined to dismiss his vision as a delirious fantasy but Charles himself continued to take it seriously even after he had made a full recovery and, without becoming overly pious or preachy, he became a reformed character. Three years passed and as the date of the prophecy approached there seemed no reason at all to fear for Charles's life. His mother Ann was worried though and asked her cousin Mary Barry to come and stay for the fateful anniversary weekend.

Travelling in a one-horse jaunting car, Mrs Barry and her two daughters were slowed by bad weather and told their driver Leary to stop at the house of an acquaintance along the way to shelter for the night. Then in the words of one daughter Ellen, describing the event in a letter sent from Spring House:

'My mother had scarcely spoken these words, when a shriek, that made us thrill as if our very hearts were pierced by it, burst from the hedge to the right of our way. If it resembled anything earthly it seemed the cry of a female, struck by a sudden and mortal blow, and giving out her life in one long deep pang of expiring agony.

'"Heaven defend us!" exclaimed my mother. "Go you over the hedge, Leary, and save that woman, if she is not yet dead, while we run back to the hut we have just passed, and alarm the village near it." "Woman!" said Leary, beating the horse violently, while his voice trembled, "that's no woman; the sooner we get on, ma'am, the better"; and he continued his efforts to quicken the horse's pace.

'We saw nothing. The moon was hid. It was quite dark, and we had been for some time expecting a heavy fall of rain. But just as Leary had spoken, and had succeeded in making the horse trot briskly forward, we distinctly heard a loud clapping of hands, followed by a succession of screams that seemed to denote the last excess of despair and anguish, and to issue from a person running forward inside the hedge, to keep pace with our progress.

'Still we saw nothing; until, when we were within about ten yards of the place where an avenue branched off to Mr. Bourke's to the left, and the road turned to Spring House on the right, the moon started suddenly from behind a cloud, and enabled us to see, as plainly as I now see this paper, the figure of a tall, thin woman, with uncovered head, and long hair that floated round her shoulders, attired in something which seemed either a loose white cloak or a sheet thrown hastily about her. She stood on the corner hedge, where the road on which we were met that which leads to Spring House, with her face towards us, her left hand pointing to this place, and her right arm waving rapidly and violently as if to draw us on in that direction.

'The horse had stopped, apparently frightened at the sudden presence of the figure, which stood in the manner I have described, still uttering the same piercing cries, for about half a minute. It then leaped upon the road, disappeared from our view for one instant, and the next was seen standing upon a high wall a little way up the avenue on which we purposed going, still pointing towards the road to Spring House, but in an attitude of defiance and command, as if prepared to oppose our passage up the avenue. The figure was now quite silent, and its garments, which had been flown loosely in the wind, were closely wrapped around it.

'"Go on, Leary, to Spring House, in God's name!" said my mother. "Whatever world it belongs to, we will provoke it no longer." "'Tis the Banshee, ma'am,' said Leary; "and I would not, for what my life is worth, go anywhere this blessed night but to Spring House. But I'm afraid there's something bad going forward or she would not send us there."

'So saying, he drove forward; and as we turned on the road to the right, the moon suddenly withdrew its light, and we saw the apparition no more; but we heard plainly a prolonged clapping of hands, gradually dying away, as if it issued from a person rapidly retreating. We proceeded as quickly as the badness of the roads and the fatigue of the poor animal that drew us would allow, and arrived here about eleven o'clock last night.'

The situation they found at Spring House was as bizarre as anything else in this tale. A wedding had been planned for the very day of the anniversary between Charles MacCarthy's ward Jane Osborne and one James Ryan (apparently Charles had tried and failed for some reason to have it postponed). This James Ryan though had some months before broken off a romance with another girl, whom he had seduced and made pregnant with the promise of marriage. Although he had given her a handsome settlement she had become unhinged by the shock and disgrace of her condition, and in the week before the wedding had been noticed lurking in the trees and bushes at Spring House. Then a couple of days before Mrs Barry's arrival Charles and James were out strolling with a friend when a shot rang out. She was aiming for her faithless lover but instead had hit Charles in the leg.

It seemed a minor flesh wound and preparations for the wedding had gone ahead, but then Charles became feverish and when the best doctors were sent for they announced that the wound had not been properly treated and that barring miracles Charles was likely to die very soon from it. So Mrs Barry and her daughters arrived to be told that he was on his death bed and was asking to see them so that he could spend his final hours alone in prayer:

'We found him perfectly calm, resigned, and even cheerful. He spoke of the awful event which was at hand with courage and confidence, and treated it as a doom for which he had been preparing ever since his former remarkable illness, and which he never once doubted was truly foretold to him. He bade us farewell with the air of one who was about to travel a short and easy journey; and we left him with impressions which, notwithstanding all their anguish, will, I trust, never entirely forsake us.'

So in this strange way Charles MacCarthy died on exactly the day he had predicted three years earlier and the poor young woman responsible was driven even more out of her mind by her bad aim, trying to the end to blame James Ryan for the murder she had committed.

Pooka

Earlier we met a kind of Irish sprite called a phouka or pooka who seemed very much like the Scottish brownie, no more or less mischievous and equally prone to adopting human households and helping with the work as long as it was treated right. But many more tales speak of the pooka's mischief and downright evil, often equating it with the devil or dhoul himself. There is a hint of such a darker side in the brownie's capacity to turn into a troublesome boggart, but it is also possible that the same name is used for quite different sprites in different regions.

The seriously scary pooka is a shapeshifter who most commonly liked to terrify people in the form of a talking black horse with fiery eyes and breath, though it can take milder form to lure the unwary into a trap. D.R. McAnally in the late nineteenth century heard of a man who went searching for treasure in a gravel pit near Clonlara in County Clare after a dream of finding gold there. When a normal-seeming pony came along he took a ride on it to shorten the way but it went rampaging across the countryside the whole night through before dropping him back at his starting point, where he was found the next day battered and unconscious. This is how they knew it had been a pooka, because they always drop their victims back where they started.

The pooka is said not to be able to seriously harm their victims as long as they are reasonably virtuous and respectful of the faeries. Their favourite victims seem in the past to have been drunkards weaving their way home alone on the country byways at night, who they forced to climb onto their backs under threat of being otherwise hoof-battered to death.

The Pooka has not always been so restrained. Before the days when Brian Boru was High King of Ireland it is said the spectre often simply killed its victims. Brian Boru got so tired of its depredations that he decided to teach it a lesson. Consulting all the ancient lore on this creature, he devised a magical bridle then set out one night in County Clare through a lonely region it was well-known to haunt.

Soon the pooka came along with its fiery eyes and mouth and fell into conversation, inviting him to take a ride on its back. The King played along but before he mounted up he slipped the magic bridle over its head so the pooka would have to go where he wanted. One limitation to this bridle was that it would only work for a radius of seven miles and the pooka was quite able to ride around half of Ireland in a night. So what Brian did was turn the pooka towards a nearby steep hill and he rode the beast round and round it up to the summit, back down and then back up again, over and over all the night long, driving it harder than ever a horse was driven before or since. Finally he gave in to the pooka's pleas for mercy and released it on condition that it no longer killed the strangers it waylaid. That hill looking northwards over Galway

Bay has been called Corkscrew Hill ever since on account of the spiral track worn into it by the pooka's hooves.

Another form the pooka commonly takes is of an evil-looking goat, also with fiery eyes. In his youth McAnally heard of one that terrified a poor country woman in the Cratloe hills of Clare around 1870, appearing to her as a 'black puck-goat with fiery eyes'.

Across Ireland the pooka is said to mark blackberries with its hoof at Michaelmas (29 September), after which they become unfit to eat.

Redcaps

Redcaps are among the most vicious of the Little People. At first sight they can look quite similar to brownies and the like, but the red in their caps is not from vegetable dye but the blood of passing strangers they have stoned to death. Redcaps live in old castles and towers, particularly along the English-Scottish border, in places where particularly wicked deeds have been done, and they feed the lingering echoes of violence with fresh bloodiness of their own. Their favourite trick is to push stones or boulders off cliffs or castle walls onto the heads of passing travellers; so it is dangerous to approach such towers alone, even in daylight. Even when in company one has to watch out for stones falling with uncanny accuracy towards your head.

Human strength counts for little against redcaps and despite their iron boots they can run terribly fast, but they can be driven off with quotes from scripture or the waving of a crucifix. They are also known as Redcombs, Bloody Caps, Dunters or Powries and you need to beware them most when their caps are looking dull because it means they are on the lookout for fresh blood to renew them.

The most infamous of this breed is said to be Robin Redcap who was the familiar or partner in wickedness of William de Soulis, the tyrannical lord of Hermitage Castle on the Scottish Borders. Folklore says de Soulis caught peasant children in order to use their blood in his black magic rituals. History suggests he may have died in Dumbarton Castle accused of plotting against Robert the Bruce, but legend gives him a much more colourful end. Tired of complaints about his infamy, Robert the Bruce is said to have told some petitioners that they could boil him if they wished but he wanted to hear no more about the man. They took him at his word and a mob stormed Hermitage Castle and dragged de Soulis to a nearby stone circle called Nine Stane Rigg, where he was wrapped in lead and boiled to death in a huge cauldron.

In Ireland the redcap is known as the fir dearg or fir darrig and is not quite as desperately violent but still full of bad will towards humans. In many tales he walks uninvited into people's homes and settles down by the hearth in his red cap and cloak. Any attempt to dislodge him or hurry him on his way results in terrible misfortunes, so the family has no choice but to put up with him as politely as they can until he leaves of his own accord.

Kelpies

The kelpie is a shape shifting faerie that often takes the form of a horse but inhabits the rivers and lakes of Ireland and Scotland, trying to lure people to their death by drowning. Sometimes it does this by wandering on the shore as a fine white horse and letting itself be caught and mounted by a passing traveller. Then it leaps into the water, drags them under and devours them. If its bridle is stolen it can be used to work magic, but if a human bridle is put on the beast, it can be tamed and put to work.

The kelpie can also take human form and lure its victim into the water in the guise of a beautiful maid or handsome young man, but their giveaway sign is that their hair is always wet and has waterweed tangled in it.

The kelpie in its water-horse form is often held responsible for lake monster legends in Scotland and Ireland. Not all kelpies were evilly inclined towards humans though. The one in Loch Garve, twenty miles from Inverness, abducted a young woman and carried her down to his house at the bottom of the lake, but only in order to make her his wife. She was happy enough with this arrangement apart from it being so cold down there and that all their food was raw.

One day as the kelpie returned home with a fine salmon for dinner, he overheard his wife saying to herself: 'I'm so cold! I'm so cold!' So, dropping the salmon he headed off for the village of Garve, changing into a fine white horse as he left the water. In the village he found the local builder who, seeing the beautiful stray horse, decided to take a ride on it. No sooner was he on its back than it galloped away back to the loch with the builder clinging on for dear life. Right into the water it charged, then dived beneath the surface and swam to its house on the bottom.

There he made a deal with the builder. If he built a fireplace and chimney, he would not only return the man to his home but give him a basket of fish whenever he wanted. And that is just what happened. The builder made a fine hearth and chimney and whenever he wanted fish for the rest of his life all he had to do was go down to the lakeside and call out to the kelpie for a basket of fish. The kelpie and his wife were happy too, and it is said that you can tell where their house is because there is a certain spot on the lake that never freezes over, no matter how cold it gets, and that is because of the heat rising from the chimney.

CHAPTER 9

Faerie Lore

Thomas the Rhymer

ONE OF THE MOST FAMOUS visitors to Faeryland was Thomas Rhymer, also known as Thomas Learmont of Ercildoune (now Earlston, Berwickshire), a village near Melrose in the Scottish Borders where he lived in a castle. Thomas was a renowned soothsayer of the thirteenth century who played an active part in the struggle to retain Scottish independence that involved Robert the Bruce, William Wallace and Edward I of England – a struggle vividly dramatised in Mel Gibson's 1995 film *Braveheart*. As with Mother Shipton of Yorkshire, many of the prophecies attributed to Thomas were written much later and after the events they describe, but enough must have proved true in his lifetime to gain him his wide reputation. He is said to have acquired his talent this way:

It was a tradition in Scotland that every First of May when the Hawthorn blossomed, the Queen of the Faeries would ride out from the west to the east with all her people in gay procession, moving from their winter abode to their summer one. The bells in the harnesses of their milk-white steeds would ring out along with their singing and laughter and enchanting music. 'The Faerie Folks' Raid' it was called, or people would just say 'there go the riders of the Shee' when they heard the sounds; and generally they kept well away because it was famously perilous to get caught up with the Good People, no matter how fair and merry they seemed. People would hide indoors with branches of rowan hung around the doors and windows to keep the faeries from stealing their children, just as during the winter raid at the start of November they guarded the house with holly and mistletoe.

The Queen herself would ride out in front in a cloak of green velvet and a dress of green silk, both adorned with sparkling jewels and golden thread. On her head was a circlet of gold with a shining gem and she was as beautiful as the dawn. Her people would follow, mostly dressed in green also and with red caps, playing golden harps and flutes, riding over the hillsides so lightly as not to leave a trace on the ground, or they would fly over the treetops through the air.

Most people hid from the faerie raid in the thirteenth century, but one May Eve under the bright moon Thomas Learmont came face to face with it on the banks of the Leader River and the Queen of the Faeries looked so radiant and beautiful that he fell to his knees and called: 'All hail, mighty Queen of Heaven! I have never before seen your equal'.

'Ah! Thomas,' she replied, 'you have named me wrong. I am but the Queen of fair Elfland, and I have come to visit you.'

Then she gave him a kiss and Thomas fell under her spell. She mounted Thomas up behind on her white steed and they galloped away with its bells jangling and all her people following on behind in wild procession. Over hill and dale they rode swifter than the wind till they came to a great desert with no sign of habitation in any direction. Then finally they came to a place where the way divided. The Queen of the Faeries bade Thomas dismount and said she would show him three wonders.

'Look,' she said, 'there lies a narrow road full of thorns and briars; it is the path to righteousness, though but few inquire after it. And see you there the broad highway that runs across the lily leven? That is the path to wickedness, though some think it the road to heaven. And see you there the bonny road that winds round the ferny hill? That is the path to fair Elfland, where you and I are bound this night. But, Thomas, you must hold your tongue whatever you hear or see there, for if you speak a word in Elphinhame you'll not return to your own country.'

She mounted Thomas up again behind her and they rode on along the third path through many rivers that rose to their knee, then through a strange dark land with no sun, moon and stars but in their ears was the roaring of the sea. At last a light appeared ahead that grew brighter and brighter till they stepped into a beautiful green country with trees and grass and flowers. In a glade they stopped and the Queen plucked an apple from a tree and gave it to Thomas saying: 'This is your reward for coming with me, eat it and you will have the power to speak truly of coming events, and men will know you as "True Thomas".' Which indeed came to be.

The Queen of the Faeries then led Thomas to her palace and clothed him in green velvet and silk. Then they feasted for what seemed to Thomas a night, and all the time he managed to hold his tongue and say nothing of the strange wonders he saw. So after the feast he was taken home again the same way and then to his wonder he found that what had seemed to be just one night had been seven years, and for seven years all his family and friends and neighbours had been wondering what had become of him.

After his return from seven mortal years in Elfland, Thomas became famous for his ballads and prophecies and he was called True Thomas because he could not tell a lie, whether he spoke of the past, present or future. Many of his prophecies came true in his lifetime and many later, and some are still waiting to be fulfilled today.

In his old age Thomas was talking one day with some lords and ladies by a river when the Faerie Queen appeared again and called to him: 'Hail True Thomas, your time has come.' So he mounted up behind on her milk-white steed and they galloped away across the ford. His companions rode after them but when they reached the far bank there was no sign of either Thomas or his Queen.

Thomas the Rhymer is said to still live among the faeries and has been seen among the Riders of the Sidhe when they gallop out from the Eildon Hills at the beginning and end of each summer, looking ancient and with flowing white hair and beard. At other times he is said to wander Scotland, mostly invisibly, going about the faeries' business. It is also said that he will return in the hour of Scotland's greatest need to aid his countrymen against their enemies, as he did when he was alive.

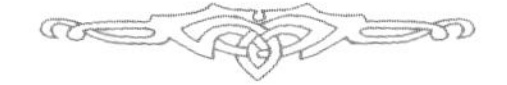

Michael Scott

Another famous friend of the faeries from the Scottish Borders in the thirteenth century was Michael Scott, a renowned wizard, architect and philosopher. He was a real enough person with a scholarly reputation across Europe, though some of the legends that have grown up around him in Scotland may be a bit fanciful.

There it is said he gained his remarkable powers this way: as a young man he was once travelling on foot with two friends to

Edinburgh. On the way they stopped to rest on a hill but were startled to hear a loud hissing. Then rolling towards them like a wheel across the moor came an enormous white serpent, which was not slowed at all by the slope but came trundling on up towards them. His friends ran for their lives but Michael was fearless even then and went to meet it with his walking staff. When it was near, the serpent uncoiled and reared to strike, eyes and fangs flashing like lightning, but Michael attacked so fiercely that soon the monster lay in three quivering pieces.

The companions went on in high spirits after this adventure and soon came to a cottage. As winter evening was setting in they knocked and asked for lodging for the night. The old wise woman who lived there welcomed them gladly, for it was a lonely spot, but when she heard the tale of their adventure with the white serpent she was troubled.

'Are you sure it was dead?' she asked.

'How could it not be?' they replied. 'We left it in three pieces.'

'Ah but it was no natural wyrm, being the size you say,' the wise woman told them. 'This has happened before. Another brave man was once attacked by it and left it in two pieces. But when he had gone the head crawled back to its stream, and after bathing there for a while it crawled back and joined itself to the other part of its body and became whole again. That is the way with these white wyrms. And after becoming whole again they lie in wait for the one who tried to kill them. Next time it attacks, you may get no warning.'

'Well, we'll take care never to go near that mountain again,' Michael declared.

'It may follow your trail,' the old woman said. 'If you want to be sure of your safety, you had best go back to where you killed it and bring to me the middle portion of its body. That way it can never make itself whole again. Hurry! before it's too late.'

So Michael went back and when he came to the place the head had indeed disappeared. Quickly he caught up the middle part of its body, which was still quivering, and carried it to the old woman's cottage in the dark, imagining all the way that something was coming after him. But he reached the cottage without trouble and was very glad to be back in its light and warmth, and for all the charms on the doors and windows that kept evil out.

The wise woman took the middle part of the serpent's body and laid it by while she gave her guests supper. After all they had been through that day the meal tasted like a feast, but their hostess was in such high spirits that after a while Michael couldn't help wondering if there was perhaps more to the business than she was letting on. So he resolved to stay alert and watch her closely. After the meal he said he felt unwell and asked if he could sleep in the chair by the kitchen fire. The woman seemed slightly put out by this but agreed readily enough. So Michael settled down in the chair and pretended to fall asleep while his friends took to their beds and were soon happily snoring.

Through half-closed eyes Michael watched the woman hang a large pot over the fire, place the portion of serpent in it and the lid on the pot. She left it to cook but after a while returned, raised the lid and prodded the meat with her finger. At this a cock crowed on the roof, startling Michael into opening his eyes fully. She noticed this.

'I thought you were fast asleep,' she said.

'I feel too ill for sleep,' he replied.

'Then you can help me with this,' she said, 'because I would dearly like to get a bit of sleep myself. Watch the pot for me will you, to see the meat does not burn; and call me when it is properly cooked. Only be sure not to touch the meat before I have tested to see that it is safe to eat.'

'I may as well have something to do,' said Michael.

'After the wyrm is cooked I will soon cure whatever illness you have,' the wise woman said with a winning smile, and then took herself off to bed.

Michael sat watching the pot, turning the meat occasionally with a ladle, and when it seemed to him cooked, he lifted it off the flames. But before calling the woman he decided to test the meat for himself, as the woman had done earlier. So he dipped his fingers into the stew and, scalded, instantly put them in his mouth without thinking. The cock on the roof crowed again even louder than before and the woman screamed with rage from her bed. Instantly a flood of knowledge poured into Michael's mind and he suddenly found he could see into the future as well as the past and present. Suddenly he also knew the cures of diseases and how to read the minds of other people, including that of the old wise woman, who he now knew for certain had been wanting this gift of enlightenment for herself.

'You didn't call me!' she screamed, rushing into the kitchen.

'I killed the serpent,' said Michael Scott. 'I had the right to taste its juice first.'

'Ah,' she replied, immediately humble, 'then I have no need to tell you of the blessings it bestows on the person who first tastes it. You are now wiser than I. You can cure diseases, see the future, command the faeries to do your will and obtain greater knowledge about the hidden mysteries than any man alive. All I ask of you now is friendship, and no anger at having tried to trick you out of this blessing.'

'That I grant you willingly,' Michael told her, and then they settled down and talked through the night till dawn, she questioning him about matters she had long wished to understand and he testing the limits of his new powers.

The next day Michael and his friends continued their journey and the tale tells of how, when at sunset they could find nowhere to shelter for the night, Michael flew them the rest of the way to Edinburgh on his walking stick, which had become his wizard's staff. The gatekeepers of the city were astonished to see them arrive with snow on their heads and shoulders, although there was none lying on the ground just then.

Among Michael Scott's many later accomplishments was the building of many bridges, dams and castles across Scotland, often overnight with the aid of the faeries.

That is how the legend says Michael Scott came by his powers. History says nothing like it, only recording that after being born in 1175 in the Borders or at Fife, he proved his talent in many fields, studying mathematics, philosophy and theology at Oxford University and also Paris. His chief fame however came from his brilliant translations of Arabic books into Latin in Toledo, Spain, including the Greek classics which had been largely lost in Europe and which later fuelled the Renaissance. This led to his adoption of Arabic dress which, together with the widespread suspicion of Arabic learning at the time, encouraged his reputation as a wizard, especially given his open interest in alchemy, astrology and sorcery in general.

The Holy Roman Emperor Frederick II recruited him as an astrologer and although he claimed there were too many variables for astrology to be a true science, he proved himself by using astrology to accurately predict the outcome of a war with the Lombard League. He also secured his place at the Emperor's court in Palermo, Sicily, by curing him of several troublesome ailments.

Scott's reputation as a wizard spread far and wide and he had the distinction of being consigned the eighth circle of Hell in Dante's *Divine Comedy,* although he is supposed in real life to have been Dante's favourite astrologer. In this circle those who in life tried to divine the future through sorcery are condemned to shuffle around with their heads twisted round on their shoulders so they can only look backwards and 'the weeping from the eyes ran down to bathe the cleft between the buttocks'. Among them is 'Michael Scott, who verily knew well the canny tricks of magical deceit.'

Border legends claim he also predicted his own death from a falling stone and took to wearing an iron cap to prevent this. But while hearing Mass in Melrose after returning from his Continental adventures, Scott was required to remove this helmet out of respect to God and a stone from the Abbey did indeed fall on his head and kill him in 1235.

In Scotland Michael Scott was almost as famous a builder as a wizard, although perhaps because his chief workers were the faeries there is not the usual distinction. One story tells how once when on the way to Inverness he came to a ford that was impassable because the river was in flood. Many other travellers were stranded on the bank and some remarked that it was a shame that no bridge had been built here yet. Michael replied that he had in fact come to build a bridge and that his workers would begin that very night. His audience laughed mockingly and went off to find shelter for the night. But to their great surprise when they returned the next day to see if the waters had subsided, they found a fine bridge newly built there, across which they could drive all their horses and cattle. And on their further travels they spread the fame of Michael far and wide.

His faerie helpers were so eager that when there was no house or bridge to build they pestered him for work. So one day he decided to give them an impossible task that would keep them so busy they would leave him in peace. So he told them to build a dam across the Moray Firth beyond Inverness and close it off from the sea. Well, far from being an impossible task, the next morning saw the job almost completed and the waters in the firth rising so quickly they threatened to flood Inverness. Michael climbed a hill and saw that the faeries had very nearly finished the task he had set them. Two promontories jutted from the north and south of the firth, leaving just a narrow gap for the waters of the River Ness to escape through to the sea.

So that night Michael commanded the faeries to undo their work, but as they were doing so a holy Christian monk came along and, suspecting they were up to mischief, made a powerful prayer to banish them. So the faeries left without completing the work and the two promontories are there to this day, the northern one being Chanonry

Point and the southern one having Fort George upon it, which guards the estuary.

Among the many other marvels credited to Michael Scott and his faerie helpers in Scotland are changing the course of the River Tweed and cutting a gash through the Eildon Hills near Melrose, a landmark that can be seen to this day from Scott's View.

Michael Scott's fading reputation was revived (along with many other Border legends) in the early nineteenth century by Sir Walter Scott in his epic poem *The Lay of the Last Minstrel*. Sir Walter claimed him as an ancestor, which may have been a fiction, but curiously enough one of his own nicknames came to be 'The Wizard of the North'.

Robert Kirk and the Faerie Commonwealth

One of the most rewarding sources of faerie lore is *The Secret Commonwealth of Elves, Fauns and Fairies* written by Robert Kirk in 1691. The author was the seventh son of the Rev James Kirk, minister of Aberfoyle in Perthshire near Loch Lomond, whom Robert succeeded as Episcopal minister in 1685 when his father died, after having been pastor in nearby Balquhidder.

In scholarly circles Kirk was most famous in his day as the first translator of the Bible and a psalter of Scottish metrical psalms into Gaelic, having graduated as a Doctor of Divinity from St Andrew's University at the age of 20. His book on faeries was almost certainly not noticed or published until 1815 after his strange tale came to the attention of Walter Scott while scouting for local colour for *Rob Roy*, and thereafter sprang into fame. One remarkable thing about his book is that it is not just a scholarly collection of regional peasant faerie beliefs, as might be expected from a man in his position. Much of it came from Kirk's direct observations of the faerie folk, working in the spirit of an anthropologist studying some shy and occasionally hostile race that he had managed to befriend.

He took their mundane reality for granted and saw no conflict between this and his Christianity. This was also remarkable because he was writing during the infamous age of Scottish witch hunts when faeries were mostly seen as belonging to the devil's party, and consorting with any supernatural beings other than angels was quite likely to end in a fiery death at the stake.

Being a seventh son was often said (not least by the Reverend himself) to be the source of Robert Kirk's 'second sight', and it would have been interesting to see what would have happened if he too had sired seven sons, but he only had two or three children. Whatever the cause, Kirk was at least a partially gifted seer who grew up in a region where this was a respected and respectable talent, and where people very strongly believed in faeries even though most could not see them.

Certain areas have always attracted tales of faeries and other supernatural beings, such as Pembrokeshire and the Gower Coast in Wales, Ben Bulben and Lough Dearg in Ireland, Carnac and the Forest of Broceliande in Brittany. Doon Hill (also known as Fairy Knowe, or Dun Sithean) near Kirk's home in Aberfoyle is one of these. A rounded, wood-crowned mound rising abruptly from a small plain, it was said to be riddled with caves where the faeries dwelt in magnificent splendour. It was here, often wandering alone at night that Robert Kirk would converse with the faeries and listen to their subterranean activities.

Perhaps he should have thought twice about writing his book though. In Celtic countries people were once notoriously wary of angering the 'gentle folk' by talking carelessly about them or revealing their secrets to strangers, and there were many tales of the devastating consequences of doing so. He died at the age of 52 just a year after completing it. Or perhaps he was taken by the faeries. What happened was that he collapsed and apparently died in May 1692 while taking one of his regular walks alone on Doon Hill, his body being found later when he failed to come home.

It was duly buried in the churchyard looking towards his favourite hill; but soon afterwards, according to the record of one of his successors in the parish, Kirk appeared to a relation in a dream, saying that he was not dead at all:

'Say to [Grahame of] Duchray, who is my cousin as well as your own, that I am not dead, but a captive in Fairyland; and only one chance remains for my liberation. When the posthumous child, of which my wife has been delivered since my disappearance, shall be brought to baptism, I will appear in the room, when, if Duchray shall throw over my head the knife or dirk which he holds in his hand, I may be restored to society; but if this is neglected, I am lost for ever.'

Well, at the christening Robert Kirk did indeed appear just as he had promised in the dream, but his cousin from nearby Duchray was so startled or amazed that he failed to throw the knife, so Kirk just drifted away and was not seen again; and it is assumed that he has been condemned to feast with the faeries ever since.

Today there is a tall pine looming above the rest on the hill's summit known as the Minister's Pine, and people hang ribbons on the bushes and branches around it for luck. Some say that his tomb is empty and that the faeries took his body as well as his spirit, but this has never been tested.

Robert Kirk opens his study by declaring his belief that constitutionally faeries are halfway between humans and angels, that their bodies were like the astral bodies later so popular with Victorian spiritualists and others. This accounted for their changeability and the faeries' ability to appear or disappear at will.

As we saw earlier, it was widely believed among all the Celtic people that faeries were some kind of fallen angel that were neither bad enough for hell nor good enough to get back into heaven. Often it was said that during the great expulsion of Satan and his rebels from heaven, many angels were carried along in the drift, then had the gates of heaven slammed behind them. Thus they were trapped in our middle world, neither joining hell nor being able to return to heaven.

Kirk said that the solidity of the faeries' astral bodies varies a great deal. Some are so refined that the only earthly sustenance they can share with humans is the spirit of distilled liquor or oil, or the scents of perfume and incense, while at the other extreme there are earthy sprites like brownies and leprechauns which can take not just the essence of grain and vegetables, leaving worthless husks behind, but can steal the actual corn or whatever itself. This kind of faerie could often be heard hammering and baking and weaving in their underground homes and were very like natural creatures except that they could disappear or change shape at will.

The faeries change their habitations every season, said Kirk, and on such Quarter Days people gifted with the second sight were liable to marvellous and often terrifying encounters. So in Scotland most people locked themselves and their livestock away, guarded with charms against the wilder faeries. Many went to church for the duration and some people, apparently, would not be seen in church the rest of the year except on Quarter Days.

Of the general organisation of the faerie world, Kirk writes: 'They are distributed in Tribes and Orders, and have Children, Nurses, Marriages, Deaths, and Burials, in appearance, even as we, (unless they so do for a Mock-show, or to prognosticate some such Things among us).' This is followed by a warning, common throughout the Celtic lands, against sharing the food at any of these feasts and funerals because mortals who do so often cannot return to their own world, or at least not without devastating changes, such as being mad or finding that a hundred years have passed.

Everything in the mortal world has its counterpart in the faerie one and the explanation of the occasional faerie raids on our herds and crops and babies is that when we have abundance, they have famine, and the reverse.

Although generally invisible to mortal eyes, faerie halls are described by those with the luck to have seen them as large and beautiful, brilliantly lit by lamps and fires that seem to burn without fuel. Women in Kirk's own time told of having been abducted to such places to nurse faerie babies, while at home a dull simulacrum took their places, going through all the motions of their normal duties but without any spark, so that their families often knew nothing of the abduction but just thought they were suffering from a loss of spirits. At the end of their duty they were allowed to return home but if by some accident, such as having splashed an eye with faerie ointment, they retained the ability to see the faeries, and revealed this to them, they were liable to be struck blind in that eye. Or else struck dumb to prevent them talking about what they have seen (this of course was at a time when most rural people did not know how to write).

To prevent nursing mothers being stolen by faeries this way, it was common in Scotland for them to sleep with a bible or a bar of iron beside them, faeries having a famous dislike of iron. Likewise, to prevent infants being stolen and a changeling being left in their stead, a bar of iron was often laid over the crib as they slept.

In their bright halls the faeries were said by Kirk to wear very similar dress to that of the humans where they lived. Their voices were clear and piping and they could speak human language if they chose. Their occupations were very similar too, the females weaving, spinning and embroidering, though Kirk did not know if this was with real wool, cobwebs or even rainbows. They were also often seen to engage in warfare, but again Kirk was unsure whether this was real or just a mimicry of human behaviour.

Kirk also said that although they live much longer than us, faeries are not actually immortal. They do die in the end, but not quite as we imagine it. It was a faerie belief that nothing actually perishes, it just passes from one state to another, just as nature appears to die in winter, only to resurface again in spring. Here we have the ancient Celtic belief in reincarnation mentioned by many classic authorities, including Julius Caesar, which is very similar to that of the Hindus and Buddhists, and probably stems from the same Indo-European root as their languages.

The faeries apparently had no religion, at least none that the

Christian minister Kirk could recognise as such, but they had an aversion to any Christian symbols, or any mention of God or Jesus.

Although repelled by iron, the faeries were said by Kirk to be invulnerable beyond the moment to human weapons because of their insubstantial bodies. In fact their medicine being so much better than ours, they suffer from no lasting or serious illnesses until their time comes to be reborn, when they simply waste away, at which point they were sometimes substituted for human babies as changelings.

Shunning iron, the weapons faeries used most often against humans and animals were 'elf-shots', little flint arrowheads that they could throw with deadly accuracy. The effect on the victim was an instant loss of vitality and faculties, generally followed by gradual decay and death. When the faeries 'took' an animal or human for whatever reason, it was usually just the essence they took, leaving the physical shell behind. The modern medical term 'stroke' describing the similar (or possibly identical) sudden loss of faculties is a shortening of 'elf-stroke' because in Kirk's day that was generally considered to be the cause.

After describing the care which country folk generally took not to disturb known faerie-hills, Kirk goes on to tell a tale he had heard on good authority in his former home (presumably Balquhidder). Around 1676 during a time of famine two women living some distance apart both dreamed on the same night of buried treasure in a mound known as Sithbruaich (literally Faerie-hill). In their dreams the treasure was first pictured and then a voice told them where exactly it was hidden. The next day they met accidentally at the place and when they dug in the spot described they did indeed uncover a vessel full of ancient coins, which they divided between them and used to buy food. There were apparently many witnesses who had seen these coins but Kirk left it to his readers to decide whether the vision had come from the faeries, angels or the restless ghost of whoever had buried the hoard.

Robert Kirk closes his study of faeries by quoting some cases collected from either the witnesses themselves or people they had spoken to. One was of a wife apparently stolen by the faeries soon after giving birth. They left a likeness behind which withered, apparently died and was duly buried. Then two years later she reappeared, convinced her husband that she was not after all dead and went on to have several more children with him. She said that during her stay with the faeries, nursing one of their infants, she at first could see very little until she came across an ointment which she rubbed in one eye. But when her hosts realised she could now see them clearly, they blew in it and she then became completely blind on that side.

Almost all that Robert Kirk had to say about the faerie beliefs of his part of the world has been corroborated by researchers and folklorists in other Celtic lands since, showing just how wide and consistent these beliefs were right up until the early twentieth century when modernism began to sweep them away.

A scholar mentioned briefly earlier who managed to capture this moment wonderfully was W.Y. Evans-Wentz in his 1911 study *The Fairy-faith in Celtic Countries*. Although later much more famous for his translations of Tibetan scriptures (including the famous Book of the Dead) this youthful investigation begun while studying at Oxford is nevertheless a classic in its field and shows a wonderful thoroughness and depth.

To gather material at first hand Evans-Wentz visited country folk in Ireland, Scotland, the Isle of Man, Wales, Cornwall and Brittany to collect stories, often sitting by a bright peat fire in some remote and humble cottage to hear tales from the most ancient and intelligent storytellers he could find. Most of these tales had passed down through generations purely by word of mouth among unlettered people but often it is possible to detect the outlines and often the very real substance of ancient legends first written down a thousand or so years earlier in manuscripts like those from which the *Mabinogion* was drawn.

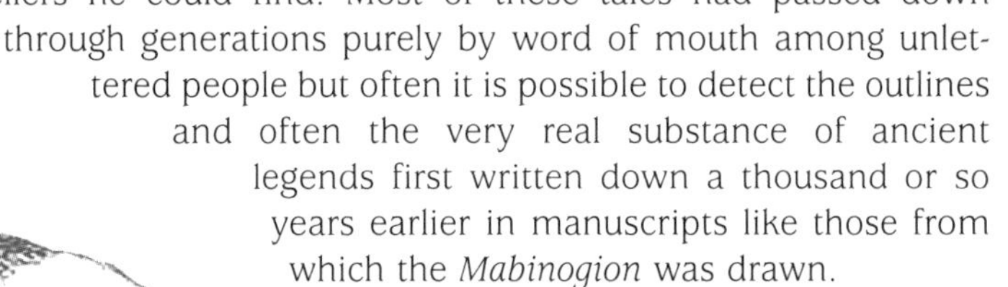

Although details often vary from place to place, much more remarkable is the consistency of most beliefs especially, for example, that regarding changelings. Through all the Celtic lands people once believed in the very real danger of babies, especially unbaptised ones, being stolen away by the faeries and usually replaced with either a husk of the infant that rapidly withered and seemed to die, or a wizened creature that would not grow at all. Local examples were readily quoted of family, friends and neighbours to whom this had happened quite recently.

Also consistent are the methods used to try and break the charm and get the original infant back. Often they involved trying to trick the changeling into speaking, in the belief that what the faeries had done was replace the human infant with one of their own that was sick or dying, or even just playing a hoax to receive the care that would naturally be given to a baby. The simplest trick was to go out as if to market or to work in the fields, leaving the infant alone in the house, then to sneak back and spy on it, when one might be rewarded with the sight of the creature dancing merrily round the cottage, singing and playing any musical instruments that came to hand with the skill that only faeries possess.

Another method, popular from Scotland to Brittany, involves setting eggshells by the hearth, filling them with water and then leaving them as if to boil. On observing this, the changeling was likely to be so bemused that it would give itself away by sitting up and saying aloud something like: 'Well, in all my five hundred years (or whatever) I never saw such a strange thing.' Whereupon it could be seized and forced into confessing the whereabouts of the true baby, often by being threatened with a red-hot poker or held over the fire.

In one Breton tale the changeling expresses its surprise a bit more poetically, saying: 'I've seen the acorn before the oak, I've seen the egg before the chicken, but never have I seen anything as strange as this!' Sometimes people reportedly dispensed with the eggshells and moved straight onto the threats, and one shudders to think of the number of sick or malformed infants who probably received this treatment. Another common remedy for changelings was to abandon them in the open where their crying would sometimes force the faeries to replace them with the original infants.

While on his travels in Brittany Evans-Wentz was told about a family plagued by changelings by renowned poet and folklorist Goulven le Scour who knew them well. A woman in the village of Kergoff, in Plouneventer had her first baby, a son who seemed perfectly bonny in all respects till one morning she woke to find him hideously changed, his back now hunched, his body twisted in other ways and his features suddenly wizened and dark. She had two more children, a girl and boy, and the same thing happened. They were born seemingly perfect and beautiful, then suddenly transformed into twisted mockeries of themselves. When a fourth child became due she was worried that the same would happen, but this time she was advised by someone who knew about such things to place in the crib a sprig of boxwood blessed by a priest, as most Breton mothers did, because the faeries were helpless against this charm. The mother did this and the fourth child apparently grew up perfectly healthy.

Unlike most changelings who either soon die or simply fail to grow as the years pass, these ones did grow and the eldest especially came to terrify the neighbourhood, trying to kill his mother several times, predicting the future and running about wild at night. The neighbours called him 'Little Korrigan' and he lived to over seventy, being reduced at the end to begging. People gave readily enough to avoid his curses.

As with changelings, when people in the Celtic lands fell into a coma or died suddenly, it was often assumed that they had been *taken* by the faeries and that there were ways to get them back. Evans-Wentz heard many examples of this, including this curious incident which was famous in the part of Ireland where he heard it:

'Father Patrick Noan while bathing in the harbour at Carns (about three miles north-west of Grange) was drowned. His body was soon brought ashore, and his brother, Father Dominick Noan, was sent for. When Father Dominick arrived, one of the men who had collected around the body said to him, "Why don't you do something for your brother Patrick?"

'"Why don't somebody ask me?" he replied. "For I must be asked to do it in the name of God." So Jimmy McGowan went on his knees and asked for the honour of God that Father Dominick should bring Father Patrick back to life; and, at this, Father Dominick took out his breviary and began to read. After a time he whistled, and began to read again. He whistled a second time, and returned to the reading. Upon his whistling the third time, Father Patrick's spirit appeared in the doorway.

'"Where were you when I whistled the first time?" Father Dominick asked. "I was at a hurling match with the gentry on Mulloughmore strand." "And where were you at the second whistle?" "I was coming over Corrick Fadda; and when you whistled the third time I was here at the door." Father Patrick's spirit then went back into the body, and Father Patrick lived round here as a priest for a long time afterwards.

'There was no such thing as artificial respiration known hereabouts when this happened some fifty or sixty years ago. I heard this story, which I know is true, from many persons who saw Father Dominick restore his brother to life.'

A Scottish Vision of the Dead

Around the same time as Evans-Wentz was collecting his tales all across the Celtic lands, Donald Alexander Mackenzie was much doing the same in Scotland, publishing the results in 1917 as *Wonder Tales from Scottish Myth and Legend*. Again he collected together many tales by illiterate nineteenth century storytellers that were virtually unchanged from versions written down a thousand years before, and some that were probably being told by bards a thousand years before that. Both collections are testimony to the remarkable endurance and fidelity of the oral storytelling traditions of the Celtic lands, having passed from the aristocratic bards and druids to enthusiastic amateurs among the peasants.

One of Mackenzie's stories encapsulates many of the basically pagan attitudes of Celtic people towards the faeries that happily survived alongside their outwardly Christian allegiances.

In Nithsdale in Dumfriesshire there once lived a poor woman who visited the dead in the Otherworld and this is how it came about. One day as she sat indoors spinning wool, her baby beside her in its crib, she heard a rustling as of leaves in the open doorway. Looking round, she saw a beautiful lady in a green silk dress standing there with a babe of her own in her arms. Smiling sweetly, she came in and asked the spinner if she would mind looking after her child for a while.

'Gladly,' the woman of the house replied, and took the baby to lie with her own. The day passed and towards nightfall she looked for the fine lady to return, but there was no sign of her so she settled the two children down for the night and went to bed herself.

The next morning she woke to find two beautiful sets of baby clothes beside her bed and some wonderful-tasting wheat cakes laced with honey. So she dressed the children and shared the cakes with them and all that day looked out for the lady, jumping up at every patter of leaves. But there was no sign of her that day or the next. Weeks passed by and she brought up the strange child as her own. Months passed and there was still no sign of her besides the refreshing cakes that often appeared in the night, and fresh suits of baby clothes now and then.

Then towards the end of the summer the lady in green reappeared. She was delighted with the obvious care that had been taken of her child but now, she said, she had come to take her home.

The woman of Nithsdale was sad. 'Of course you have every right,' she said, 'but I have come to love her almost as dearly as my own.'

'Then come with me,' said the faerie lady, 'and I will show you where we live.'

She led the way to a green hill not far away. When they were halfway up the sunny slope she said a few words in a strange tongue and the turf bank suddenly lifted up to reveal a door which opened for them and then closed behind when they had entered.

The woman from Nithsdale found herself in a bare, dim underground chamber. The faerie lady laughed at her disappointment, then took from her belt a crystal phial filled with dark green liquid. 'Now you shall see my home,' she said. She carefully tipped three drops of the liquid into her guest's left eye and said: 'Now look again.'

The woman looked and was filled with wonder because now she saw a beautiful land stretched out before her with green hills and forests and sparkling streams. There was a glittering lake and between the hills a plain of barley ripe for harvesting. The faerie then tipped three drops of the liquid in the woman's right eye and now she saw men and women gathering fruit from the trees and harvesting the corn. What is more she recognised many of them as friends and neighbours who had passed away.

'What are they doing here?' she asked the faerie. 'I know some of them.'

'They are working off their misdeeds in life,' said the faerie. Then she passed her hands over the woman's eyes and the vision disappeared, leaving them standing in the dim cave once more. Then after giving her gifts of rich cloth and healing potions, the faerie led her out of the mound again and bade her thanks and farewell.

The woman of Nithsdale went home and life carried on much as before save that she was richer now after selling the cloth and also she often saw the faeries coming and going in the countryside around. For a while she kept this talent secret but one day she greeted one of the faeries as they passed.

'Which eye do you see me with?' asked the faerie.

'Both,' replied the woman.

The faerie breathed into her eyes and vanished, and from that day she lost the power of seeing them, but she was happy enough and her baby grew up into a beautiful maid with a touch of the faeries about her.

Angus and Bride

Donald Alexander Mackenzie also came across some remarkable tales whose roots reach right back to the very earliest days: stories about Dark Beira.

Beira was said to be the mother of all the gods and goddesses in Scotland, just as Dana was of all those in Ireland. She was also responsible for fashioning most of the mountains, lochs and valleys of Scotland with her magic black axe, raising the mountains both as stepping stones for getting about the country and as homes for her many quarrelling sons, who were giants. Their battles are responsible for most of the random boulders found at the foot of these hills, because they were in the habit of throwing them at each other. Beira's own home was on or within Ben Nevis.

Beira was a triple goddess who every year passed through the three ages of woman – maiden, mother and crone. In her crone aspect she was Dark Beira, Queen of Winter, terrible and gloomy, her anger as bitter and merciless as the North Wind.

Back in the days when the world was still taking shape and the seasons had not yet settled into their familiar pattern, Dark Beira ruled the world and kept it in continual cold and darkness. In her stone castle she also held captive a beautiful young princess named Bride. Old Beira was jealous of the princess and made her life a misery. Dressed in rags like Cinderella, she was made to work among the servants at the humblest tasks, and fault was found with everything she did.

Then one day Dark Beira gave Bride a brown fleece and told her to wash it in the stream till it was pure white. Bride took the fleece to an icy pool beneath a waterfall and washed it all day, but by the end it was still as brown as in the beginning, though her hands were numb with cold.

Beira scolded her for being a useless hussy and told her to go back to the pool the next day and try again, and every day after that till the fleece was as white as snow. So every day after that Bride went to the Waterfall of the Red Rock and scrubbed the brown fleece and it seemed to her this sad and pointless labour would continue till the end of time; but one day an old man with a long grey beard came by and stopped to ask who she was and why she was weeping so bitterly. Bride told him and he took pity on her.

'Give me the fleece and I will make it white for you,' he said, 'for I am Father Winter.'

Taking the brown fleece, he shook it three times and it turned white as snow, and when he returned it to her he gave her something else as well, a bunch or pure white snowdrops.

'If Beira scolds you,' said old Father Winter, 'give her these flowers, and if she asks where you found them, tell her they came from the green rustling fir-woods. Tell her also that the cress is springing up on the banks of streams, and that new grass has begun to shoot up in the fields.'

Then he took his leave and Bride returned to the castle and laid the gleaming fleece before Beira. She hardly glanced at it but glared in sudden anger at the snowdrops in Bride's hand.

'Where did you find those disgusting flowers?' she screeched.

As she had been told, Bride said: 'The snowdrops are now growing in the green rustling fir-woods, the cress is springing up on the banks of streams, and new grass is beginning to shoot up in the fields.'

'Get out of my sight,' Dark Beira screamed, 'this is evil news you bring.'

Bride left with a light step, feeling that her life would soon change for the better, and she was right although it was hard to see at first. Summoning her eight chief hags, Beira despatched them on their shaggy goat steeds to all corners of Scotland to smite the land with tempests and gales and biting frost. She rode out herself too with her magic axe, with which she whipped up the oceans and brought terror to every living thing in the land.

Now the reason Dark Beira kept Bride prisoner was not just envy of her youth and beauty but because she knew that Bride might one day be the cause of her downfall, bringing about the end of her frosty reign. Her son Angus Og, the ever-young, had fallen in love with Bride after seeing her in a dream. Angus Og lived far away over the ocean in the Green Isle of the West, also known as the Land of Youth where it was always summer and age had no power. In his dream Angus had seen a beautiful maiden weeping by a pool. He asked an old man standing by in his dream who she was and why she was so unhappy, and the old man had told him about Bride and how she was held prisoner and cruelly treated by Beira.

When he woke, Angus went to his father, the King of the Green Isle, and asked him where he might find his dream maiden. The King told him that Beira kept Bride prisoner because she knew that the day Angus married her he would become King of Summer and she the Queen, and Beira's harsh reign would be over. Angus decided to set out immediately and because Scotland was locked in the snows of the wolf month (February) he borrowed three days from August, his own month and sent them on ahead of him. Then he mounted his white steed and rode eastwards over the waves, over the Western Isles and landed in the Grampian Mountains as bright dawn was breaking, his golden tunic shining and his crimson mantle spread out across the sky. An ancient bard seeing his arrival raised his harp and sang:

'Angus hath come – the young, the fair
The blue-eyed god with golden hair
The god who to the world doth bring
This morn the promise of the spring;

'Who moves the birds to song ere yet
He hath awaked the violet
Or the soft primrose on the steep
While buds are laid in lidded sleep;

'And white snows wrap the hills serene
Ere glows the larch's vivid green
Through the brown woods and bare. All hail!
Angus, and may thy will prevail.'

Angus searched everywhere but could find no trace of Princess Bride. She however saw him in a dream and knew he had come looking for her. When she woke she wept tears of joy and wherever her tears fell, violets sprang up as blue as her beautiful eyes.

Dark Beira was furious when she heard Angus had come searching for her captive. She raised a great storm to drive him back to the Green Isle, but Angus fought against it and carried on his search till finally he found the castle where Bride was held, and he met Bride herself in the forest nearby. Violets and primroses blossomed in the warmth and bright sunshine Angus had brought with him, trees burst into leaf and birds into songs of joy.

•

'Beautiful princess,' said Angus, 'I saw you in a dream weeping tears of sorrow.'

Bride replied: 'Mighty prince, I saw you in a dream too, riding over hills and through glens in beauty and power.'

'I have come to rescue you from Queen Beira, who has kept you all this long winter in captivity.'

'To me this is a day of great joy,' Bride said.

'It will be a day of great joy to all mankind ever after this,' Angus replied, and indeed the first day of spring at the start of February has been called Bride's Day in Scotland ever since.

Through the woods came a company of faeries who greeted Angus and hailed Bride as Queen of the Summer. The Faerie Queen waved her wand and Bride's rags became a white wedding dress sparkling with gems and with a jewelled clasp at her throat. Then the Faerie Queen led the couple into her underground palace within the forest for a marriage feast and all the land thrilled with the joy of that union, which was the first Festival of Bride.

The joy did not last, however. When Dark Beira heard of the wedding and the joy that was spreading through the land, she struck the ground so hard with her magic axe that it froze solid as iron again. Then she scattered her eight hags on their shaggy goats to the corners of the kingdom again to make war on Angus with tempest and storm, while she mounted her black horse and rode to the mound of the Faerie Queen. Angus and Bride fled on his white steed to the Green Isle in the west while the faeries locked all the doors of their palaces and winter once again gripped the land.

From the Green Isle Angus made many raids on Beira's realm and each time the sun shone and the land struggled to bring forth life, and each time he was driven away again by fresh storms. Beira's gales lashed the land and froze the herds on the hills and the birds in the trees. Often it seemed that she was invincible but gradually she and her hags weakened under Angus's repeated assaults till finally he drove the hags away to the north. Beira chased after them and roused them for one final battle against Angus to destroy him once and for all.

Out of the frozen north they rode in the midst of a black tempest. Also Beira borrowed the three missing days from the start of February, just as Angus had done from August, and sent them on ahead in the form of three black hogs that devastated the land and sea, killing cattle, sheep and humans alike. These days were later called the Three Hog Days and days like them at the end of winter are still called that now.

But then a great weariness came over Beira as she saw Angus kill the black hogs and scatter her hags. Finally she lost the will to fight and a great longing came over her to visit the Spring of Youth in the Green Isle. So she turned her black steed northwards and fled, resting awhile on the Isle of Skye before heading westwards out over the ocean.

That same day, the first of May, Angus brought Bride to Scotland and they were crowned King and Queen of summer and they rode from south to north and from east to west, accompanied by a warm breeze that melted the last of the snow and ice and breathed life into the grass and flowers and trees. Crops grew in the fields and the beasts multiplied. Wherever they went, Angus played on his golden harp and his songs spread love and joy wherever they were heard. Birds that were the kisses of lovers flew around his head, darting away sometimes to inspire thoughts of love in others.

When softly blew the south wind o'er the sea,
Lisping of springtime hope and summer pride,
And the rough reign of Beira ceased to be,
Angus the Ever-Young,
The beauteous god of love, the golden-haired,
The blue mysterious-eyed,
Shone like the star of morning high among
The stars that shrank afraid
When dawn proclaimed the triumph that he shared
With Bride the peerless maid.
Then winds of violet sweetness rose and sighed,
No conquest is compared
To Love's transcendent joys that never fade.

Beira meanwhile in the Green Isle drank at the Fountain of Youth and became young again and as beautiful as Bride, but she aged quickly over the summer. By autumn she was a grim crone again and returned to seize power over the land, driving out all the bright joys brought by Angus and Bride, and drawing cold and darkness down out of the north. And that has been the way of it ever since. Each spring Dark Beira does battle with Angus Og until at last she retires to the Green Isle to renew her youth; and each autumn she returns and wrests control of the land from him again, so that he and Bride have to retreat.

PART 4

The Celtic Twilight

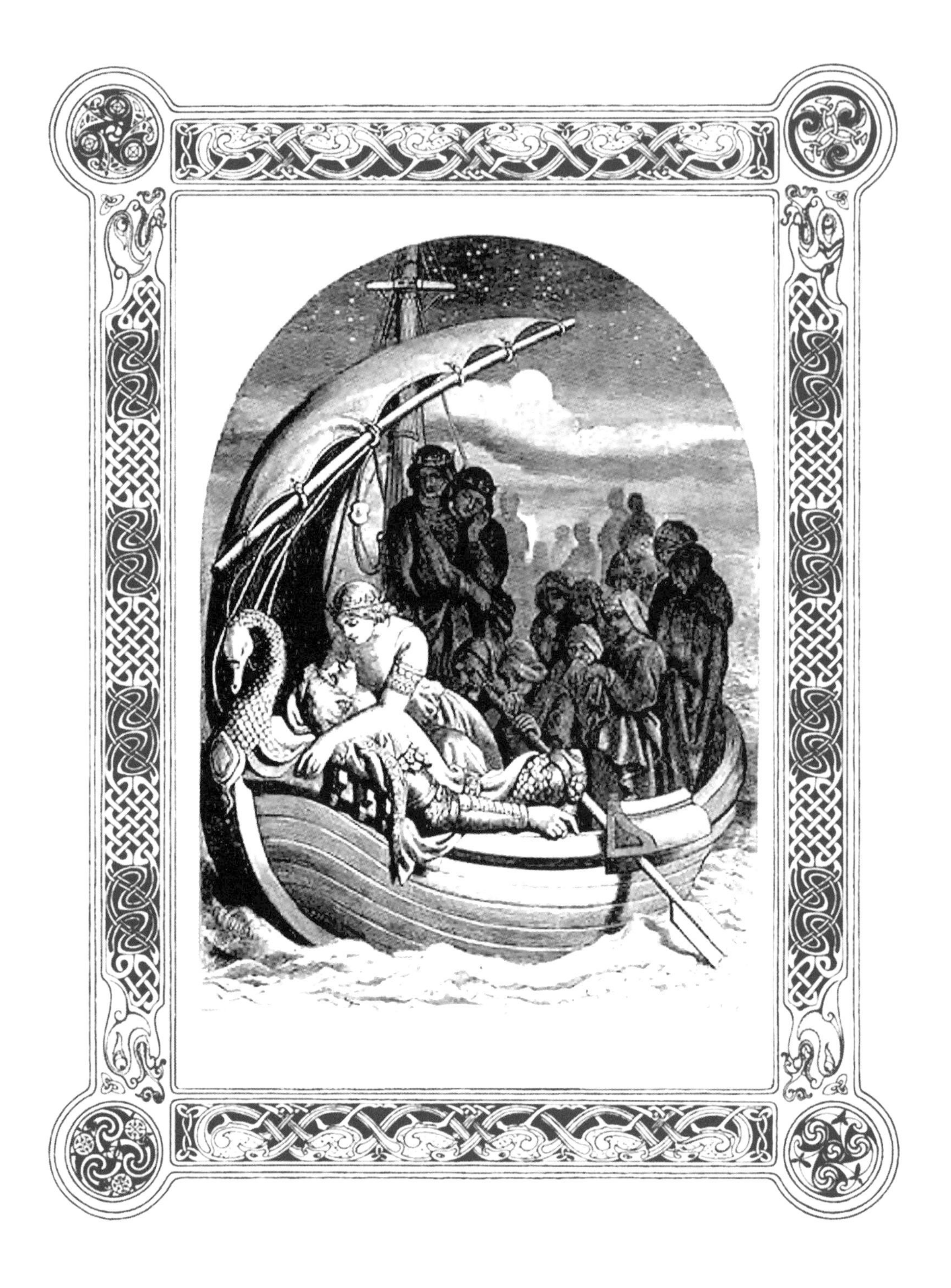

CHAPTER 10

Enchanted Islands

When the Celtic faeries withdrew from our world into their parallel one within the faerie hills, it was a place that to human visitors seemed as spacious and as full of game and forests and plains as the one above ground, and even more full of wonders and treasures. Here the Tuatha had their faerie kingdoms with occasional wars and dramas very much like those of the Sons of Mil above ground; but they also had another land off in the Atlantic to the west, the Land Under the Sunset. This was the island or islands of Hy Brasil, possibly identical with Tir na nOg, the Land of Eternal Youth, which has many other names too such as the Land of Promise, Land of the Living, Land of Delights, the Green Isle and the Happy Plain.

To the British Celts Hy Brasil was possibly identical with the Isle of Avalon and classical scholars have also related it to the fabled Garden of the Hesperides in Greek myth, which were also islands situated somewhere towards the sunset where magic apples grew and there was no sorrow or death. Marie de France in her Lays tells the tale of Lanval, a Breton knight in the days of King Arthur, who fell in love with a faerie maid and mounted up on her horse behind her to ride off to the Otherworld:

On the horse behind her
With full rush Lanval jumped.
With her he rides away to Avalon
According to what the Briton says
Into an isle which is very beautiful.

There is a tradition in the west of Ireland that Hy Brasil becomes visible on the horizon in the direction of the sunset every seven years, and many independent witnesses have testified to this through the ages right up until a century or so ago. When Evans-Wentz was collecting stories in Ireland he was told that the summer of 1908 had been a particularly good one for sightings, with many educated witnesses of a normally sober and rational tendency. Otherwise the island only seems to show itself when its inhabitants choose, or when trouble threatens Ireland.

Nevertheless, so certain were people of its existence that for several hundred years it was shown on many Atlantic charts as a real place. One of the earliest examples was in 1325 when Genoese cartographer Dalorto positioned it west of Ireland. The 1597 map opposite by Giovanni Magini, shows the twin island further south and marked as 'Brafil'. It is commonly described as being a circular island more or less bisected by rivers.

It is quite possible that the mythical Hy Brasil gave its name to the South American country of Brazil due to its legend having spread among Celtic sailors from Ireland and Britain down to Celtic Galicia in north-west Spain, and from there down into Portugal which took possession of the South American country. Although there is another theory: from the fifteenth century one of the Azores was often called the Brazil Island on Portuguese charts, probably taking its name from a type of wood found there that was used to make red dye, and it is very possible that this name was transferred to the South American colony later because even more of the same type of wood was to be found in that vast country, and it became a valuable commodity in Portuguese trade. Whatever the truth, Hy Brasil and the South American country of Brazil apparently both existed on British Admiralty charts until 1865 when the island was finally erased due to lack of confirmatory evidence.

In 1684 the Irish historian Roderick O'Flaherty wrote of Hy Brasil: 'From the Isles of Arran and the west continent [i.e. Irish mainland] often appears visible that enchanted island called O'Brasail and, in Irish, Beg Ara. Whether it be a real and firm land kept hidden by the special ordnance of God, or the terrestrial paradise, or else some illusion of airy clouds appearing on the surface of the sea, or the craft of evil spirits, is more than our judgments can pound out.'

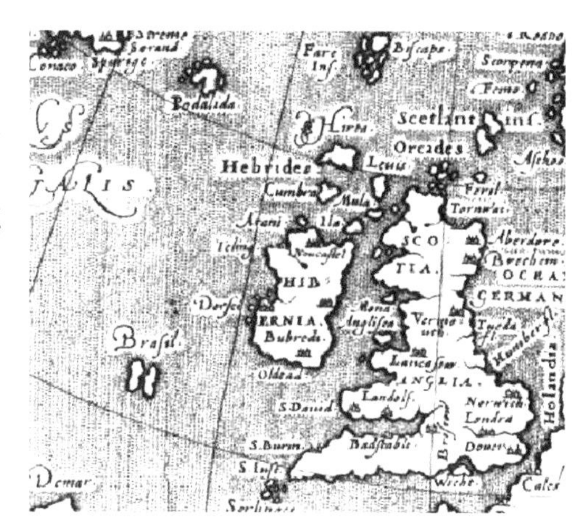

O'Flaherty goes on to tell of a witness then still living who claimed to have visited Hy Brasil for two days some years earlier. It apparently came about like this: in April 1668 he had a row with his wife and left home, wandering from village to village in a black mood. Then in 'Iross-Ainhagh, in the south side of the Barony of Ballynahinshy [Ballynahinch] about nine leagues from Galway by sea' he met three strangers who forcibly bundled him into a boat and ferried him out to a strange island. Being able to speak both English and Irish, they told him it was Hy Brasil and he was able to confirm this by picking out the Aran Islands, Golam Head and other familiar landmarks far away on the Irish coast. Then after a couple of days he woke feeling very ill on the coast near Galway with no idea how he had got back there, and had to recuperate for a few days at a friend's house.

Another of O'Flaherty's recorded tales about Hy Brasil was this: 'Some few generations ago, the crew of a fishing boat passing an island which they did not know, landed thereon to refresh themselves. They had no sooner landed than a man appeared and told them they had no business there as the island was enchanted. They therefore returned to the boat, but as they were going away the islander gave one of them a book with directions not to look into it for seven years. He complied with the request and when he opened and read the book he was able to practice surgery and physic with great success. This man's name was Lee, and the book remained as an heirloom with his descendants.'

A third circumstantial account he gives again offers no very solid evidence for the existence of the fabled island but does tell us much about the strength of belief in it at the time. 'In the western ocean, five or six leagues from the continent there is a sandbank about thirty fathoms deep in the sea. It is called in Irish, Imaire Bay, and in English, the Cod-fishing Bank. From this bank about twenty years ago, a boat was blown southwards by night; next day about noon the occupants spyed land so near them that they could see sheep within it, and yet durst not, for fear of illusions, touch shore, imagining it was O'Brasail, and they were two days coming back towards home.'

The Voyage of Bran

One of the most famous visits to enchanted islands in ancient legend is that recorded in the simple and beautiful poem *The Voyage of Bran, Son of Febal* translated into English in 1895 by Kuno Meyer from versions in several manuscripts dating back to around 1100 AD. The tale begins when Bran goes out wandering alone one day from his castle. After a while he hears sweet music behind him. He turns to see who is playing, but whichever way he turns the music still seems behind him. Soon he is so lulled by it that he falls asleep, as is often the way with faerie music. When he awakes he finds beside him a silver branch with white blossoms, and so pure is the silver that it is hard to tell the branch from the flowers.

He returns to his royal home with this treasure, then later at the feast a strangely-dressed woman appears in the midst of the host as if by magic and sings them a song telling of the beauties and joys of the land across the sea from which she has come:

Splendours of every colour glisten
Throughout the gentle-voiced plains.
Joy is known, ranked around music,
In southern Mag Argatnél.

Unknown is wailing or treachery
In the familiar cultivated land,
There is nothing rough or harsh,
But sweet music striking on the ear.

Without grief, without sorrow, without death,
Without any sickness, without debility,
That is the sign of Emain
Uncommon is an equal marvel.

A beauty of a wondrous land,
Whose aspects are delightful.
Whose view is a fair country,
Incomparable is its haze.

Ending with the exhortation:

Do not fall on a bed of sloth
Or let intoxication overcome you;

Begin a voyage across the clear sea,
If perchance you may reach the Land of Women.

Then she leaves as mysteriously as she arrived, and as she disappears the silver branch springs from Bran's hand into hers, despite him holding onto it with all his might.

The next day Bran sets sail with three companies of nine men. After two days they meet a man coming the other way, riding a horse-drawn chariot across the waves as if they were a meadow. He introduces himself as Manannan mac Lir and says he is on his way to Ireland after a long absence to father a son who will become a great hero. He intends to sleep with the fair Caintigern, whose husband Fiachna will accept Manannan's son as his own and call him Mongan mac Fiachna who will in time become King of Ulster.

He will delight the company of every fairy-mound,
He will be the darling of every goodly land,
He will make known secrets – a course of wisdom –
In the world, without being feared.

He will be in the shape of every beast,
Both on the azure sea and on land,
He will be a dragon before hosts at the onset,
He will be a wolf in every great forest.

He will be a stag with horns of silver,
In the land where chariots are driven,
He will be a speckled salmon in a full pool,
He will be a seal; he will be a fair-white swan.

After prophesying much more about the glorious son he is off to sire, Mannanan ends:

Steadily then let Bran row,
Not far to the Land of Women,
Emne with many hues of hospitality,
You will reach before the setting of the sun.

Bran and his men sail on and come in time to an island where they see many people on the shore. But when they try to address them, all these people do is laugh and gape and fool about as if they have lost their wits. Bran sends one of his men ashore to try and get sense out of them but as soon as he touches shore he becomes as foolish as the rest and they can get no sense out of him either. So they sail on and leave him behind on the Island of Joy to be collected on the way back.

Soon they come to the Island of Women, or so they guess because only women come down to the harbour to greet them.

'Come ashore, O Bran son of Febal,' calls their leader, who is the lady who visited Bran's court with the silver branch. 'Welcome is your arrival.'

After what happened at the other island Bran hesitates, but then the woman throws a ball of thread straight at his face. When Bran instinctively puts his hand up to shield himself, the ball sticks firmly to it, and by that means the leader of the women pulls his coracle in to shore. Then she leads him and his companions to a large and gracious hall where a feast is laid ready. Soft beds too are laid out for each man, each in its own chamber and each with its own beautiful chambermaid to share the bed. No delight is lacking in the Isle of Women and no matter how much they feast, there always seems as much left over.

Finally though, after what seems about a year, homesickness seizes his men. Bran is in no hurry to leave but gives way in the end. The lady of the silver branch warns them that they will regret their choice; but if they must go they should beware of stepping ashore in Ireland.

So they head for home, collecting their friend (with some difficulty) from the Island of Joy on the way. Finally they approach the shores of Erin and a crowd comes down to greet them.

'Who are you?' they call.

'Bran mac Febal,' Bran replies.

'We've never heard that name,' they say, 'save in old legends which say he sailed away into the west and was never seen again.'

Then Nechtan mac Collbran, who is the most homesick of them all, leaps from the boat to wade ashore. But the moment his feet touch the soil of Ireland he crumbles to ashes.

So now they understand the warning they were given and no-one else tries to follow Nechtan's lead. Before sailing away, Bran tells the audience the tale of their adventures then turns the boat about and nothing more is known of his wanderings.

In Irish and British Celtic tradition Manannan mac Lir's Land of Promise was usually said to be situated far out in the western Atlantic; but the High King Cormac mac Art reached it simply by riding into an enchanted fog near his own castle at Tara, and others by simply entering a faerie mound. Clearly distances and geography are fluid in the faerie Otherworld and it is quite possible that all theories are true at the same time because of that. Certain places have always been considered gateways to the Otherworld, places where you step from one dimension into another in a manner quite familiar in modern Science Fiction. It's quite possible that in the Celtic perception of long ago Manannan's kingdom was quite static in the Tuatha's realm but with gates to many different places in ours, including some far out in the ocean but others quite near at hand.

One such place was long supposed, even in Irish annals, to be the Isle of Man which is named after Manannan who had his faerie castle on South Barrule where he feasted with his company and from time to time wreathed the island in fog when raiders threatened. Sometimes also when raiders succeeded in landing he would raise a phantom army in the mist so that wherever there was one warrior to defend the island there would seem like a hundred. And if even this failed, he would descend upon them in the form of a fiery three-legged wheel hurtling down the mountain into their midst and scattering them.

In gratitude for this protection the islanders would bring tributes of rushes to him every Midsummer's Eve (St John's Eve) and have a great celebration in his honour with blazing bonfires and inflammable bales of rushes which they lit and rolled down the hills in his honour:

The rent each paid out of his hand
Was a bundle of green rushes every year
And that was on them as a tax
Throughout the country each St John's Eve

Some went up with the rushes to
The great mountain up at Barrule
Others would leave the grass below
With Manannan, above the Keamool

(The Keamool is believed to be the hill of the Tynwald or Manx Parliament, the oldest continuous parliament in the world.)

These celebrations continued into modern times, even though

Manannan is said to have been banished by St Patrick. The story goes that Patrick and some monks were caught up in a wild storm in the Irish Sea and ran ashore on the rock off the west of the Isle of Man that has been called St Patrick's Isle ever since. The next day they walked ashore at low tide and decided that since Providence had brought them here, they would set about converting the people to Christianity; which they did with great success, at the same time educating them in better ways of spinning and weaving and agriculture.

When Manannan heard what was going on he was furious. It was too late to hide the island in fog or send contrary winds because these pacifist invaders had already landed, creeping humbly in under his guard. It was no use summoning hundreds of phantom warriors out of the mist because the monks were completely unafraid and saw them for the illusions they were. So finally Manannan changed into his fiery, three legged wheel form and rolled down the mountains towards Patrick and his monks. But all Patrick did was begin to chant the prayer he had fashioned, which is now called St Patrick's Breastplate which begins:

I arise to-day
Through the strength of heaven:
Light of sun,
Radiance of moon,
Splendor of fire,
Speed of lightning,
Swiftness of wind,
Depth of sea,
Stability of earth,
Firmness of rock.

This prayer has an ancient structure similar to the druid spells recited by Amergin when the Sons of Mil landed in Ireland, and it has been dated by linguists to at least the seventh century when it was already attributed to St Patrick; so this may well be true. It is said to be the prayer which carried him through his first serious challenge to the druids at Tara.

All Patrick's monks chanted along with him and between them they raised an invisible shield that Manannan could not pass. So he changed back into his usual form and then flew back to his mountain in a wild storm that shook the whole island. And when the storm cleared his faerie castle had vanished from South Barrule.

That is how the story goes anyway, told from the Christian perspective. In Manx folk tales Manannan is usually presented as a great wizard who once ruled the place. But although his daily and immediate presence on the Isle of Man ended with St Patrick, when the mists closed in around the island afterwards people still said that Manannan was pulling on his cloak, and that when storms raged he was angry. Manxmen continued to have bonfires on Midsummer's Eve and roll fiery wheels down the hills in his honour, and his three-legged wheel is still to be seen on the Manx flag with the Latin motto saying: 'Whichever way you throw me I stand'.

This three-legged cross, (trinacria, triscele or triskelion), is a very ancient symbol across Europe dating back to the Bronze or early Iron Age in Italy. It is also the emblem of Sicily (though with a Gorgon's head at the centre) where, as in the Isle of Man, it is often interpreted as showing the islanders' readiness to repel the invaders who have repeatedly threatened it from all sides. Like the swastika originally, it is usually seen as a symbol of the sun and is always shown rotating in a clockwise (or sun-wise) direction when representing the positive aspect of the sun, and anti-clockwise (as in the Nazi symbol) when representing evil.

St Brendan's Voyage

It was not just the pagan Irish who believed in magical islands far out in the Atlantic. When Christianity came along, it absorbed the notion along with so much other faerie lore. One of the most famous Irish saint's Lives is that of St Brendan the Navigator, who in legend sailed the Atlantic for seven long years in his finally successful search for the Land of Promise (or, as he preferred to call it, the Land of Promise of the Saints).

Although like many other Irish saints a body of myth has grown up around him, St Brendan was a real person who was born in 484 near Tralee, County Kerry. One of his spiritual tutors was St Ita, sometimes called the 'Brigid of Munster', who taught him for five years before he completed his studies under St Erc and was ordained in 512. Over the next eighteen years he founded two monasteries at Ardfert and at Shanakeel (or Baalynevinoorach) below what came to be known as Brandon's Hill in his honour, on the Dingle Peninsula. This was where he set sail from on his famous voyage which is assumed to have begun around 530. In later years his fame grew so great that new monasteries had to be founded nearby at Gallerus, Kilmalchedor, and the Blasket Islands to cope with the pilgrims and students who came flocking to Ardfert and Shanakeel seeking Brendan's spiritual guidance.

After his quest for the Land of Promise, Brendan's life is again quite well documented. Around 550 he founded a monastery at what is now Coney Island in County Clare, then for three years he did missionary work in Britain and Brittany, visiting Iona and leaving his name at Kilbrandon near Oban and Kilbrennan Sound. Back in Ireland he founded many more churches and monasteries, the most famous of which was Clonfert Abbey in Galway around 560, where he was buried in 577 at the ripe old age of 93. One of his sailing companions is said to have been St Malo, a Welsh saint who gave his name to the Channel port in Brittany.

So popular was Brendan that towards the end he was afraid that his more extreme devotees would make off with his body after death. So when he did die on a visit to his sister Brig, a nun in Annaghdown, his body was smuggled secretly to Clonfert (the 'Meadow of Miracles') in a luggage cart, where he was buried in the cathedral.

Brendan's fame and popularity as a living saint in his own day was more to do with his missionary and monastic endeavours than his quest for the Land of Promise, but the sea journey is what made him famous across Europe as the ninth century written account of it in Latin was translated into English, Flemish, German, French, Italian and other tongues. Over a hundred Medieval Latin copies still survive. In these Brendan the Navigator is said to have been inspired for his journey by the visit of a kinsman and fellow monk who had seen the fabled land with his own eyes. This monk, Barinthus (Barrind) said that he had paid a visit to his son Mernoc who was Abbot of a monastery called the Isle of Delights off the west of Ireland. At his arrival: 'the monks poured from their cells like a swarm of bees to look at us. The cells were scattered far and wide over the island, but the monks lived in close spiritual union . . . they all ate at the same table and sang the Divine Office in common.'

Incidentally the little circular stone cells he describes are still often called beehive cells and there are many examples still to be seen on the south-west coast of Ireland. However, to continue, that night Barinthus and his son took a walk along the island shore and Mernoc suddenly suggested they take a boat and sail westwards to see if they could find the fabled Land of Promise. And this they did. Soon a great mist gath-

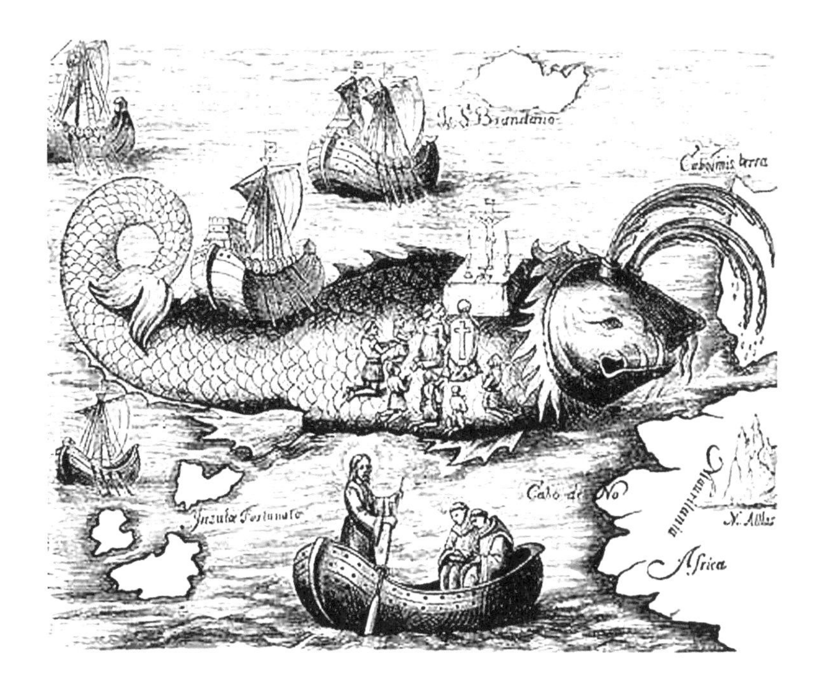

ered around them so dense they could not even see the front of their boat. Then after a couple of hours they came to a bright light and suddenly found themselves on a spacious, green and fruitful shore.

They explored the island for fifteen days without reaching the far shore and: 'all the plants we saw were flowering plants and every tree was a fruit tree; the very stones beneath our feet were precious.' On the fifteenth day they came to a river flowing from east to west and were just debating whether to try and cross it when a man with a shining aura appeared. He greeted them and told them that they could not cross the river, which divided the island in two, and would have to turn back. He also said that it was indeed the Land of Promise of the Saints, as they may have noticed from not having needed any food or drink or sleep during their stay. Also that the land had perpetual light provided by Jesus himself. So Barinthus and Mernoc returned to their boat and sailed back to the monastery on the Isle of Delights where Barinthus learned that his son often disappeared on such trips and returned with the fragrance of paradise on him.

This was the tale that is said to have inspired Brendan for his own great journey with a number of companions that varies from seventeen to 150; but for them it was to be no mere sail of a few hours through fog. It took seven long years according to the legend, during which time they visited many strange and magical islands (some repeatedly) and met many strange creatures.

The most famous and commonly illustrated story is where they land on a bare island, set up an altar and light a fire, only to have the island suddenly come to life under them – because it was in fact a whale that Brendan dubbed Jasconius or 'big fish'.

Among the other islands they visit most are clearly imaginary, such as the rock where Judas Iscariot was imprisoned in perpetual torment, but several islands have been identified, suggesting a kernel of truth to the legend and that the surviving story is probably a wildly exaggerated record of Brendan's real journey. Iceland is a likely source for the episode of Brendan's visit to the Gates of Hell; and Greenland, the Faeroes, Shetlands, the Azores, Canaries, Madeira and the West Indies have all been suggested as possible locations for other episodes. The description of an island like a pillar of crystal has also been interpreted as the confused memory of meeting an iceberg. As to the location of the Land of Promise itself, North America has often quite seriously been suggested as a possibility.

The brief description of what Brendan finds in the Land of Promise after his seven-year voyage exactly matches that of his kinsman Barthinus, except that it takes his party forty days to reach the great dividing river. There they also meet an angelic stranger who says that it took so long for them to reach the paradise because God wanted them first to witness all the wonders of the deep. Then he bids them to load their vessel with precious stones and fruit and go home, which they do.

In 1976 Tim Severin built a replica ancient Irish coracle and sailed it to Newfoundland to prove that such a journey was at least possible. In the late 1980s there was great excitement in West Virginia about the possible discovery of ancient Irish ogham inscriptions in stone. According to a 1983 article in *Wonderful West Virginia* magazine by Dr Barry Fell: 'The West Virginia Ogam texts are the longest Ogam inscriptions recorded from anywhere in the world. They exhibit the grammar and vocabulary of Old Irish in a manner previously unknown in such early rock-cut inscriptions in any Celtic language.' Other academics are more sceptical however, some dismissing his arguments as 'delusional'.

Whether Brendan ever really did find his promised land out in the Atlantic is debatable but what is certain is that his method of navigation (i.e. just letting his boat drift freely according to the winds and currents) was a quite common practice. Celtic monks were greatly inspired by the Desert Fathers who took to the wastelands of the Middle East and Africa for their solitary meditations. Around Ireland they took to near-barren islands on the same principle, but many went further still. Seeing the ocean as their own equivalent of the sandy desert, it became quite common practice for monks to take to the open ocean either singly or in groups like Brendan's; and once out at sea they would simply entrust themselves to the elements in the full confidence that God was steering them. It is impossible to know how many lost their lives this way, but it would not be all that surprising if some did indeed wash up on the shores of America.

The Voyage of Teigue

Although much of the Latin account of Brendan's journey is obviously fanciful, the belief that he had reached the Land of Promise was strong enough for 'St Brendan's Isle' to be shown on many charts of the Atlantic, often at the same time and separate to Hy Brasil. This separateness was deliberate because despite their obvious similarities, the Christian writers wanted to make very clear that their promised land was quite different to the old pagan one where feasting, hunting, fighting and other carnal pursuits were enjoyed. One story does manage to reconcile the two concepts quite neatly though, and that is the tale of the Voyage of Teigue in *The Book of Lismore*.

Teigue was a prince of West Munster and heir to its throne. One day his wife and many others were stolen away by pirates so Teigue and his followers set sail to catch them. But it was spring and they ran into a fierce storm. For nine weeks it drove them around the Atlantic till finally the storm died and they came to the most beautiful island they had ever seen, with 'red-laden apple-trees, with leafy oaks too and hazels yellow with nuts in their clusters'. They also found 'a wide, smooth plain clad in flowering clover all bedewed with honey.'

In the middle of the plain were three hills, each crowned with a magnificent palace. The first palace they came to had walls of white marble. They were graciously welcomed and entertained by a faerie lady who told them that the palace was home to all Ireland's kings from Heremon, the son of Mil, to Conn of the Hundred Battles.

The second castle had walls of gold and again they were entertained by a faerie lady also dressed in gold who told them that the place was the world's Fourth Paradise. The third palace had walls of silver and there they met Connla, son of Conn of the Hundred Battles. Connla and his faerie bride were dressed in green, and she told Teigue that long ago she had fallen in love with Connla and so had arranged for him to join her in this place where, sustained only by a magic apple that perpetually renewed itself, they were gifted with eternal youth and happiness. When she and Connla walked on clover it barely bent beneath their weight.

When Teigue asked who lived in the golden palace the faerie maid replied that no-one did yet and that it was reserved for all the Christian kings of Ireland that were yet to be, including Teigue himself. Then many other faerie maids joined them and one gave Teigue an emerald cup which had the virtue of turning any liquid poured into it into the finest wine. She warned him to take good care of it because he would die soon after losing it; then she would bury his body but: 'thy soul shall come with me hither, where till the Judgement's Day thou shall assume a body light and ethereal.'

As they boarded their boat to leave, the maiden asked Teigue how long he thought he had been in that happy place. 'A day,' he replied, because that was how long it had seemed and there had been no night. But she told him it had been a year, during which time they had felt no hunger or thirst or tiredness, because that was the virtue of that land. Teigue and his men then set sail and when they shortly looked back there was no sign of the land they had just left: 'for incontinently an obscuring magic veil was drawn over it.'

CHAPTER 11

The Revival

Star of descending night!
Fair is thy light in the west!
Thou that liftest thy unshorn head from thy cloud:
Thy steps are stately on thy hill.
What dost thou behold in the plain?
The stormy winds are laid.
The murmur of the torrent comes from afar.
Roaring waves climb the distant rock.
The flies of evening are on their feeble wings:
The hum of their course is in the field.
What dost thou behold, fair light?
But thou dost smile and depart.
The waves come with joy around thee:
They bathe thy lovely hair.
Farewell, thou silent beam!
Let the light of Ossian's soul arise!

Poems of Ossian by James Macpherson, 1773

IN THE EUROPEAN ROMANTIC PERIOD of the nineteenth century, many legends and ideas which had been banished from the world by the Age of Enlightenment and Industrial Revolution were triumphantly reborn in literature and art, among them faeries in all their ancient splendour. The magical world of King Arthur and his fey half-sister Morgan, Tristan and Isolde, Parsifal, Aoife and their kindred sprang to life again as vividly as in the Middle Ages, in response to some hunger that the pragmatic spirit of the day failed to satisfy.

The late eighteenth and nineteenth centuries saw an explosion of interest in Europe in both its living faerie traditions and those preserved in ancient tomes. The Brothers Grimm sparked a general passion for collecting folktales before they were lost, and often folklore was used as a tool for nation building. A shining example of this was the masterly piece of scholarship by Elias Lönnrot in Finland who synthesised the country's national epic, the Kalevala, from a mass of native legends, significantly helping to forge a national identity after centuries of domination by first Sweden and then Russia which had almost swamped the native culture.

In the Celtic lands such folklorists were especially well rewarded because of both the still vibrant storytelling tradition and the extensive ancient literature, especially in Ireland and Wales. Scotland was rather lacking in such ancient writings until in the 1760s James Macpherson caused a sensation by publishing *The Poems of Ossian* which he claimed to have translated from old Gaelic manuscripts he had discovered in the Western Isles, an epic cycle of Scottish poems from the early Dark Ages. In them Ossian, a blind bard, sings of the heroic life and deeds of Fingal, who is the same person as Finn mac Cumhal of Ireland and Ossian (Oisin)'s father.

These poems had a massive cultural impact on the Romantic movement across Europe, especially in Germany through translations by Goethe and Herder. They also helped ignite the Celtic revival, inspiring Walter Scott to make his own large contribution to the nineteenth century Scottish renaissance. Napoleon is said to have taken an Italian translation of the poems into battle because it was among his favourite books. The city of Selma, Alabama, was named after Fingal's home in the poems and Mendelssohn helped spread the word with his Hebrides Overture (Fingal's Cave) composed at the age of twenty after a stormy visit to the Isle of Staffa where this natural marvel stands. Jean Dominique Ingres in 1815 painted one of his most moody and romantic pieces *The Dream of Ossian*, one of a series inspired by the poems, and Byron was also greatly influenced by them.

Sadly it was all a great hoax. Arguments raged back and forth for a century but in the end even the poems' greatest admirers had to admit that there was no original manuscript and although Macpherson had drawn on real folklore traditions, the poems as he presented them were mostly his own composition.

One of the earliest doubters was Samuel Johnson who made some investigations during his own journey to the Scottish Western Isles and declared his opinion in 1775 that the poems had been faked, or worked up from a few mere fragments. Macpherson challenged this but was unwilling to produce the original Gaelic manuscript he claimed to have discovered. He argued that it would be too expensive to publish the original and anyway it was beneath him to meet his critics on their own petty level. And many people wanted to believe Macpherson, and continued to do so for decades.

After Macpherson's death in 1796 Malcolm Laing in an appendix to his *History of Scotland* (1800) was another sceptic who dismissed the ancient origins of the poems but this did little to dent their popularity because they are in fact very well written. It is impossible to say now how great their impact would have been if Macpherson had been honest from the outset and simply published them as poems in an antique style, much as Tennyson published his equally influential Arthurian *Idylls of the King*, but the *Poems of Ossian* are nevertheless still considered one of the landmarks of Scottish literature because of their influence, and many of the incidents in the poems have been duplicated in other collections of Scottish folklore such as J.F. Campbell's massive *Popular Tales of the West Highlands*, taken from illiterate peasant storytellers who had heard nothing of Macpherson.

The *Poems of Ossian* may have been faked but plenty of genuine ancient Celtic material came to light during the nineteenth century in the form of oral tales collected from peasant storytellers and translations from medieval manuscripts. Walter Scott did an enormous amount to popularise the history and traditions of his native Scotland, along with other authors such as George MacDonald. In Ireland an army of academics and enthusiasts set about rescuing the national heritage but a few names stand out particularly, such as Thomas Crofton Croker and Samuel Lover for their collection of living folktales and Kuno Meyer and Whitley Stokes for their translations of old manuscripts into English which, even within Ireland, enabled them to reach a far wider audience than before. And then, like some triple incarnation of Dana or Brigid there are the three Ladies: Guest, Wilde and Gregory.

Lady Charlotte Guest (1812 – 1895) was born at Uffington House in Lincolnshire, daughter of the ninth Earl of Lindsey, Albermarle Bertie. Her father died when she was only six and she was unhappy when her mother remarried, retreating into her studies by learning Arabic,

Hebrew and Persian by the age of twenty. She escaped home by marrying an industrialist, John Josiah Guest who owned the Dowlais Iron Company in Merthyr Tydfil, and was the local elected Member of Parliament. Besides having ten children and helping run the company, Charlotte learned Welsh and began translating medieval songs and poems from Middle Welsh, culminating in her classic translation of the *Mabinogion*, the first into English which enabled it to reach a wide audience for the first time. Although criticised for her censoring of the more racy passages and superseded by more recent and probably more accurate translations, Lady Guest's version is still popular and has its own distinct charm.

Lady Jane Wilde (1821 – 1896), also known by the pen name 'Speranza', was the wife of Sir William and mother of the precocious Oscar. She was a gifted poet and linguist as well as a folklorist and a passionate believer in Irish independence, although after her husband's death in 1879 she lived much of the time in London where she gathered a circle of Irish writers around her, including George Bernard Shaw, W.B. Yeats and of course her son Oscar, whom she misguidedly forced to stay and face trial rather than fleeing to France, saying that if he fled she would never speak to him again. When he was jailed her health declined rapidly and she died without him being allowed to visit her deathbed. Her chief collection of folklore is *Ancient Legends, Mystic Charms, and Superstitions of Ireland* (1887).

Isabella Augusta, Lady Gregory (1852 – 1932) was one of the driving forces of the Irish Literary Revival also known as the Celtic Revival which stimulated interest in traditional Irish literature and culture and helped pave the way for Irish independence. Together with W.B. Yeats and Edward Martyn she also encouraged new writing that built on the old traditions and founded the Abbey Theatre to stage plays by the likes of J.M. Synge (*Playboy of the Western World*) and Sean O'Casey which examined the Irish predicament. Although born into an aristocratic Anglo-Irish family with strong ties to Britain, it was her Irish roots that preoccupied her increasingly and led to her changing her political stance from mild Unionism to fervent Republicanism. Among her many collections and translations of Irish lore were: *Cuchulain of Muirthemne* (1902), *Poets and Dreamers* (1903), *Gods and Fighting Men* (1904), *A Book of Saints and Wonders* (1906), *The Kiltartan History Book* (1909) and *Visions and Beliefs in the West of Ireland* (1920). She also wrote more than forty plays which she put on the Abbey Theatre, but few are still performed or even read today.

Another leading light of the Celtic revival with two of the above Ladies was William Butler Yeats (1865 – 1939) who as both a poet and a scholar was a tireless promoter of the Celtic world view with its particularly mystical slant. Like Gregory he was Anglo-Irish but a passionate Irish nationalist and wrote many poems in support of that cause. Yeats was a great promoter of the idea of the Celtic Twilight, which was the title of a collection of prose essays he published on the theme in 1893 and revised and expanded in 1902.

The term Celtic Twilight may seem a strange one for what was actually a renaissance, conjuring as it does the Twilight of the Gods, the Germanic account of their decline and fall. Yeats's 'twilight' does not mean that kind of decline but rather the liminal mood of dusk and dawn in which it is easy to imagine the boundaries between worlds dissolving and faeries stepping out of their world into ours, and vice versa. Many of the tales in his book came from one Paddy Flynn, an old peasant acquaintance of his in Sligo. Yeats almost filled a notebook with this old sage's stories and sayings, but had to end it abruptly when: 'a friend of mine gave him a large bottle of whiskey, and though a sober man at most times, the sight of so much liquor filled him with a great enthusiasm, and he lived upon it for some days and then died. His body, worn out with old age and hard times, could not bear the drink as in his young days. He was a great teller of tales, and unlike our common romancers, knew how to empty heaven, hell, and purgatory, faeryland

and earth, to people his stories. He did not live in a shrunken world, but knew of no less ample circumstance than did Homer himself.'

In *Celtic Twilight* Yeats tells a tale which shows how strong the country belief in faeries still was in his own day in the West of Ireland. Around 1890 a small girl disappeared on the western slopes of the notoriously faerie-haunted Ben Bulben mountain in Sligo. The rumour immediately spread that the faeries had taken her and when the local constable was called, he not only started the practical measure of a house to house search but sent some people to the field where she had disappeared to burn all the ragweed (bucalauns) there, on the grounds that ragweed was sacred to the faeries. They spent the whole night burning clumps of weed and sure enough in the morning the little girl was found safe and well. She said the faeries had carried her off a great distance on one of their horses till they came to a wide river upon which she had seen one of the searchers, a particular older friend who had long tried to guard her against the faeries, riding the waters in a cockleshell. Whereupon the spell had broken and she had found herself back in the field where she had started.

As to the truth of this story Yeats is circumspect, commenting that perhaps it is sometimes good to believe things one does not understand because there may be some strange truth hidden in them i.e. if they had not set fire to the field perhaps the girl would not have been safely found. This kind of double vision Yeats also found very common in regard to religion where completely pious churchgoers could quite comfortably talk of the Virgin Mary and faeries in the same breath, seeing no contradiction. The reality of faeries was simply and widely as taken for granted as the weather.

As was the danger of being carried away by them, either by force or through rashly consuming their faerie food. Wherever he went in Sligo, where he partly grew up and often returned to later in life, Yeats heard tales of faerie kidnappings from either the victims themselves or, more often, from people who had known them. Sometimes their absences had been brief, as with the little girl, but often it had been for seven, fourteen or even twenty-one years. Some victims had returned with their wits shattered but many seem then to have carried on perfectly normal lives. New brides and babies were the most popular and closely guarded targets, but it could be anyone.

In connection with kidnappings Yeats describes a certain white square in an inaccessible limestone cliff on the southern face of Ben Bulben overlooking Sligo city. This spot, clearly visible in his day, was

famous as one of the main gates by which the 'gentle folk' would stream out of the mountain at night to go rampaging across the country: 'All night the gay rabble sweep to and fro across the land, invisible to all, unless perhaps where, in some more than commonly "gentle" place – Drumcliff or Drum-a-hair – the night-capped heads of faery-doctors may be thrust from their doors to see what mischief the "gentry" are doing. To their trained eyes and ears the fields are covered by red-hatted riders, and the air is full of shrill voices – a sound like whistling, as an ancient Scottish seer has recorded.'

Drumcliff, incidentally, is where Yeats is buried, looking towards that southern face of Ben Bulben and its faerie gate. Another famous portal was Heart Lake about five miles south of the city, so named because of its shape. It was a gloomy pond and its faeries were considered more dangerous than most, so some of the local men decided to drain it. As they were about this, one of them suddenly shouted that he saw his home on fire. The others looked around and each equally thought he saw his own cottage going up in flames. They all ran home but it was just a faerie 'glamour' and there were no flames at all when they got there. The draining was abandoned and in Yeats's day a half-dug trench was shown to visitors as evidence of the tale.

Yeats also heard a sad story there of a young man who was on his way home in the evening to his newlywed bride when he met her on the way amid a merry company. She welcomed him to join the revelry, only warning him not to eat or drink anything, and set him to playing cards with three of them. He did so with no idea that they were faeries until he saw the chief of the band carrying his wife away. Suddenly he knew what was happening and sprang up, but it was too late because she and the rest just melted into the shadows. Then as he drew close to home he heard the keening of mourners and learned that his bride had died shortly before.

Yeats however did not just record the faerie visions and encounters he heard from others. Like Robert Kirk he had some direct experiences of his own, though he was reluctant to talk about them. In the second edition of *Celtic Twilight* though, he recalled an incident from many years before in Sligo when he had been out with a couple of friends to whom he was related, a brother and sister, collecting the reminiscences of an old peasant. It grew dark as they were walking home through the countryside and this, combined with having their imaginations excited by the wonder tales they had been listening to, was perhaps an explanation for what followed. Or maybe, he speculated, the combination of circumstances merely opened them to the kind of consciousness prevailing in the countryside that enabled its peasants to see into the faerie dimension so much more clearly than those whose minds were overlaid with city-dwelling and education.

Anyway, what happened was that first of all the sister saw a light moving slowly across the road. The other two saw nothing but a while later they passed an old church and the foundations of an old town that had been destroyed by Cromwell. They stood there looking out over the fields for a while when they saw: 'a small bright light on the horizon, as it seemed, mounting up slowly towards the sky; then we saw other faint lights for a minute or two, and at last a bright flame like the flame of a torch moving rapidly over the river.'

This was no faerie cavalcade but a strange enough incident in itself, especially in those days. Such lights were commonly seen near known faerie sites long before the invention of electricity or the easy distribution of fireworks. The incident was followed by a number of strange events at the house where they were staying. First, when Yeats and the sister were sitting quietly alone in a room he heard a sound like that of peas being thrown against a large mirror there; and as he looked straight at it Yeats heard the sound again, though there was nothing to be seen. Later when on his own he heard a loud knock as if a large stone had hit the panelling by his head but again saw nothing. He continues: 'And after that for some days came other sights and sounds, not to me but to the girl, her brother, and the servants. Now it was a bright light, now it was letters of fire that vanished before they could be read, now it was a heavy foot moving about in the seemingly empty house.'

He wondered if somehow they had drawn home with them from the old town where they saw the lights some supernatural creatures that lingered there.

Yeats also gives an interesting insight into the many stories of people being abducted by pookas in the form of horses and taken for wild rides through the night. Although it gives comfort to the sceptic by providing a rational explanation for a magical phenomenon, it does not really explain the phenomenon away because 'glamour' has always been one of the faeries' chief weapons.

The story concerns an old rath at the inland edge of the flat and grassy Rosses peninsula just north of Sligo town. The place had many strange incidents associated with it and was avoided by locals, especially at night: 'One night a farmer's young son came from one of them and saw the fort all flaming, and ran towards it, but the "glamour" fell on him, and he sprang on to a fence, cross-legged, and commenced beating it with a stick, because he imagined the fence to be a horse, and that all night long he went on the most wonderful ride through the country. In the morning he was still beating his fence, and they carried him home, where he remained a simpleton for three years before he came to himself again. A little later a farmer tried to level the fort. His cows and horses died, and all manner of trouble overtook him, and finally he himself was led home, and left useless with "his head on his knees by the fire to the day of his death".'

CHAPTER 12

Modern Faerie Encounters

The Cottingley Faeries

ONE OF THE MOST sensational proofs of the reality of faeries seemed to come in 1917 when two English girls took two photographs showing themselves with various dancing winged faeries. The girls were Elsie Wright aged 16 and her cousin Frances Griffiths, 10, who lived in the village of Cottingley in West Yorkshire, on the edge of Bradford. Because of the war, Frances and her mother had come to live with their relations, leaving her father behind in South Africa serving the war effort.

One day in July 1917 Elsie borrowed her father's plate camera to take a picture of her cousin and when he came to develop the portrait he was at first puzzled and then amazed by some small, pale winged shapes in the foreground. He took them at first for birds or wrapping paper and was astonished by the girls' claim that they were some of the faeries they had often claimed they saw while playing at Cottingley Beck, the stream at the foot of their garden; which indeed is just what they looked like on closer inspection – little female faeries with butterfly wings dancing and playing instruments. Mr Wright was not overly impressed though, and certainly never guessed he was looking at what was to become one of

the most famous photographs in the world. He suspected a trick by the girls, bearing in mind that his daughter Elsie was a gifted artist who had been going to Bradford Art College since the age of 13 and was fond of painting faeries. She had also briefly worked at a photographer's shop in Bradford, where she could easily have learned a few tricks.

A month or two later Frances took another photo, this time of Elsie with a prancing goblin-like elf but still the parents were unconvinced. They unsuccessfully searched the girls' room for evidence of trickery and even though none was found, banned them from using the camera again. The girls stuck firmly to their story though. In a letter to a friend in South Africa Frances mentioned in a matter of fact way how friendly she and her cousin had become with the faeries of Cottingley Beck, remarking how odd it was that she had never seen faeries in Africa and wondering if maybe it was too hot for them there, even though those in England only came out in bright weather.

The girls' photos and stories of faeries became family lore and that might have been the end of it had Elsie's mother Polly not taken some interest in esoteric matters. Two years later she attended a lecture on faeries at the Theosophical Society in Bradford. Afterwards she mentioned the two photographs, which sparked immediate interest. Copies of them circled ever higher through the ranks of Theosophy till finally in early 1920 they came into the hands of a leading light, Edward L Gardner. He began using them in his lectures, rumours of which in turn reached the ears of the enormously popular and influential Arthur Conan Doyle, the famous author born in Edinburgh to Irish parents. He happened to have already been commissioned by the *Strand* magazine for an article on faeries for their 1920 Christmas Edition and saw a possible way of turning his piece into a bombshell.

Doyle obtained the pictures from Gardner and after some investigation they gave him a spectacular headline for his article: 'An Epoch-Making Event – Fairies Photographed.' This was followed by an uncritical resume of the girls' own account of how the pictures were taken, with the full backing of Conan Doyle's forensic reputation as the creator of Sherlock Holmes (who incidentally was also launched in the *Strand* magazine). Doyle declared that after thorough investigation of both the girls and their photographs he considered them all completely genuine. All copies of the magazine were sold within days, kick-starting a controversy that was to last intermittently for over sixty years.

Conan Doyle was not completely gullible, although certainly dazzled by the sensation he knew the pictures would cause. The genuineness of the photographs was vouched for by, among others, a leading expert in fake photography, Harold Snelling, whose opinion after closely examining the plates was: 'These two negatives are entirely genuine, unfaked photographs of single exposure, open-air work, show movement in the fairy figures, and there is no trace whatever of studio work involving card or paper models, dark backgrounds, painted figures, etc. In my opinion, they are both straight untouched pictures.'

His contact Edward Gardner also visited the girls on Doyle's behalf (he was on a trip to Australia at the time) and reported that he was satisfied as to their honesty. Then to strengthen their case, he lent the girls two cameras and before long they produced three new faerie photos which inspired Conan Doyle to write a second article in the *Strand* the following year, followed by a book *The Coming of the Fairies* in 1922, which looked even further into the story, as well as reviewing other faerie sightings around the world.

All this caused a sensation and arguments that raged around the world for decades. Doyle's reputation as a rational thinker was severely dented, but he went to his grave in 1930 still convinced that he was right and his critics wrong. The girls, now grown into women, long continued to maintain that the pictures were real, though playfully evading too many direct questions.

Then finally in 1981 and 1982 they were interviewed by Joe Cooper for *The Unexplained* magazine and Elsie admitted that all five photographs had been faked and they had based their faeries on illustrations by Claude Shepperson for a copy of *Princess Mary's Gift Book* owned by Frances. Frances herself admitted that most of the pictures were faked but claimed that one had been real (possibly because Elsie had set it up without telling her). She claimed though that there really had been faeries by the Cottingley waterfall despite the fraudulent pictures. They had only faked the photographs to try and prove the reality of what they saw there.

That Conan Doyle (and through him much of the world) should have been duped by two young girls was a matter of wonder to Elsie Wright's father while he was still a sceptic himself, and happy to tell investigating journalists so. But when corresponding with the great man himself he kept quiet about his doubts.

After Cottingley

It is often suggested that Doyle's judgement was clouded by his eager embrace of Spiritualism, especially following the death of his son during the Great War. Although not directly connected, Doyle saw that proving the existence of faeries might be very useful in proving the reality of other non-material entities, such as the souls of the dead. He did not approach the Cottingley Faeries with his critical faculties switched off, but was just a bit too eager to accept the evidence he wanted to hear, and deaf to the rest – such as, even more obvious to our eyes than those at the time, the contemporary way in which the faeries in the photos dressed and bobbed their hair. There were many critics at the time who pointed out the obvious, but Arthur Conan Doyle's word carried more weight.

The girls' story also tallied closely with 'true' tales of faerie encounters which he had already been gathering for his *Strand* article. At one point Doyle even speculates in print that it was perhaps more than coincidence that the pictures came his way just when they did, clearly suspecting supernatural intervention. He was plainly in the mood for miracles to counter the rational materialism he feared was swamping the world. As he opens the first chapter of *The Coming of the Fairies*: 'The series of incidents set forth in this little volume represent either the most elaborate and ingenious hoax ever played upon the public, or else they constitute an event in human history which may in the future appear to have been epoch-making in its character. It is hard for the mind to grasp what the ultimate results may be if we have actually proved the existence upon the surface of this planet of a population which may be as numerous as the human race, which pursues its own strange life in its own strange way, and which is only separated from ourselves by some difference of vibrations.'

He also had a background interest in faeries, not only through his Celtic origins but thanks to his uncle Richard Doyle with whom he was quite close. Although now most famous for his iconic cover for *Punch* magazine which was used for over a century,

Richard Doyle was more famous in his day as a faerie artist, having illustrated *The Fairy Ring: A New Collection of Popular Tales* in 1846 and *Fairy Land: Pictures from the Elf World* in 1869, along with many other fairy-tales which Conan Doyle knew well from childhood.

Among the examples of faerie witnesses besides the Cottingley girls, Conan Doyle quotes from the 1913 *A Book of Folklore* by renowned folklorist, author and hymn-writer Sabine Baring-Gould (1834 – 1924). As a folklorist Baring-Gould was generally content to report what he heard from others but was also happy to describe any personal experiences relevant to whatever he was discussing; as in the atmospheric introduction to his *Book of Werewolves*. In *A Book of Folklore* he opens the chapter on pixies and brownies with some interesting personal observations:

'In the year 1838, when I was a small boy of four years old, we were driving to Montpellier, on a hot summer day, over the long straight road that traverses a pebble and rubble strewn plain on which grows nothing save a few aromatic herbs.

'I was sitting on the box with my father, when to my great surprise I saw legions of dwarfs of about two feet high running along beside the horses – some sat laughing on the pole, some were scrambling up the harness to get on the backs of the horses. I remarked to my father what I saw, when he abruptly stopped the carriage and put me inside beside my mother, where, the conveyance being closed, I was out of the sun. The effect was that little by little the host of imps diminished in number till they disappeared altogether.

'When my wife was a girl of fifteen, she was walking down a lane in Yorkshire between green hedges, when she saw, seated in one of the privet hedges a little green man, perfectly well made, who looked at her with his beady black eyes. He was about a foot or eighteen inches high. She was so frightened that she ran home. She cannot recall exactly in what month this took place, but knows that it was a summer day.

'One day a son of mine, a lad of about twelve, was sent into the garden to pick peapods for the cook to shell for dinner. Presently he rushed into the house as white as chalk, to say that whilst he was engaged upon the task imposed upon him he saw standing between the rows of peas a little man wearing a red cap, a green jacket, and brown knee-breeches, whose face was old and wan, and who had a grey beard and eyes as black and hard as Sloes. He stared so intently at the boy that the latter took to his heels. I know exactly when this occurred, as I entered it in my diary, and I know when I saw the imps by looking into

my father's diary, and though he did not enter the circumstance, I recall the vision today as distinctly as when I was a child.'

Baring-Gould attributed the immediate physical cause of all his three examples as being sun-stroke, before going on to consider why such circumstances should produce similar hallucinations, not just in his own family but in the faerie-believing population at large. His own theory was that it was not because there was any reality in the creatures themselves, just that in hallucinations the imagination draws on images previously seen in books or heard of in fireside tales.

Conan Doyle was impatient with this rationalisation and went on to quote a less hesitant witness, Violet Tweedale (1868 – 1936), an author of real and imaginary ghost stories that he applauds for her courage in daring to speak out publicly, overlooking her apparent habit of sometimes passing off imaginary ghost stories as real:

'I had a wonderful little experience some five years ago which proved to me the existence of fairies. One summer afternoon I was walking alone along the avenue of Lupton House, Devonshire. It was an absolutely still day – not a leaf moving, and all Nature seemed to sleep in the hot sunshine. A few yards in front of me my eye was attracted by the violent movements of a single long blade-like leaf of a wild iris. This leaf was swinging and bending energetically, while the rest of the plant was motionless. Expecting to see a field-mouse astride it, I stepped very softly up to it. What was my delight to see a tiny green man. He was about five inches long, and was swinging back-downwards. His tiny green feet, which appeared to be green-booted, were crossed over the leaf, and his hands, raised behind his head, also held the blade. I had a vision of a merry little face and something red in the form of a cap on the head. For a full minute he remained in view, swinging on the leaf. Then he vanished. Since then I have several times seen a single leaf moving violently while the rest of the plant remained motionless, but I have never again been able to see the cause of the movement.'

Another witness Conan Doyle quoted in his book (and probably a much more trustworthy one because of his position) was the Rev. Arnold J. Holmes who wrote:

'Being brought up in the Isle of Man one breathed the atmosphere of superstition (if you like to call it), the simple, beautiful faith of the Manx fisher folk, the childlike trust of the Manx girls, who to this day will not forget the bit of wood and coal put ready at the side of the fire-place in case the "little people" call and need a fire. A good husband is the ultimate reward, and neglect in this respect [may lead to] a bad husband or no husband at all. The startling phenomena occurred on my journey home from Peel Town at night to St. Mark's (where I was Incumbent).

'After passing Sir Hall Caine's beautiful residence, Greeba Castle, my horse – a spirited one – suddenly stopped dead, and looking ahead I saw amid the obscure light and misty moonbeams what appeared to be a small army of indistinct figures – very small, clad in gossamer garments. They appeared to be perfectly happy, scampering and tripping along the road, having come from the direction of the beautiful sylvan glen of Greeba and St. Trinian's Roofless Church. The legend is that it has ever been the fairies' haunt, and when an attempt has been made on two occasions to put a roof on, the fairies have removed all the work during the night, and for a century no further attempts have been made. It has therefore been left to the "little people" who claimed it as their own.

'I watched spellbound, my horse half mad with fear. The little happy army then turned in the direction of Witch's Hill, and mounted a mossy bank; one "little man" of larger stature than the rest, about 14 inches high, stood at attention until all had passed him dancing, singing, with happy abandon, across the Valley fields towards St. John's Mount.'

Such sightings are far from rare today, though probably much less common than in the Celtic countryside a century or more ago. In *Fate* magazine in May 1977 Cynthia Montefiore of Somerset told of how she was in the garden with her mother who was demonstrating how to take cuttings from rose trees. She stood behind one with her daughter on the other side, when:

'Suddenly Mother put a finger to her lips to indicate silence and then pointed to one of the blooms. With astonishment, I saw what she was seeing – a little figure about six inches high, in the perfect shape of a woman and with brilliantly coloured diaphanous wings resembling those of a dragonfly. The figure held a little wand and was pointing it at the heart of a rose. At the tip of the wand there was a little light, like a star. The figure's limbs were a very pale pink and visible through her clothes. She had long silvery hair which resembled an aura. She hovered near the rose for at least two minutes, her wings vibrating rapidly like those of a hummingbird, and then she disappeared.'

Montefiore then commented: 'Perhaps the most surprising aspect of the experience was the way in which the little creature we both saw corresponded in practically every detail to the archetypal fairy of folklore and nursery stories. I know now that these descriptions are firmly founded on reality.'

A while later she also saw a garden gnome: 'I was sitting reading under a tree when my eye was caught by a sudden movement in front of me. A little figure, about eighteen inches tall, ran from the lawn on my left, across a path and onto another lawn, finally disappearing under a young fir tree. The sturdily built figure seemed to be dressed in a brown one-piece suit. I was not able to see the face because it was turned away from me. I immediately jumped up to investigate the area around the fir tree but there was no longer any sign of this gnome.

'Not long after this episode, a man friend of the family, who was obliging my mother by digging in the vegetable garden, saw the self-same gnome and described it to me . . .'

There are many more recent examples and a good place to find them, as mentioned in the Introduction, is the Fortean Times. The magazine regularly hears from people claiming to have encountered faeries or leprechauns without seeming to have any obvious axe to grind. One correspondent said that learning to see them was analogous to learning to see the 3D Eye pictures for which there was a craze in the 90s – one has to learn to kind of un-focus normal vision and then the hidden form suddenly becomes visible. This is not so different from what my artist friend felt, that in certain places he felt sure there were faeries present but on the edge of vision and could not be looked at directly. It is also close to Yeats's notion that seeing faeries required a certain unfocussing not of the eyes but consciousness or receptiveness, something quite easy for children and many country folk of his day, but not for minds that have been drilled for a lifetime in the opposite direction.

The internet also has many forums where people share countless recent sightings of faeries and other supposedly imaginary beings. Of course it's impossible to know how many of these are genuine because it is easy enough simply to make up a story, but it seems unlikely that all claims are false. Being considered 'away with the faeries' is still generally not taken as a compliment and it takes a certain courage to stand up and be counted. Many other well documented examples of encounters with faeries of all kinds throughout the twentieth century can be found in Janet Bord's 1997 book *Fairies: Real Encounters with Little People*.

Then there are the modern phenomena of UFO sightings and alien abductions, which have a remarkable amount in common with faerie encounters, if one strips away the Science Fiction 'glamour' – being transported to wonderfully strange places by little people, time slips, coming back disorientated or even a little mad, the absence of any tangible proof of what has happened. Even the strange lights accompanying alien abductions were common with faerie ones. Being shapeshifters perhaps faeries, like angels, simply adapt their appearance to human expectations. Perhaps there has been no great fall-off in the number of faerie sightings at all; but that is a whole other story.

Conclusion

WHY ARE FAERIES RELEVANT TODAY? This is a question I was asked a few times while writing this book; and if I was careless enough to mention what I was working on in the wrong company I received some very strange looks. I could see the question written in the bubble over their heads, 'What's a grown man in the twenty-first century doing spending his time writing a book about fairies?' and beside this caption a little illustration of Tinkerbell or one of Cicely Mary Barker's pretty little Flower Fairies.

The question was never actually asked outright and if it had been, all I probably would have replied is: because it's something that interests me. Which is true enough, if rather lame. The whole subject of Celtic mythology and its evolution into a faerie-faith that lived on alongside Christianity right into the twentieth century and to some extent beyond has fascinated me for years, and I leaped at the chance to do something substantial about it here, thanks to my publisher Cameron Brown.

Hopefully though, the subject has some relevance beyond simply my personal interests. Despite the general impression, faeries seem not to have totally disappeared from the modern world and one can still read about encounters with them in the news, or of construction projects in Ireland grinding to a halt because of some faerie bush or mound blocking the way. Whether brushes with faeries are just projections of the unconscious or meetings with some objective reality is a tricky question, and possibly an irrelevant one because who can doubt that ideas shape our world just as much, if not more, than objectively tangible forces of nature?

When I was in the closing stages of this book there was a lovely correspondence in the Fortean Times about an article by Patrick Harpur (FT209:54-55) on the common phenomenon of 'pixilation'. This has nothing to do with digital images but is a term coined, or maybe just remembered from childhood, by the author's mother and is probably related to the West Country term 'pixie-led' for unaccountably losing your way when it lies clearly before your eyes. Pixilation in his essay is the disappearance of vital objects like keys, tickets or rings, and their later mysterious reappearance in an obvious place that the losers are sure they have already searched. In the old days this was put down to mischievous house pixies or other sprites, and the solution was not to carry on searching ever more frantically but to stop still and ask 'Them' politely to return the object. Whereupon it almost always miraculously reappears.

The same charm seems just as effective today, going by examples Harpur quotes in his article and others in the following correspondence. It does not seem necessary to name the powers though two correspondents said the same charm works just as well when addressed to the Catholic St Anthony of Padua, who among other attributes is the patron saint of lost articles.

So, some at least of the old faerie beliefs seem as alive as ever, at least to some people. The interesting question is whether anything at all has changed about the faeries apart from our perceptions of them, being increasingly cut off from the natural world as we are by both consciousness and technology. Even if we happen to live in the countryside we rarely experience it as our rural ancestors did, occasionally finding ourselves stranded by nightfall on some remote track with nothing but the light of the sky to show the way. Now if we have to travel such paths by night we have cars or at least torches to hold back the spectre of the pooka and other demons of the night.

Many years ago I visited my parents one Christmas in their isolated Sussex village. Emerging from the closest train station that evening I saw a bus just about to leave which passed near the village, so I hopped on, to save calling the family to pick me up. It would mean half a mile or so walk the other end I knew, but that seemed no problem. Only when the bus dropped me off and hummed away did I realise I'd been living in the city too long, because it was pitch dark. Apart from the bright dwindling bus there was not a speck of light to be seen anywhere. I waited for my eyes to adjust but it made absolutely no difference. Not being able to see your hand in front of your face ceased to be a stale metaphor, because even after five or ten minutes and looking up at the sky it remained a simple statement of fact.

Well, being in a festive mood I decided to take this as a challenge and began feeling my way along the kerb towards a lane that was the back way to the village, helped by the lights of the occasional passing car. I knew the way well enough so this was a purely technical challenge which I took as a lesson in what it must be like to be struck blind. Entering the lane though was another matter altogether. It was one of those Sussex lanes, still surprisingly common, which are only wide enough for one car and in which the trees on either side meet overhead; a tunnel through the woods in fact, with no solid kerb to guide one's feet. If there had been a bright moon this may not have been too bad, because being winter most trees would have been bare, but in the pitch dark and with the soft rustling and creaking of trees all around it was like entering a different, ancient and not at all comforting world. There were no real dangers, I was well aware of that. The worst was perhaps bumping into a deer in the dark, which was quite possible there, and maybe enough to bring on a heart attack in itself, but not because there was any real danger from the beast itself, who would probably also have one. The curious thing was that even knowing that the only dangers were imaginary made them no less alarming. There felt a terrifying danger of bumping into something from the Otherworld that had been released by the dark.

Suffice it to say that after a hundred yards or so I picked my way shakily back to the road and waited for the next bus back to town and made the phone call. Nothing of a supernatural nature happened at all, but it was a useful lesson in how shallowly below the surface lie all kinds of creatures we have considered in this book.

More concrete though, as far as the objective reality of the faerie world goes, was the curious incident of the leprechauns who invaded my computer. A few years ago while writing a book about leprechauns I made a little joke about their skill as tinkers, saying how until recently (when affluence has disposed of most of them) many an old tractor in the west of Ireland was kept going well beyond its natural span by the tinkering of leprechauns; but that they had not begun to come to grips with computers. Soon afterwards my computer crashed. I made no immediate connection between the two things, and as it kept crashing I called in my computer genius friend Terry to fix it, as I often did then. He was baffled because there was nothing obviously wrong and although he did what he could, the computer kept on crashing after he left. As I was close to deadline I had no choice but to plough on, saving

the text every few minutes to pre-empt the next crash. The curious thing was that it was not just that particular file that was unstable. Just typing the word 'leprechaun' onto my computer, even when sending an email or using any other program, was enough to trigger a crash. So what I had to do was finish the book without typing that word again and after the book was safely packed off I had to wipe the computer and start afresh, which seemed to do the trick, and although I had my fingers crossed, I heard of no problems from the publishers.

The rational explanation is that while rootling around on the internet to see what other people had to say about leprechauns I picked up a mischievous virus linked to the word 'leprechaun' but it's hard to imagine why anyone would create such a thing and I've not heard of anyone else having a similar problem. My friend Terry remains convinced that the leprechauns did it and occasionally tells people about the computer he once knew that became haunted by leprechauns; but of course no-one believes him any more than they believe in leprechauns themselves.

You'll notice though that I've not made any little sarcastic jokes about leprechauns in this book that they might take in a disparaging way, especially with regards to them and computers. And the same goes for the rest of the faerie folk . . .

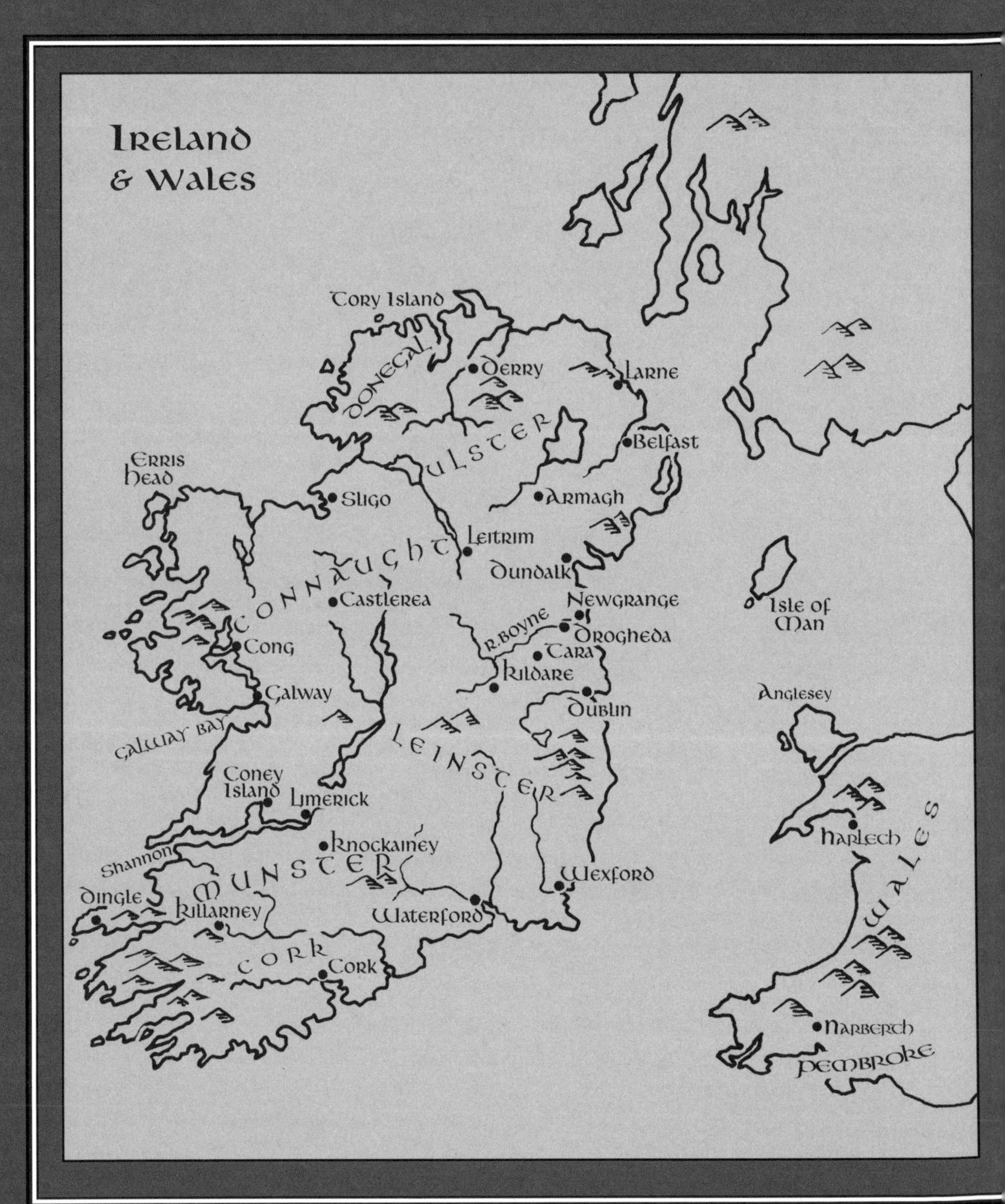

Ireland
& Wales
Tory Island
Donegal
Derry
Larne
Ulster
Belfast
Erris
Head
Sligo
Armagh
Leitrim
Connaught
Dundalk
Castlerea
Newgrange
Isle of
Man
R. Boyne
Drogheda
Cong
Tara
Kildare
Galway
Dublin
Anglesey
Galway Bay
Leinster
Coney
Island
Limerick
Harlech
Knockainey
Shannon
Munster
Wexford
Wales
Dingle
Killarney
Waterford
Cork
Cork
Narberth
Pembroke